For my daughter,
Miniator Malekpour

Acknowledgments

This book could not have been written without the support and assistance of Dr. Jamshid Malekpour (Gulf University) and Dr. Roger Hillman (Australian National University) who read the manuscript and offered numerous suggestions. They were truly a source of inspiration. I must also mention Arne Sjostedt who assisted me in polishing the manuscript. Finally my thanks goes to those directors and actors (too numerous to mention by name) who generously provided me with their films and photos.

Contents

Preface

The Iranian cinema is attracting increasing global attention and "is having its golden age."[1] However, despite "an almost ubiquitous and increasingly winning presence at the premier international film festivals,"[2] Iranian cinema is still largely unknown and underexposed. Western viewers find most films difficult to fully understand, as there is not enough written material about the films and the filmmakers to put the movies in context. Consequently, they cannot follow and understand, historically and aesthetically, Iranian cinema, in particular its connection to the Islamic Revolution of 1978/79, which changed Iran into a theocratic state. It is also important to remember that traditionally, "Islam disapproves of the visual arts and music in general and in particular disapproves of any representation of the human form."[3]

Among those writing about Iranian cinema in recent years, two groups have been identified, both using extreme approaches to the subject. The first group attempted to convince the readers that the new Iranian cinema was created after the Islamic Revolution, due only to the circumstances that emerged after the revolution and with the support of the Islamic regime. These writers, needless to say, have enjoyed the support of the cinema authorities, both in and outside the country. These writers strongly deny the impact — and in some cases the very existence — of the new wave in Iranian cinema that began before the revolution, labeling many pre-revolution filmmakers as either pagan Marxists or corrupt royalists. The best example of this type of writing is *Cinemayeh badaz Enghelab*.[4] The second group argued that the new Iranian cinema was created before the Islamic Revolution, and the filmmakers who brought Iranian cinema international recognition after the revolution were those who made films before the revolution. According to works such as *Cinemayeh pasaz Enghelab*,[5] the Islamic regime took advantage of this group of

1

filmmakers to claim that the credit for creation of the new cinema should
be given to the revolution and the regime. In the eyes of these writers,
those who argue that the Islamic Revolution had a share in the development of the new cinema are supporters of a fanatic regime. I tried, therefore, not to fall into either of these extreme schools of thought, but to
modify these claims and to recognize the new Iranian cinema as a movement that started in the 1960s and continues to the present. My purpose
in writing this book was to follow the development of the new Iranian
cinema, showing its personality in connection with social and political
forces within the Iranian society by studying and analyzing the works of
those filmmakers who contributed to the movement. As the development
of the new cinema was largely a reaction against commercial cinema, I
devote a chapter to the latter, in order to provide necessary context.

Knowledge of a few other points about this work will also benefit the
reader. This book is about the new Iranian cinema before and after the
Islamic Revolution of 1979. To cover the stated subject and at the same
time avoid confusion about the periodization, the book is divided into
five chapters; two chapters are devoted to the new cinema before the revolution and two to the new cinema after the revolution. However, as a few
filmmakers who worked before the revolution continued to work afterwards, the placement of discussion of their works is based upon the films
which made them recognizable in the movement. Therefore, filmmakers
like Mehrjui (*The Cow*, 1969), Kimiai (*Qasar*, 1969), Taqvai (*Peace in the
Presence of Others*, 1970) and Bayzai (*Downpour*, 1971) are studied as filmmakers of the new cinema before the revolution, despite their working
and making films after the revolution. Similarly, filmmakers such as
Kiarostami (*Where Is My Friend's Home?*, 1987) and Naderi (*The Runner*,
1985) who made many films before the revolution are placed in the post-
revolutionary cinema because the films that made them icons of the new
cinema were made after the revolution and under the circumstances of the
post-revolutionary cinema. Each director's entry is titled with his name,
and the title of his most important contribution to the body of New Wave
movies. The original, Persian titles of films are used upon the first appearance, accompanied by the translation in parentheses. Thereafter, for ease
of recognition, the translation is used as the movie title. (The translations
in most cases are the titles under which the films were released in the
West.) The filmography that follows the text is alphabetized by the English-
language title with which readers will be most familiar.

There are three recognizable waves in the new Iranian cinema. The
first one started in 1969 and lasted until the Islamic revolution in 1979,
while the second wave, and the most important in my view, began around

1984 and kept roaring to 1997. This book is about these first two waves. Therefore I do not extensively discuss filmmakers such as Majid Majidi (*Color of Heaven*, 1999), Jafar Panahi (*The Circle*, 2000) and Tahnineh Millani (*Two Women*, 1999), among others. I believe these filmmakers and many more belong to a third wave, which began around 1997, the result of a thriving new social and cultural environment that followed the election of moderate president Mohammad Khatami, in 1997. The development of a reformist movement allowed a less restricted and censored approach towards social and cultural issues, and the attendant filmmakers and their work merit, indeed require, further research before they can be fully appraised.

I decided to use Persian materials as my primary sources to provide an Iranian point of view for analysis of films; this perspective is the most important structural figure of my research.[6] Western reviews in most cases have been written only based on a single subtitled film from any given filmmaker and do not put the film in its proper context. These reviews ignore historical, social and cultural subtexts of a film, particularly in connection with the other works of the same filmmaker, but also the broader social and cultural context of the Iranian cinema.

While this work may not provide answers to all questions about the new Iranian cinema, it will serve, hopefully, as a primer to the subject, providing a history of the work from its beginning until the end of the second wave, in 1997, and further research and a subsequent volume will bring it to the present. Needless to say, any approach to an artistic or literary work is, after all, a matter of "taste" and "attitude," and how differently these two elements can be used and interpreted.

Introduction:
Early Iranian Cinema

Attempts to invent an instrument capable of projecting "moving pictures" cannot be allocated to a specific moment in time or to particular individuals. The creation of cinema spanned a period of several years and included the cooperation of many people around the world. However, two major events, which occurred in New York and Paris, had a significant impact upon the introduction of cinema to the world.

The first took place in New York in 1894 when Thomas Edison who had patented the "Kinetoscope"[1] held public exhibition, the first public viewing of a motion picture. The second event occurred in Paris in 1895, when the Lumière brothers showed enthusiasts their "Cinematograph."[2] These two events informed the world of this new invention and drew the public's interest towards cinema. It is due to this that most cinema critics and historians did not acknowledge any progress previous to these two events and consider this the embryonic beginnings of cinema.[3] Shortly thereafter, the Cinematograph was accidentally brought to Iran; within five years of its invention Iranians had been introduced to this new phenomenon.

When one of the Iranian kings, Mosafaredin Shah from the Qajar dynasty[4] traveled to France in 1900, he saw the Cinematograph. He was so amused by this new invention that he immediately ordered Mirza Ibrahim Khan Akasbashi, the chief photographer of the King's Court, to purchase the equipment. The entire incident was accounted in Shah's travel journal:

> July 9, 1900. Today we ordered Akasbashi to ready the equipment for our viewing. They went and set up the equipment by dusk. We went to the

place, which is close to the inn in which our servants eat lunch and dinner. We sat. They darkened the room. We viewed the equipment. It shows many things, which is extremely astonishing. We saw many landscapes and buildings and the falling of the rain and the Seine River and so on and so on in the city of Paris.[5]

During his travels in Europe, and two weeks after his introduction to the cinematograph, he traveled to Onstand (Belgium) to attend the Flower Festival. Akasbashi also accompanied the Shah with the newly purchased filming equipment and filmed the festival. About this historical event, the Shah wrote:

Today is the Festival of Flowers and we have been invited to visit. His Excellency Prime Minister and also the Minister of Court were accompanying us. It was a very interesting festival. All the carriages were adorned with flowers, and the inside of the carriages and the wheels were filled with flowers, so that the carriages were not visible. The ladies were in the carriages and paraded in front of us with bouquets of flowers. And Akasbashi was busy filming the event.[6]

From this evidence, we may deduce that Mosafaredin Shah was responsible for the importation of the first film equipment into Iran, and that Mirza Ibrahim Khan Akasbashi was the first Iranian cinematographer.[7]

In Iran, the cinematograph became, for a period of time, a source of entertainment for the Royal Family and the Royal Court. It was several years before the general public gained access to cinema. During this time, Akasbashi, at the Shah's order, made several films in Tehran. The first was of the lions of the Royal Zoo in Farah-Abad.[8] The second was a mourning procession of the month of Muharram in Sabzeh Meydan.[9] He also occasionally filmed weddings and celebrations within the Royal family, however all of these films have been lost.

Besides Mosafaredin Shah and Akasbashi, Mirza Ibrahim Sahafbashi must also be mentioned as a significant contributor to the progress of early Iranian cinema. Sahafbashi was one of the great intellectuals and pro–Constitutional activists of his time, and due to his occupation as an antique trader he was able to travel extensively. On one of his trips to Europe, in 1897, he attended several theatre productions in London, Paris and Berlin, but he also saw "moving pictures" in London.[10] Because he traveled to London three years before Mosafaredin Shah went to Paris, it is likely that he was the first Iranian ever to have seen cinema and mentioned it in his travel journal:

Tammadon Cinema, established in 1928 in Tehran.

Another equipment which has been invented and is working with electrical power, is able to project everything as it is in real life. For example, it shows the American falls exactly as it is or an army of soldiers marching or a moving train in full speed and this is an American invention.[11]

From his writings it is evident that Sahafbashi was introduced to the Kinetoscope, invented by one of Thomas Edison's colleagues, W. K. Dickson, in 1890. Apparently he purchased a kinetoscope and brought it back with him upon his return to Iran. However, he did not begin using it until years after Mosafaredin Shah bought his cinematograph. His delay was likely due to the social, political and religious climate in Iran, which at the time was not disposed towards nor accepting of such new Western inventions.

In 1903 Sahafbashi started the first cinema open to the general public in Iran, at the back of his shop. One year later, in November 1904, he opened a second cinema, on Cheragh Gas Avenue, in which he showed short French comic films and American news footage, which were bought from the Odessa and Rostov markets in Russia.

One of the French films was about a garbage collector who, while sweeping the streets, was run over by a steamroller and flattened. He was run over again by another machine, this time becoming short and fat, and so on. Another film was about a chef who found skeletons and ghosts in his kitchen cupboards.[12] The news footage pieces were about the Transvaal Wars in South Africa.

The films were shown at night and most patrons were rich aristocrats, with very few ordinary people attending. Apart from the fact that the purchase of a ticket was out of reach for the majority of people, most viewed this new phenomenon as a Western influence and therefore an agent of corruption, and a threat to traditional Iranian values. This view undoubtedly was supported by religious people, including Sheyhk Fazlollah Noori, who was a high clergyman. Another reason for the lack of support for Sahafbashi's cinema was his pro–Constitutional views. Sahafbashi was one of the few people of the time who welcomed any new phenomenon, and who would make people aware of the dictatorship of the Qajar kings. This led to constant confrontation between Sahafbashi and government officials; the government retaliated by causing him personal difficulty, as well as hindering the operation of his cinema. This negative environment, which was created by both the government and the religious faction, ultimately led to the closing of the cinema and Sahafbashi's imprisonment.

After his release from prison he sold his cinema equipment, his shop and factory. In 1907 he and his family left Iran on a self-imposed exile to

Karbala (in Iraq) and afterwards to India, where he finally settled down for good. He left the difficult task of the expansion and promotion of cinema in Iran to those who were not interested in its social and political impact but were more concerned with the commercial aspects of the business. Roosi Khan was among those who, after Sahafbashi, took on the challenge.

Mehdi Roosi Khan (Ivanov) was the student of Abdullah Qajar, the chief photographer of Muhammad Ali Shah's court. He was originally from Russia. In 1907 Roosi Khan opened his own photography shop; the same year, two Russians showed two films in the Mirror Hall of the Golestan Palace in honor of Prince Ahamad Mirza.[13] Both films were accompanied by a gramophone, and both lasted two hours. These same two Russians, whose names are unknown, later showed several sessions of films to well-known aristocrat families in their houses and at their weddings. The support for the Russians' films led to Roosi Khan's purchase of a projector and fifteen rolls of film (which were 500 to 1000 meters each) from the Pathé Company in Paris. He showed these films mostly in the royal harem-house and the houses of aristocrats. He also began showing films in his own photography shop, advertising them in the daily newspaper, *Sobeh-Sadeq*:

> Roosi Khan's Photography Shop in Alaodollah Avenue will show the new motion pictures using the Cinematograph, which is the new invention for the display of moving pictures.[14]

In 1908 he turned the existing backyard of Darolfonoon College into a new theater, placing seating within the yard and covering it with a blue cloth for protection from the heat. This venue was able to seat two hundred patrons and showed short films every afternoon. Among these was a short film about the Japan-Russia war and the 1904–5 wars. He also employed a violinist and a pianist to promote his cinema. The following year Roosi Khan went to Russia and brought several films back to Iran. Because of the popularity of his business, Roosi Khan decided to open another cinema. He rented the upper level of the Farous Publications on Laleh Zar Avenue, and there he screened French comic films, mostly those of Max Linder, one of the leading comic actors of the time.[15] Compared to previous venues, the new theater was very large, with the capacity to hold 300 to 500 patrons. In addition, for the first time in Iran, the light for the projector was provided by an arc lamp.

A year later, in 1909, Roosi Khan filmed the Ashura mourning procession of Muharram[16] and sent it to Russia to be developed. Due to political and religious reasons this film was never shown in Iran; in Iran, it was impossible to show such a religious ritual in the cinema, because movies were prohibited by religion. Roosi Khan, the second Iranian cinematographer, after Akasbashi, was consequently unable to display his work in his home country.

In the same period, a man named Aghayov stepped onto the scene, establishing a new cinema in the back of a shop in Naseri Avenue (present Naser Khosro). This small cinema had only 20 seats. In the tradition of Abel and Cain, Roosi Khan and Aghayov, pioneering brothers in the history of Iranian cinema, soon began a fiercely jealous competition which ultimately led to conspiracies by both parties. The popularity of Roosi Khan's Darolfonoon Cinema, which was located close to the Aghayov Cinema, led Aghayov to employ goons to attack and severely injure one of Roosi Khan's employees. Roosi Khan took the matter to his Russian friend, Lyakhov, who was the chief of police in Tehran. Lyakhov used his power to imprison Aghayov in the Kazak prison of the Russian embassy. Roosi Khan also hired one of Lyakhov's men as a security guard for his theater. Still, the tension continued. Aghayov who was also influential, hired a lawyer and had Roosi Khan put in jail. Ironically, the Abel and Cain of Iranian cinema spent time in the same jail together!

After his release from prison, Roosi Khan closed the troublemaking theater at Darolfonoon and opened a new one in the Darvazeh Qazvin suburb. At his new establishment, most of the films shown were Russian. Roosi Khan, who unlike Sahafbashi was not a freedom fighter but instead was a supporter of the Qajar dynasty, preferred his patrons to be aristocrats and especially anti–Constitutionalists. But since pro–Constitutional activists were also in search of entertainment and viewed cinema positively, they did not boycott Roosi Khan's cinema. At the height of the pro–Constitutional movement, in 1909, the theater would be occupied by pro–Constitutionalists one night, and by anti–Constitutionalists the following night. This compromise continued until Muhammad Ali Shah, who was against the Constitutional movement and was trying to maintain his absolute power, lost the battle against pro–Constitutional activists. In 1909 he had to take refuge in the Russian embassy, and subsequently fled Iran.

The victory of the Constitutionalists made the situation difficult for Roosi Khan, and he closed his cinema in Darvazeh Qazvin and made significant changes at the Faroos cinema, but eventually he was forced to close that one as well. In 1909, with the flight of Mohammad Ali Shah from Iran and the climax of the pro–Constitutional uprising, Roosi Khan's shop was looted. He was forced to leave for France in 1912.

Roosi Khan and Aghayov can be credited with establishment of commercial cinema in Iran. They were both Russian, and most likely Christian Orthodox. Other than Sahafbashi, no Iranian Muslim had the courage to engage in the business of cinema at a time when the prevailing religious and political attitudes were opposed to the activity.

Following in the footsteps of Roosi Khan and Aghayov, Ardeshir Khan next became the leading figure in Iranian cinema. Ardeshir Khan-e Armeni (Armenian) was a textile trader who traveled to France in 1900, where he was introduced to the cinematograph. He worked for a while at the Pathé Company, and upon preparing for his return to Iran, he purchased a bicycle, a gramophone and a film projector to take back.[17] Like Sahafbashi, Ardeshir Khan did not tell anyone of his purchase. With the victory of Constitutionalists there was a great change in the political and religious atmosphere of the country, and in 1913, he opened a theater on Allaodolleh Avenue. He called his cinema Tajadod (Modern), and its opening supported a new wave of modernism initiated by the pro-constitutional activists. Like Roosi Khan, he also employed a pianist and a violinist to play during the screening of the films. When the audience was small, he himself played the piano, while also explaining the scenes in the motion picture. In his theater the guests were treated to ice cream and refreshments during summertime, and in winter patrons were offered tea and sweets, creating a friendly atmosphere for the audience. However, after some time the offerings became repetitive because Ardeshir Khan was unable to purchase new films. His business declined, and Ardeshir Khan was forced to close his theater in 1913, the same year it opened. He returned three years later, however, and in 1916 he once again opened the cinema, with renovations. He advertised the reopening in *Etelaat*, a newspaper:

> New and important show! Soon in the Allaodolleh Avenue, opposite the Pars Inn, a new cinema called "Modern Cinema" will be opened. The films shown in this cinema are from the battlefields of the recent European wars. Audiences will enjoy the viewing of these films immensely.[18]

Modern Cinema had no more than eight rows of seats, with a maximum capacity of eighty people. The small screen (approximately 3.5 by 2 meters) was made of white cotton. Only fifteen minutes of silent films were shown each day, and as electricity was not available in that part of the city, a kerosene lantern served as the source of light for the projector.

Ardeshir Khan was also responsible for the establishment of the first open-air cinema in Iran. He rented a park, situated between Aramaneh and Amiriyeh Avenues, and began to show films there. He also opened a cinema for female audiences only, with the cooperation of Khan Baba Motazedi, but unfortunately the cinema was closed soon after its opening due to a difference of opinions between the partners. Social issues, like the appearance of women in public places, probably contributed to the closing of the cinema. Ardeshir Khan remained active in the cinema industry until 1925.

Around 1920 the industry expanded to other parts of Iran and many people in various capital cities around the country began opening theaters, although many did not stay open long. Ali Vakili, a businessman and graduate of the Alliance School in France, was very active in the establishment of cinemas during this period. He was very welcoming towards the new art form, and believed that to achieve progress, one must move with the times. On one of his trips to Baghdad in 1924, he bought a projector and several films. He rented the Grand Hotel salon and opened it as Grand Cinema. This salon, with a capacity of 500, was not very different in terms of equipment and facilities from other theaters. Like Ardeshir Khan, Vakili also opened a cinema solely for female patrons. He transformed the Zoroastrian Girl's School theatre hall into a cinema and placed various advertisements in newspapers to attract female patrons:

> Good news for ladies: In Zoroastrian Cinema, the famous series of Ruth Roland,[19] the world renowned artist, will be shown for the respected ladies. The viewing of amusing actions of a young female like Ruth Roland is necessary for ladies. On 10th May 1928, Zoroastrian Cinema will provide a complementary ticket for every lady who purchases a ticket.[20]

Although Reza Shah Pahlavi, after gaining power in 1921 and the establishment of the Pahlavi dynasty in 1925, was eager to improve the social and cultural situation for women in Iran, the social structure of Iranian society still did not allow women to venture outside the house in order to go to the theatre or cinema. Such social activities were limited to only those women from well-educated and modern families. Due to ongoing religious and social restrictions, these first attempts to establish cinemas for women were unwelcome and consequently failed. This did not deter Vakili and he began to think of other ways to attract women to the cinemas. For example, he separated men and women into two sections, and gave the balcony to the women. He advertised this new change in a newspaper:

> The announcement of "Grand Cinema" and the entry of women: The Founder of Grand Cinema, in order to serve you has dedicated a section especially for the respected ladies and therefore tonight invites all locals to view new and unequaled films. And in honor of the attendance of the respected ladies, the first and second parts of the famous series "The Copper Bullet" will be shown for the first time in one night. The entry door

for respected ladies is from Grand Cinema, and for the gentlemen from Grand Hotel. The employees of Grand Cinema and also the officers of Police Department will refuse entry to inappropriately dressed ladies and troublesome youth.[21]

Vakili's advertisement generated little response, and the balcony was often empty. Ladies chose not to attend this new cinema, or were prohibited from attending by their husbands, fathers and brothers. Vakili, undiscouraged, established a new cinema, called Cinema Sepah, and also undertook efforts to publish Iran's first film magazine. In 1928 he was granted a license by the Ministry of Cultural Affairs, and in 1930, publication of *Cinema va Namayeshat* (Cinema and Theatre) began. After the publication of the second issue of *Cinema va Namayeshat*, however, Ali Vakili retired from the cinema industry altogether.

The first important silent Iranian news footage was produced by Khan Baba Motazedi, Iran's third cinematographer, between 1925 and 1931. He learned the art of cinematography while studying electrical engineering in France. For a time while in France he was employed with the Gaumont Company as a cinematographer, and upon his return to Iran, he brought a film projection system and all the other equipment required to screen films. Between 1925 and 1931 he produced several pieces of news footage, the most important of them capturing the establishment of Constitutional Parliament in which the monarchy was passed from the Qajar dynasty to the Pahlavi dynasty. His second important film was about the coronation ceremony of Reza Shah Pahlavi in 1926.[22] In early 1928, he followed the example of Ardeshir Khan and established the San'ati Cinema for female audiences. Unfortunately the cinema was destroyed in a fire few months later. During the fire *The Thief of Baghdad*[23] was showing. The fire was said to be caused by faults in the electrical wiring, however with the evidence that emerged later and the repeated fires in other cinemas, it is apparent that this incident and similar ones were the work of anti-cinema groups. (The most horrific of these fires was the burning of Cinema Rex in the city of Abadan during the Islamic Revolution in 1977; more than six hundred people lost their lives). The San'ati Cinema was probably burned because it raised the ire of those who were opposed to cinemas in general, and furthermore, because it actively sought women as patrons.

After the San'ati Cinema fire, Khan Baba Motazedi established the Pari and Tammadon cinemas. He gave the right side of the salon to the women and the left to the men. Apart from this, Motazedi and Vakili also translated the captions into Persian in order to attract a greater number of patrons. This was the first attempt to create subtitles in Iran, in the language of the audience, but unfortunately due to the illiteracy of many of

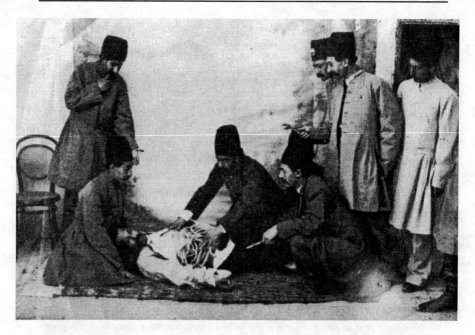

A scene from one of the films of Akasbashi, the first cinematographer in Iran (1900–1904).

the patrons the effort did not have the desired effect. Later, the dubbing of films became routine in Iran. To solve the problem of the patrons' illiteracy, Motazedi employed someone to read the captions out loud for the audience (similar to the early Japanese cinema). At the time most cinemas in Tehran screened films starring Richard Talmadge, the American actor who was famous for his wild actions.

The first school for cinema in Iran was opened by Avance Okaniance (Okanian) in 1930. Okaniance was a Russian-Armenian immigrant who studied in the School of Cinematic Art in Moscow and in 1930 emmigrated to Iran.[24] He soon became active in the film industry, and with the support of one of his countrymen, Grisha Sakvarlidze, opened a school for cinema studies:

> Madreseh Artisti Cinema (Artistic School of Cinema) will open on Allaodolleh Avenue on April 15, 1930. The school has both male and female specialised teaching staff, and there are special classes for ladies.[25]

The advertisement did not attract many students, and so Okaniance placed a second one in the same newspaper. After the second advertisement, one hundred and fifty students enrolled in the school, but no women were among them. Okaniance, who like most intellectuals of his time was eager to involve women in the art of cinema, again advertised the establishment of his school, hoping to attract them.

Okaniance taught various courses, including music, acting, cinematography, gymnastics and dance. But over time the number of students declined, and women did not welcome the school either. Apart from social and religious barriers, two other factors were working against his school. One was the popularity of theatre art, which in those days attracted the attention of most intellectuals and art lovers. The Kermanshahi School of Drama and Shahrdari Theatre were training theatre actors in 1931, and women were participating in both schools. It seems that few intellectuals were drawn to cinema, with the exception of Ibrahim Khan Sahafbashi, a pro-democracy activist who became aware of cinema in its first days. As a result of this lack of interest among Iranian intellectuals and artists, the cinema industry fell into the hands of businessmen who had no artistic knowledge or passion for the new medium, and unfortunately it continued that way for years. Only in the 1950s was this tradition overcome; the arrival of two young educated artists, Farrokh Ghaffari and Hoshang Kavoosi, signaled a change, and paved the way for artists such as Golestan and Rahnema, who started the new wave of cinema in Iran.[26]

Okaniance's lack of proficiency in the Persian language may have been a factor in the failure of the school. This language gap made understanding the subjects difficult for the students. Together, these factors doomed Iran's first school of cinema to a short life. However, this did not deter Okaniance; he moved his institution to Shaykh Avenue and again started teaching cinema courses, though with fewer students. The teaching program consisted of acting based on the American method (possibly method acting); photography; cinema technique; acrobatics; Swedish exercises; boxing; fencing; ballet; Oriental dance; and European dance.[27]

In 1930, after the first term of school was finished, Okaniance directed the first full-length silent Iranian movie, *Abi va Rabi (Abi and Rabi)*.[28] His friend Grisha Sakvarlidzeh, owner of Cinema Mayak, was an investor in the film, which met with mixed reactions from the public. However, the production of an Iranian film by an Iranian group (even though the producer and director were foreign), was a focus of great attention and was a source of motivation for others. In 1931, the *Abi and Rabi* print was destroyed in a fire at Cinema Mayak, and a second copy of the film has never been found.

Eighteen students graduated from Okaniance's school in 1932, after its second term. Okaniance then thought of making another film, but he was unable to find a producer. Finally he decided to sell shares for his film to artists and was able to raise the money. Thus the first cooperative production in Iran's cinematic history, *Haji Agha Actor Cinema Mishavad* (*Haji Agha Becomes an Actor of Cinema*) was made. This comic film was about a religious man who was opposed to movies. His daughter and son-in-law, both cinema students, began filming him in secret. They then tricked him into going to a theater, where he saw the film of himself. He applauded both himself and cinema, having become a converted fan of the new technology. The film was a representation of cinema's place in Iranian society and the clash of two social groups, represented by Haji Agha the traditionalist, and his daughter and son-in-law the modernists. The clash of the two social groups is won by the modernists, who convince Haji Agha that the modern invention is both good, and necessary for progress.

After the screening of *Haji Agha*, Okaniance's film school began its third semester. F. Jabar Vaziri, who had just finished studying acting in America, was hired to use her skill and knowledge to teach female students. The third semester was not a success; when it failed to attract students, Okaniance closed the school forever and emigrated to India. He left the task of making Iran's first feature-length drama to one of his students, Ibrahim Moradi.

Bolhavas (*Fickle*), made in 1934 by Moradi, is about a village man who meets a girl in a weekly market in northern Iran; he marries her and they settle down in the village, but after some time he becomes ill and travels to Tehran for treatment. In the city, he meets and falls in love with another woman, and forgets his wife back in the village. When his first wife hears what has happened, she attempts suicide, but a man from the village saves her. After time her husband realizes his mistakes and yearns for the village life, but he is too late: when he returns home to be with his first wife again, she rejects him.

Fickle illustrates the fickleness of man, but it also depicts the differences between urban and rural life and contrasts the values found in each. The purity, honesty and simplicity of rural life and the brutality, complexity and harshness of urban life were illustrated in the film. The subject was new for its time, but the novelty did not translate to and was not a success at the box office. Its failure may be due to the fact that it was a silent film, and by this time many foreign films with sound were showing in cinemas. Iran's first drama fared poorly, but its failure did not stop Iranian cinema from proceeding along its slow path. It was soon revived by another filmmaker who was working outside Iran, but within the Iranian culture, making movies for the Iranian people. The result of his work would be the first — and most important — sound film in the history of Iranian cinema.

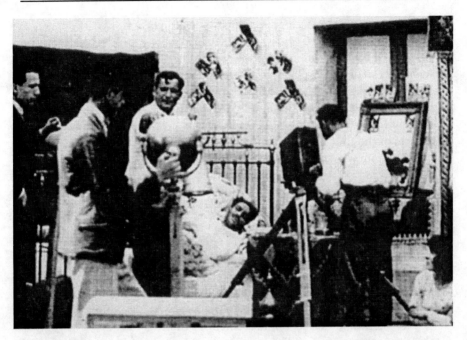

A shooting scene from *Bolhavas* (*Fickle*), starring Amir-Fazli and Tabesh, directed by Ibrahim Moradi in 1935.

After helping to stage and performing in a few Iranian theatre productions, Abdul-Hussien Sepanta went to India in 1927; there he was introduced to Ardeshir Irani, the owner of the Imperial Film company in Bombay. This meeting and Sepanta's subsequent visit to the studio ignited his love for cinema. Sepanta's attraction to and study of filmmaking fired in him a desire to produce a Persian-language film. He discussed this new idea with Ardeshir Irani, who welcomed it warmly. With the guidance and assistance of Ardeshir Irani, Sepanta began to write a script which in 1933 was made into a film called *Dokhtar-e Lur* (*The Lur Girl*).[29] Making the film proved a difficult task for Ardeshir Irani and Sepanta. One of the main problems was finding a competent actress who could also speak Persian. After some time they discovered Rouhangiz Kermani, who could speak Persian (although with an accent), and asked her to be in the movie. Rouhangiz Kermani's appearance in the film was a pivotal point not only in the history of Iranian cinema, but also for the women's freedom movement in Iran: for the first time, an Iranian woman allowed herself to be filmed without a veil. Rouhangiz established forever her place in history as the first actress in the history of Iranian film. The film was 35mm and in black and white, and used the optic system for its sound.

In the movie Jaffar, a government official, meets Golnar, a dancer at a highway teahouse. Golnar was taken from her family by a group of thieves who raided her city and then forced her to work and dance in the teahouse. Jaffar and Golnar fall in love and together plan to fight with Goli Khan, the gang leader, and to bring them to justice. They find the gang's hideout and are able to end their days of looting. While the central theme of the film is the love of Golnar and Jaffar, certain social and cultural aspects of the time are also illustrated.

The film was screened in Cinema Mayak on December 22, 1933, and was received very warmly by people. At the time films being shown in theaters were changed twice a week, but *The Lur Girl* was screened for 37 days. After its first screening at Cinema Mayak, the film played at Cinema Sepah for another 13 days. Its success can be attributed to its being the first Persian-language sound film, and also to the fact that it was technically better than those silent films made in Iran. The film presented love as its central theme, which also attracted audiences. The appearance of an Iranian woman without a *hijab* (veil) in a film also contributed to its success. This was a pivotal point both in the history of the country's cinema and for the women's freedom movement in Iran.

After the success of *The Lur Girl*, the Ministry of Moaref (Culture), which in those days was responsible for cultural affairs, asked Sepanta to make a film on the life of Ferdowsi (one of the greatest Persian poets)[30] in order to celebrate the millenium of his birth. Ardeshir Irani, who had profited greatly from the production of *The Lur Girl*, immediately announced his desire to participate in this new production. The film was made quickly; when it was presented to Reza Shah Pahlavi at a private screening, he ordered the removal of few scenes connected to the treatment of Ferdowsi by Sultan Mahmood Ghaznavi. Reza Shah did not wish to support the slightest criticism of past Iranian kings, even those that reigned a thousand years ago.

Sepanta was forced to cut those scenes, and he re-edited the film. Sultan Mahmood, who was obviously the cause of Ferdowsi's pain and suffering, was depicted in the new version as a just and art-loving king. As a result of this censorship, the title character in *Ferdowsi* lost a great deal of his identity. This occurrence was the first and most crucial event in the establishment of a powerful censoring body for Iranian cinema. This body has survived to this day and always had (and still has) powerful control over Iran's film industry.

Ferdowsi was finally ready for release after many changes, but unlike *The Lur Girl*, it was not a success. *Ferdowsi* only lasted three days on the screen. In the film, Sepanta played the role of Ferdowsi, and Nosratollah

Sepanta in *Laila va Majnun* (*Laila and Majnun*), directed by Abdul-Hussein Sepanta in 1937.

Mohtasham played the role of Sultan Mahmood; Mohtasham later became one of Iran's most famous actors. The success of *The Lur Girl* and the failure of *Ferdowsi* led Sepanta to return to love as a subject.

He next made *Shireen va Farhad* (Shireen and Farhad), an adaptation of a famous classical Persian love story written by Nezami Ganjavi in the 12th century. The film was made in 1935, and told the story of distant lovers who had to fight, even against nature, in order to reach each other. To reach Shireen, who was living in the king's castle, Farhad made a tunnel in the mountain, barehanded and alone. One of the film's most important features was its music, which was specially composed for the movie. It was actually a musical, as all of the dialogue was sung, making *Shireen and Farhad* the first musical in the history of Iranian cinema. Unlike when making *The Lur Girl*, Sepanta had no problem finding female actors this time. Fakhri Vaziri played the role of Shireen, while Sepanta himself played Farhad.

Sepanta's fourth and last feature film, made in 1936, was *Laila va Majnun* (Laila and Majnun). This film was another adaptation of a famous classical love story by Nazami Ganjavi.

Laila and Majnun are denied the right to marry each other by Laila's father, and only in death are they united, resting together in the cemetery.[31] The film took one year and eleven months to be finished. Every shot was carefully designed with special attention to details. About the movie and Sepanta's work Farrokh Ghaffari wrote:

> His versatile style of writing is admirable.... I saw a shooting screenplay from him that showed how precise and careful he was. He had designed every shot with details. Even after the new movement in Iranian cinema, and after the production of *Toofan-e Zandeghi* (The Storm of Life)[32] until today, this sort of attention to all details has not been seen in Iranian cinema.[33]

Sepanta was the first Iranian filmmaker who knew and respected all the principles involved in the process of making a movie. He always had a complete shooting script in his hands and knew exactly what he was going to shoot. He always had drawings of every scene, and knew which angles he wanted to use. Although love and romance were central themes of his films, he took every opportunity to show social and cultural life of Iran and its people. Editing was an important element of his work. It is evident that through all stages of film production, from scriptwriting to shooting the scenes, editing was Sepanta's major concern. Perhaps had the next generation of Iranian filmmakers followed in Sepanta's footsteps, investing the same care in their work, Iranian cinema might not have wasted so many precious years in finding its national identity; in form and context, a truly *Iranian* cinema would not come to be until after the Islamic Revolution of 1979.

I

The Development of the Commercial Film Industry

Avance Okaniance's *Abi and Rabi* (1930) is known as the first true product of an Iranian film industry.[1] Thus Iranian cinema is a seventy year old industry, of which nearly fifty of those years passed during the reign of Pahlavi dynasty (1925–1979). Those years coincided with the years of development and globalization of cinema. The golden years of American movies in the 1940s and 1950s, the masterpieces of the neo-realist school of Italian cinema in 1950s, and the new wave (Nouvelle Vague) of French film in the 1960s were among the most important events in world cinema in those years. Due to the absolute domination of the Pahlavi regime over all aspects of culture and economy in Iran, and in particular due to the establishment of very harsh censorship of films, Iranian cinema did not likewise progress in those years. As the film industry became international, its products crossing borders and transcending cultures, Iranian cinema absorbed negative elements from the commercial films of Hollywood and Indian. As a result, Iranian movies did not reflect the true national or cultural identities of the country.[2] This type of cinema, a genre later labeled Film Farsi, operated as a "dream factory" for the majority of the audience, and dominated the Iranian film industry for over forty years.

During the Film Farsi period (1934–1978) Iranian popular cinema had no aim other than copying the commercial elements of the two big producers of films, the American and the Indian film industries. The result was low-quality movies for audiences who were becoming more and more addicted to such fare, losing any taste or demand for anything different.[3] Consequently, Film Farsi, due to the lack of an artistic creativity both in form and context, did not truly reflect the norms of life of Iranians or the artistic taste of the society.

21

The majority of Iranian films in this period were made only to entertain the audience, giving them something to dream about and helping them to forget the bitter realities of their lives.[4] This dream factory was manufacturing its products, primarily in keeping with the regime's cultural policies, and secondly, in line with the will of producers who were only concerned about the box office. The regime wanted films showing what was in essence the opposite of the country's social realities, distracting the people with fantasies that also undermined any ideas or sense of criticism and judgment. The main goal of such cinema, which was controlled completely by a governmental board of censorship, was to keep the audience happy and grateful for what they had and to keep them silent about what they did not have. The producers, on the other hand, were manufacturing films in order to make more money and to monopolize the industry. The cooperation of these two forces during the reign of the Pahlavi dynasty produced Film Farsi and its easily consumable cinematic confections, but this was far from the type of cinema that a filmmaker like Abdul-Hussein Sepanta would have envisioned when he made *The Lur Girl* in 1933. An indicator of the nature and characteristics of Film Farsi is the fact that, in 1968, Manocher Vosooq had leading parts in ten Iranian films.[5] In 1970, director Reza Safaie made six films, with the average time of production for each film around twenty days.[6] This quickly produced, unvarying output was representative of the type of cinema which developed in those years and became the norm for Iranian filmmaking. With this in mind, one can discuss and analyze the different periods of cinema during the Pahlavi dynasty.

The years between 1936 and 1947 have been considered a time of stagnation in Iranian cinema. In this period, the harsh censorship of the regime coupled with the economic, social and cultural consequences of the Second World War, were among the leading causes of a stifling recession in Iranian cinema.

Reza Khan Pahlavi, who took power in Iran through a coup d'etat backed by the United Kingdom in 1921 and in 1925 named himself as the Shah of Iran, was a nationalist dictator who wanted to modernize Iran based on a Western model, regardless of the traditional values of Iranian society.[7] Parallel to his many reforms aimed at transforming the country from a feudal to a modern one, a very strong and dangerous inner conflict between the society's modern and traditional values was also in progress. One reform which was absolutely necessary for the continued development of cinema in Iran was the freedom of Iranian women to study and to work. These rights were denied women by a male dominated society for ages. Under the new regime, Reza Shah Pahlavi gave Iranian women the right to come out of their houses and to go to school and to work. It is important to keep in mind that before 1937, Iranian women were not even able to go to markets unless they were accompanied (or guarded) by male members of the family.[8] They were not allowed to go to movie theatres, or to work as actors in films. Therefore, the women's movement was vital for the development of cinema in Iran. In line with modernization of the country and with the support of intellectuals like M. Forooqi and H. Taqi-Zadeh, Reza Shah Pahlavi passed a law in 1937, granting women freedom to unveil in public and to be admitted to Tehran University. Before the Women's Movement of 1935–36, an Iranian woman participated in only one film made in Iran, *Haji-Agha* (1932), by Okaniance. Judging by the name of that actress, Asia Ghostantanian, it is apparent that she was Armenian (Christian) and not Muslim.[9] The first Iranian Muslim woman who acted in a film was Ghodsi Partovi, who had the leading female role in *Fickle*, made in 1935. Her participation in that film, undoubtedly, was the fruit of the Women's Movement.

The struggle for emancipation of women, encouraged by the regime, was a positive move for Iranian cinema, but any hope of real progress soon vanished. The same regime soon imposed harsh censorship upon the new and fragile industry, discouraging the private sector from coming forward and investing in movie making. Laws passed in 1930, 1934 and 1935 put Iranian cinema solely into the hands of the Department of Police.[10] The scope of censorship imposed by the Department's officers was so immense that after a while, Iranian filmmakers lost any control over their work. The police officers not only cut scenes that they thought were politically or ethnically unsuitable, they changed entire plots and even wrote new scripts for movies. The end of *Agha Mohammad Khan Qajar* (directed by N. Mohtasham, 1954) was changed completely by the board of censorship after three days of screening in Tehran cinemas. They sent the film back to the studio, where the producer had to change the destiny of the King. Instead of being killed by two of his companions, as in the original version and based on historical fact, the King, in the new version, drops his sword and goes to fight the enemies of the country barehanded. Nilla Cram Cook,[11] who was in charge of the board of censorship in 1942 in Iran, writes:

> It would be hard to say whether Hollywood or Reza Shah's police censor played the more villainous role in stunting the growth of native drama. I had an opportunity to judge the pernicious influence of the latter when in 1942, as an employee of the Iranian Government, I took over the censorship of Iranian theatre and cinema. The censor was a policeman who posed as a dramatic critic, dedicated to the service of the Shah.... This censor had access to the Palace because it was he who borrowed films for the royal

previews, and so for years he pretended to represent the imperial views....
This censor also fancied himself a critic. On one occasion he authorized
The Merchant of Venice for production only with a "connecting scene" of
his own because the author had "forgotten to insert it." *Hamlet* he banned
altogether because "it suggested ways in which to murder a king."[12]

Apart from the establishment of the board of censorship, the main
body for censoring films, indirect censorship was also experienced in Iranian cinema after the coup d'etat of 1953, when the military returned the
Shah to power with the help of the CIA.[13] For several years, after the coup,
the government was ruled by generals and army officers; some of them
entered the theatre and cinema industries in order to impose the cultural
policies of the government upon both. These officers worked as producers, writers and directors. Apart from the army-owned studio,[14] Lieutenant Deram-Bakhsh established a studio, Shahriyar, and Lieutenant Shab-
Pareh established Ray Studio. Though the studios were apart from the
army, both had the same goals as the army policymakers. Most of the films
that they made had a common aim: the promotion of nationalistic feelings of the people in order to secure their support for the monarchist
regime, and the army which was behind that regime.

One of those films was *Mihan-Parast* (*Patriotic*), made by Lieutenant
Deram-Bakhsh in 1953. It falsely portrayed Iran's involvement in the Second World War, as well as her terrible defeat. When a retired army colonel learns that his son has been killed on the battlefield in defence of the
motherland, he asks his son-in-law to join the army and fight for the country, as had his lost son. His son-in-law refuses to join the army, but the
colonel and his daughter voluntarily, join the army and go to the battlefield, where the colonel is wounded and hospitalized. When the son-in-
law learns of this he feels ashamed, and decides to join the army. Soon after
his arrival upon the battlefield, the enemy army is defeated and the motherland is saved. The colonel, his daughter and son-in-law return home
victorious and continue living together as happily as ever.

Nationalism and defense of the Iranian homeland are the nominal
themes of the film, but its real goal was to praise the army for what it never
did, or failed in doing, during World War II. Iran announced her neutral-
ity in the Second World War, but the allied forces needed to use Iran as a
bridge to take supplies and ammunition to the Soviet Union. British forces
from the south and Soviet forces from the north invaded Iran on August
26, 1941, and captured most of the country within 24 hours. They forced
Reza Shah's abdication, turning over the throne to his son, Muhammad
Reza Pahlavi. The Iranian army was a powerful force inside the country
and consumed a great portion of the budget every year, yet it did not resist

the invasion, and within a few hours the soldiers put down their arms and left the trenches.[15] It was a disastrous and shameful defeat for an army that ruled the country with an iron fist. For this reason, the army, after gaining power through the coup d'etat of 1953, inserted itself into theatre and cinema: it needed to reestablish its image in the minds of the people. *Patriotic* is an early example of exactly the sort of film that would result from the government's intervention in the film industry.

Both *Patriotic* and another army product, *Noql-Ali,* despite their sentimental and patriotic stories, were unable to attract audiences and failed at the box office. This formula's failure forced one of the army film producers, Colonel Shab-Pareh, to use seventeen songs in a historical film (*Aroos-e Dejleh,* 1955) in a desperate attempt to attract audiences.

The invasion by the allied forces was not all bad for Iranians. The invasion and the change of the king created a semi-democratic environment, and political parties, intellectuals and artists began to raise their voices after years of repression in an absolute dictatorship. This newfound freedom of speech loosed the creativity of writers and artists, freeing them from the yoke of government censorship. This allowed Iranian theatre to flourish between 1945 and 1952. This period is considered the golden years of theatre in Iran, and came about due to the democratic atmosphere created after the Second World War. Alas, this new political environment did not see similar progress for Iranian cinema, nor did movies flourish, unlike theatre and literature. The Iranian economy was depressed and uncertain, and no producer dared to risk investing in films. Iranian currency, the rial, was so down against other currencies that prospective producers couldn't afford equipment and materials from abroad needed to make films that had any chance at the box office. At the same time, two other factors were inhibiting the growth of Iranian cinema. One was the interest of Iranian artists in theatre, and the other, the uncertainty about the future of the country, specifically whether or not it would fall into the hands of the Soviet Union. For these three reasons, despite the semi-democratic political atmosphere, little of significance happened in the film industry from 1941 to 1948.

It was only in 1948 that a producer and filmmaker, Ismael Koshan,[16] made a film, *Tofan-e Zandeghi* (*The Storm of Life*), considered by Iranian film critics as the first step of Film Farsi or Iranian commercial cinema.

The main characters, Nahid and Farhad, meet at a concert of the National Society of Music and fall in love. Nahid's father is not happy about his daughter's new love, and he forces Nahid to marry a rich man. Nahid's father is a businessman of a certain sort, one who gained quick riches in the unsettled market experienced by Iran after the Second World

War. This quick wealth turns him into someone who judges everything from a financial viewpoint. After his love is forced to marry another, Farhad dedicates himself to his profession and soon becomes wealthy and well-known. In contrast, Nahid's husband squanders everything on his lavish lifestyle. Finally, Nahid leaves her husband and returns to Farhad, and they begin a happy new life together.

On the surface the film is a standard melodrama in both theme and plot: A poor boy and a rich girl fall in love; at first, it seems they're doomed to forever be apart, but in the end, everything turns upside down, the boy and girl are united, and the audience leaves the cinema relieved and happy. But there is a difference between this film and the other melodramas that were produced soon after. In *The Storm of Life* one can see how the story is linked to social situation in Iran at the time. The film portrayed characters and a society that were deeply influenced by the political and economic consequences of the Second World War, the coup d'etat and social uprisings. Melodramas made after *The Storm of Life* had little connection with the realities of Iranian society. The film, however, was a failure both in terms of its box office earnings and artistic values. The film was of generally poor quality, and the acting was exaggerated. There were even fixed frames with no movement at all. The movie had its problems, but it's worth noting that it was made after years of depression in Iranian cinema, and in a financial climate where no producer dared to risk his money in an industry without a promising future.[17] A review, published anonymously in *Etellaat Haftegi* in 1953, noted these very problems:

> *The Storm of Life* was the first Film Farsi, and was shown for thirty-nine nights. This film was produced by Dr. Koshan of Mithra Film. The lack of experience and shortage of equipment hurt the quality of the film so badly that the most optimistic people were convinced that it was still too early for us (Iranians) to make movies. The only person who did not lose hope and did not change his way was Koshan himself.[18]

The use of well-known singers and popular songs in Iranian movies became commonplace because of this film's influence. However, most Film Farsis used these songs in an irrelevant way, while *The Storm of Life* used them in connection with the story and characters. Using the setting of the Music Society as the meeting place of Nahid and Farhad made the use of the songs even more effective.

As the anonymous critic stated, Koshan was not disappointed or deterred by the failure of *The Storm of Life*, and he made his second film, *Sharmsar* (*Disgraced*), in 1950. *Disgraced* has a very important place in the history of Iranian cinema; it became the pattern from which many Iranian films that followed were made. The theme and the plot of *Disgraced*, as well as its commercial elements, such as song and dance and violence, soon were adopted by many Film Farsis.

In *Disgraced*, Mariam is a girl from a village, who is engaged to Ahmad. A man from the city, Mahmood, seduces and disgraces her. She runs away from her village and her family and goes to the city, where she is forced to work in such places as cabarets, which had bad reputations as places for women to work. But she soon becomes a famous singer and secures a good life for herself. Eventually the three, Mariam, Ahmad and Mahmood, come face to face, and Ahmad (who still loves Mariam) kills Mahmood in an act of vengeance. Ahmad and Mariam return to the village, marry and begin a happy life together.

Disgraced was a family melodrama that dealt with the sensitive issues of honor and disgrace in a traditional society, one that felt its values threatened by new, alien elements of Western society. The theme of the film (the clash of cultures), better technique (in comparison with *The Storm of Life*) and especially the use of a famous singer[19] and her songs made the film successful at the box office and provided a model for other filmmakers to follow.

The creators of Film Farsis quickly realized that the use of a few elements ensured success: those elements were song and dance, and sex and violence.

Violence and Sex in Iranian Films

Violence and sex as cinematic staples resulted from the influence of Hollywood, and often they were adapted to the Iranian way of life to better appeal to their audience. At the time, filmgoers came mainly from the lower classes of Iranian society, and were more likely to be unfamiliar with Western cultures.

The Western invasion of Iran in the 1940s brought more than military machines. It also introduced elements of foreign cultures, in particular their films, which introduced Iranians to new lifestyles that sharply contrasted the centuries-old traditional Iranian way of life. One can gauge the speed of cultural invasion in those years by comparing the number of American films shown in Iranian cinemas with the number of Iranian films shown. In 1941, 250 films were shown in Iranian cinemas; of these films, 60 percent were from America, 20 percent from Germany, 5 percent from France and 5 percent from the Soviet Union.[20] By 1950, the American share of the Iranian film market was more than 80 percent.[21] American films were dominating Iranian cinemas, and not surprisingly, their influence upon Iranian films was strong. Sex and violence, common in movies from the West, gradually found a solid place for themselves in most Iranian films through this cultural invasion.[22]

The familiar elements found in American movies were adapted by Iranian filmmakers to suit their prospective audience. First it was in the form of gangs that were mainly in the business of drug trafficking and controlling cabarets and restaurants. The gangs in Iranian films had a completely American appearance because there was no similar tradition in Iranian society. As in American films, the boss wore a grey-striped business suit, had a few hit men around him, and also had a fiancé with hair dyed gold, an exact copy of the blonde women often seen in American films. Both a public engagement and golden hair were unusual in Iranian society, but American films and their Iranian counterparts soon introduced them to moviegoing Iranians. *Yek Ghadam ta Margh* (*One Step to Death*), made in 1961 by Samuel Khachekian, is about a gang that is planning a big robbery. One member of this gang is a young woman (a concept that was completely foreign to Iranians), and the boss also carries a gun (carrying a handgun was not usual in Iran either, even by criminals). In *Faryad-e Nimeh-Shab* (*Cry at Midnight*), made by the same filmmaker in the same year, a young man, Amir, is in need of money to marry Mariam. He cannot find a way other than to join a gang, which is in the business of printing fake bank notes. The boss's fiancée falls in love with Amir, but Amir still loves Mariam and he rejects her advances. The boss finds out about his fiancée's love for Amir, and a fight breaks out among the three. The boss and his fiancée are killed in the shooting and Amir returns to Mariam.

The negative effect of these films had on youth was even acknowledged by the censors, who usually were much more lenient concerning the presentation of sex and violence than they were of any criticism of the political and social system of Iran. On the influence of American films on juvenile crime in Iran, Nilla Cram Cook, who was in charge of censorship, wrote:

> The influence of American films was not limited to the theatre. In 1943 the Minister of the Interior, a jurist and former Prosecuting Attorney, conducted an investigation which demonstrated that many cases of juvenile crime on record in Iran, and many of delinquency, had been inspired by American gangster films. It is perfectly true that these films end on a moral note, but this is a thin apology for the techniques taught and activities suggested to impressionable minds. Under the guise of "crime doesn't pay," audiences and regions in Iran for the first time were being introduced to the existence of an organised underworld.[23]

Iranian gangster films that were heavily influenced by their American equivalents were popular only in the 1960s. The violence, still mirror-

Korechian, Arman, and Fardin (left to right) in *Cry at Midnight*, directed by Samuel Khachekian in 1961.

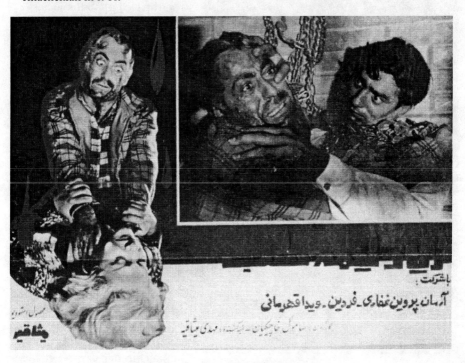

Arman and Fardin in *Cry at Midnight*.

ing the content of American films, still had a firm place in most films in the 1970s. Violence in the work of Iranian filmmakers was presented differently, even if it was directly inspired by American cinema. In most American films, the gun was the favored weapon of gangsters and other outlaws, while in Iranian cinema, in keeping with tradition, the knife was the weapon of choice.

Parveen Ghaffari in *Cry at Midnight.*

Sex did not find its place into Iranian movies as easily as did violence. Iran has been an Islamic society for the last hundred years, and its traditional religious values remain strong today. It was, and still is, hard to show nudity and sex scenes in films. It was only in the 1960s and 1970s, due to the westernization of the country imposed upon the society by the Pahlavi regime, that sex finally began to appear in Iranian films. Unlike violence which was presented in ways very similar to that found in Western films, sex had to be adapted and modified much more heavily in order to be presentable in films. Sex was presented under the veil, or *chadoor*.[24] This is the reason that many Iranian actresses of the '60s and the '70s wore sexy miniskirts, along with chadoors: In most of the films of this period, the actresses waved their chadoors, revealing their naked legs. Sex scenes required a different solution. Iranian filmmakers presented sex in the form of rape or sexual assault of women by the bad guys. One of the first Iranian films that used such scenes, and in which the actress appeared nude on-screen, was *Lezat-e Gonah* (*The Pleasure of the Sin*), made in 1964 by Siamak Yasami. In the film a man rapes a young deaf woman; upon viewing the movie, it is obvious that the rape scene is a flimsy excuse for showing the actress naked. The scene turned the actress, Forozan, into one of the superstars of Film Farsis. In harmony with antireligious policy of the Shah's government, the censor allowed such scenes to remain in the film, and encouraged other filmmakers to use sex in their films as well. Because the rapist was inevitably punished, there was a moral message to the whole that, in the eyes of the censors, made the presentation of nudity in this manner acceptable.

Dance was also used as a device to present sex to the audience. Most Film Farsis had a couple of dance scenes, which usually took place in cabarets or cafés. The dances were presented either as an Arabic belly dance or as Iranian Baba-Karam[25] dance. In both dances, the uncovered body parts of the dancers and their shaking breasts and hips were the central focus of the camera. The art of choreography or the artistic presentation of human movement was never a consideration. In every film these scenes used the same narrative technique: a low-angle camera would show the naked legs of the dancer, and then circle around her while zooming in on different parts of her nude body.

The use of sex in Iranian films reached its peak in the 1970s, when Iranians for the first time saw the naked body of a male actor in *Brehan-e ta Zohr ba Soraat*. Directed by K. Haritash in 1976, this film met with lots of criticism, even from pro–Western critics and audiences. This criticism demonstrated the degree of masculinity in Iranian society. The critics argued that showing the naked bodies of women was not immoral, while showing men's bodies was. In truth, there was no difference in the attitudes of the filmmakers and the critics, as neither had any qualms about objectifying women and using sex to attract male audiences.

Song and Dance

Song and dance entered Iranian cinema through influence of Indian films, and soon became a special ingredient of every Film Farsi. Soon, it was impossible to think of making a Film Farsi without at least four song and dance scenes. The song and dance routines were added to every film regardless of whether they were relevant to the story or characters. A cursory viewing of many of these films makes it clear that most filmmakers used these scenes arbitrarily.

Even though the number of Indian films shown in Iran was considerably less than the number of American films, Indian movies' impact was greater because of the closeness of the two cultures. Especially influential were both the melodramatic structure and the excessive use of music and dance in Indian films.

The characters and the stories of most commercial Indian films, commonly known as Hindi Films, are taken from Indian and Persian traditions. Kathryn Hansen writes:

> Of the many performance sites at which this transformation occurred, the Parsi theatre had the greatest impact on the evolution of modern and regional drama as well as popular cinema in South Asia.... Until the 1870s, the plays were written mainly in Gujarati, the first language of the Bombay Parsis. Their plots were initially based on martial legends from the Persian *Shahnameh*.[26]

Shahnameh or *The Book of Kings* was written by Firdausi in A.D. 994 and is regarded as the greatest epic poem of the Persian language. Many characteristics of its heroes, battle scenes, and its storytelling techniques found their way into many Parsi plays in India, and those plays eventually helped shape the evolution of popular cinema in India. Because of the cultural connections between Iran and India many elements of Hindi films, including song and dance, were more familiar and palatable to Iranian audiences than what they found in movies from countries whose cultures were very different.

In most Hindi films, song and dance is used to express either the sadness or happiness of a character or an event. The same technique has been used in most Film Farsis, although there is a significant difference between the two, which is related to the different place that music and dance occupies in Iranian and Indian culture. In Indian culture, music and dance are regarded as holy forms of art, and have special places in traditions and rituals. In the Islamic Iranian culture, music and dance have been suppressed and banned, for the most part, by religious authorities. The religious restriction presented music and dance from developing and finding a legitimate place in Iranian society. Furthermore, these art forms have been targeted on some occasions as the means of moral vitiation. This attitude prevented the Iranian film industry from using the genre of the musical, unlike Indian cinema. Music and dance in Iranian cinema became solely instruments of entertainment, useless as a means to reflect either the aesthetics or the cultural identities of Iranian society.

The use of songs in Film Farsis did attract more people to the theaters. It worked so well that audiences began to come to the movies to hear the songs and see the famous singers rather than to see the films. After a few years, these films were so successful and preferred by audiences that distributors of foreign films started to use the same technique, hoping to attract even more customers. It was no surprise, then, to see a song by an Iranian singer inserted right in the middle of *Ben Hur*.[27]

Forozan, a popular actress who appeared in many Film Farsis.

Until the 1970s, most Iranian films were black and white, but the popularity of color song and dance scenes in Indian films forced Iranian filmmakers to adapt. They began to film the dancing and singing in color, and would then edit them into the black and white films. One of the first films to use this method was a huge success: *Ganj-e Gharoon*. In the film, a single song-and-dance scene was in color, and audiences flocked to the theater. The leading actress, Forozan, danced and sang in different modes and different costumes, including in Indian dress, to satisfy the tastes of the entire audience. While she was dressed in *sari* (traditional Indian dress), she danced, poorly, imitating an Indian dancer, to a dubbed Iranian adaptation of an Indian song. This film, and in particular this scene, shows the extreme impact that Indian films had on the Iranian film industry, which, with other factors, would mean the loss of a sense of national identity in Iranian cinema.

One of the reasons the audience was so interested in seeing such scenes was related to the socioeconomic background of most filmgoers. The audiences of Iranian films consisted largely of people from the middle and lower classes of the society, and they couldn't afford to go to the cabarets to see popular performers. For some, it wasn't the expense but rather religious conviction that kept them from visiting places such as cabarets. Consequently, the cinemas were a better option for both groups. The songs, dances and reliance upon a melodramatic stories appealed to audiences, but the movies were never a reflection of reality.

Filmmakers used two standard techniques to present singing and dancing in most Film Farsis. In one, they would first film famous singers or dancers in the cabarets where they usually performed, and then edit the scenes into the film simply by having one of the characters go to the cabaret to have a drink or dinner. Delkash and Vigan were among the famous singers who "appeared" in many Iranian films in this way. These two singers grew so popular among cinemagoers that producers soon began to feature them as the star of the movie.[28] Jamileh and Shahrzad were two popular dancers who appeared in dance scenes in many Films Farsis; but would later join the cast of many films.[29]

When leading actors and actresses realized that singing or dancing could make them more popular among audiences, they too started to sing and dance in films, miming the words of the songs. Since all of the Film Farsis were dubbed and most actors' and actresses' own voices weren't used, dubbing the songs did not create any problems. After a while, audiences accepted the dubbing, and many believed that the actors were actually performing the songs. One of the actors who used this method and became a superstar of many Film Farsis was Fardin; he owed much of his popularity to a singer named Iraj, whose popular songs attracted many people to theaters. The actress Forozan, through the voice of the singer Ahdiyeh, similarly gained popularity.[30] The songs were recorded and played during the shooting, and the actors then lip-synced the lyrics. The actors became so dependent on the singers that if for any reason an actor could not engage the services of their counterpart, it could hurt both a film's performance and the actor's popularity.

Even though the Film Farsis have been divided into categories according to subject matter and character type found in the films, all were made using a fixed formula. Each film had a superstar as the protagonist, who became involved by accident in a conflict with a bad guy, and inevitably the hero had to save someone (usually a helpless, young beautiful woman who had been deceived or caught by a villain). The hero would dispense justice with iron fists, delighting the audience. The audiences fantasized about being either the rescuer or the rescued. The formulaic films were always decorated with fight scenes, dancing, singing and one or two characters who provided comic relief vital in such melodramas. Good examples of this film formula include *Ganj-e Gharoon* (The Treasure of Gharoon) and *Raghase Shahr* (The Dancer of the Town). *The Treasure of Gharoon*, made in 1965 by Siamak Yasami, became the most successful Film Farsi and

Fardin, a popular actor of Film Farsis.

consequently was used as the model for many films thereafter.

The movie is about a rich man named Gharoon, who throws himself in a river to commit suicide. A young worker, Ali, is passing by and saves him. Ali takes Gharoon to his house and the two become friends. Gharoon does not reveal his true identity, but instead starts living and working with Ali and his older friend, Hassan, who sells children's toys in the streets. Ali accidentally gets involved with a girl named Shirin. Shirin comes from a very rich family, and she hates the man who has proposed to her. She has no choice but to marry him because her father is after the man's fortune, which in fact doesn't exist because her suitor is a charlatan. Because Shirin doesn't want to marry the con man, she lies to her father, telling him that she

Fardin (top), Forozan (left) and Arman (center) in *The Treasure of Gharoon* (*Ganj-e Gharoon*), directed by Siamack Yasami in 1965.

has been seeing the son of Gharoon, widely considered the richest man in the country. Shirin tells her father that Gharoon's son is coming from India very soon, and that she will introduce him to the family. Shirin temporarily deceives her father and saves herself from being married to the charlatan. She then finds herself in a difficult situation, since she has to introduce someone as Gharoon's son, the heir to a fortune who wants to marry her. Shirin is forced to ask Ali to let himself be introduced to her father as Gharoon's son. At the end, Ali realizes that he is in fact the son of Gharoon;

years ago, before he grew rich, Gharoon divorced his wife (Ali's mother) and kicked both mother and child out of his house.

In this melodrama, the structure and driving elements are based on accident and destiny, and the director is trying to portray two classes of society in stereotypical frames. Shown first is the unhappy world of Gharoon, in which money is everything and success is founded on corruption. Ali belongs to the second world and is a hard-working person with a big heart. In the opening scene, Gharoon, wearing black glasses to hide his sad eyes, is sitting behind a big dining table. The only food on that big table is a piece of toast and a glass of water: due to health problems including high cholesterol, high blood pressure and ulcers, Gharoon cannot have anything else. The obvious cliché relayed by the scene is that money can't

Forozan and Malekmoteai in *The Dancer of the Town* (*Raghase Shahr*), directed by Shahpour Gharib in 1971.

buy happiness or health. This scene is in direct contrast to the one in which Gharoon is saved from the river and taken to Ali's house, where he is forced to dine with people not of his social class. They eat a fatty traditional meal (with plenty of meat and beans and bread), while their songs and dance ridicule the problems of the wealthy — including having high cholesterol and ulcers.

Gharoon, in spite of being the richest man in the country, is unhappy because he kicked his wife and only child out years ago and now he is sick and close to death. He realizes he has no one to take care of him or inherit his wealth. His working-class son, in contrast, seems more fortunate than the father. Ali is a kind person with a happy face; he sings and dances at every occasion, and advises people not to care about the problems of life but to be happy with what they have. This is exactly the happy face presented to audiences by Film Farsi. Movie audiences consisted largely of people of the same social class as Ali, and they found the messages reassuring.

The Treasure of Gharoon, with its simple structure and melodramatic theme, worked as a sedative for audiences that were faced with numerous social, economical and cultural problems. Male moviegoers pictured themselves with Forozan (who played Shirin) in their arms, and imagined that they, like Ali (played by Fardin) might miraculously discover themselves to be the lost heir to untold riches. This is the patent structure and pattern of Film Farsi, and *The Treasure of Gharoon* is a textbook example.

Two factors were involved in the creation of the genre. The first one was the social, cultural and economic confusion that resulted from rapid westernization and modernization of Iran in the 1960s and 1970s. Pouring petro-dollars into the country, the pro–Western government had no understanding of or respect for the traditional values of the people. Because the government had no realistic plan for the transformation, it caused tremendous social upheaval, along with economic chaos. The government's actions, disconnected as they were from the will, wishes and ways of its people, threatened Iran's national identity.[31]

The second factor that shaped the formation of Film Farsi was the internationalization of the cinema. While open borders helped the development and expansion of cinema around the world, in Iran, with its highly traditional society and weak, dependent economy, influences from abroad caused many problems, within both the society and the Iranian film industry. Internationalization in Iran, and the Iranian cinema, was often synonymous with Americanization, and this, in many ways, had a harmful effect on Iranian society. American films opened Iranian popular entertainment to depictions of actions and behavior that, before, would have conflicted with the people's traditional values. Among these were movie scenes with sex, alcohol, bars, cigarettes, and gangs. Concepts like fashion, in the Western sense, were also new to Iranians, where traditional dress was the norm, and a reflection of long-held values.

Film Farsi became the main attraction of Iranian cinema in the 1960s and 1970s, yet nothing to do with the national or cultural identity of the people of Iran. Iran's ancient civilization, the Persian Empire, and particularly its Aryan elements, and the features of Islamic Shi'ism have been the main sources of a sense of national identity in Iran for centuries. The struggle between good and evil, or light and darkness, from the ancient religion of Mazdaism, and the concept of martyrdom from the Shi'a Islamic tradition, reflect the spiritual side of Iranian national identity. Socially and politically, that identity has been bound to a resistance against those who would use absolute power to deny people justice. Economic insecurity has had a profound effect on Iranian national identity, as the traditional structure has failed to create a productive economy with low unemployment. For many, the miracles of life in Film Farsis were similar to the thin hopes to which they clung in order to endure the hardships of daily life. A sense of pride for what they were, a sense of disappointment for what they are today and a sense of hope for the future — not in this world, but in the other — were the main characteristics of the Iranian national identity, and these no Film Farsi could portray. It was only with the advent of a new movement in the Iranian film industry that filmmakers began to express these ideas in their work.

The problem with Film Farsi came not only from its content, which failed to reflect the everyday life of Iranians, but also from the generally poor quality of the work. Even a movie made purely for entertainment, devoid of any social message and lacking any sophistication, can have merit if it is well made. The majority of Film Farsis were made so cheaply that they might be called an insult to their audiences. A Film Farsi usually had a few master shots, lasting up to twenty minutes each, taken through a normal lens in a fixed position, cut with only a few close-ups. There was no lighting for the most part; the source of light in interior scenes was commonly a couple of projectors located behind the camera. As a result the shadows of actors and objects can be seen everywhere. Zooming in was the favored method of getting close to a subject; traveling with the camera, a more sophisticated technique, was seldom used. Poor subjects coupled with poor technique characterized Film Farsi, yet its success with audiences left no incentive for the Iranian film industry to experiment or evolve. The new style of Iranian cinema arose primarily as a reaction to Film Farsi, the dominance of which hindered economic, social and artistic development within the Iranian cinema. The new cinema was not born in isolation, however; it was influenced by other cultural and cinematic movements and influences, including French New Wave, Italian neorealism, and world literature.

II

The Pioneers of
the New Cinema

In most countries, art house and other forms of alternative cinema emerged as reactions against mainstream commercial film industries in connection with a variety of artistic, social and historical movements trends. The same is true in Iran. The *new wave* cinema in Iran, which started in the 1960s and continued until the Islamic revolution, arose as a reaction to the mainstream commercial cinema, the Film Farsi. The new wave was a natural response from filmmakers looking for new ways to express themselves, and to artistically mirror the national and cultural identity of their society. This was unknown in commercial films, which had no agenda other than to mimic commercial American and Indian films and bring audiences into the theaters, never considering the structure of society or its traditions and beliefs. It's worth noting that the Iranian new wave helped mainstream commercial cinema despite being a reaction against Film Farsi. A few directors of the new wave migrated to commercial film production, taking with them the experience and skills gained in the new wave movement.[1] Some commercial filmmakers tried to change their films due to the influence of the new wave. In any case, the first steps towards change were not easy, and at every stage the new wave filmmakers faced many difficulties. These difficulties were due primarily to Iran's faltering economy, and to the cultural background of the audience. The early revolutionary filmmakers were rarely given sufficient budgets to make their films. The producers were not willing to risk investing in films that did not guarantee commercial success. These same filmmakers had to fight the anti-artistic taste of the Iranian audience. Attracted by the action, sex, and melodrama of commercial films, the majority of the Iranian cinema audience (like many other audiences around the world) were unwilling to support films that challenged

39

them with new ideas and didn't conform to their expectations. For these reasons and many more, including censorship and a lack of freedom of expression, early new wave filmmakers were unable to sustain a continuous movement. Flaring like sparks in the darkness, the early works of Iran's pioneer filmmakers would take many years to finally build into the coherent movement now recognized as the New Iranian Cinema.[2]

In the creation of the new wave of Iranian cinema, three people were most influential. As filmmakers, as theoreticians, or as members of government cinematic bodies, these three men had undeniable influence on the movement, becoming one voice in spite of their differences for the wave of change. Farrokh Ghaffari, Abrahim Golestan and Ferydoon Rahnema were artists who defined the new wave cinema movement. Two of them — Ghaffari and Rahnema — were educated in France, and were well acquainted with French cinema, especially the French new wave. The third, Golestan, though he was educated in Iran, had studied the Italian neorealist cinema and was also well acquainted with world literature, being an avant garde novelist himself. There is little doubt that the new wave in Iranian cinema, which is also known as a cinema of the intellect, was generated under the shadow of French new wave cinema and Italian neorealism. The three filmmakers, while differing in attitude and technique, shared a common goal: to work against commercial cinematic forms, and create films that expressed not only new ideas, but also the values and traditions of the society they were portraying.

Farrokh Ghaffari: Shabe Qossi (The Night of the Hunchback)

Farrokh Ghaffari, who went to Europe when he was young and studied in Belgium and France, started to study film seriously in Paris. During this time, he gained practical experience working in the cinema. He also worked as a film reviewer for magazines like *Variety*.[3] He returned to Iran in 1949, where he became an influential figure in the development of Iranian cinema. His most important achievement was the establishment of Iran's Cinematheque. The importance of the Cinematheque is almost inexpressible, as it was there that most of the filmmakers of the new wave were trained, it being the only place where they were able to see a range of films from different countries that were not shown in commercial cinemas. The establishment of the Cinematheque by Ghaffari and his colleagues was a very important step towards the creation of the new types of Iranian cinema.[4]

In 1955 Ghaffari made a short film under the title of *Bombast* (*Dead-end*), with the cooperation of Ferydoon Hovayda, an Iranian film critic and novelist living in France. Next, he made a documentary entitled *Iranian Miniatures*, using the resources in the Paris National Library. This film was the first in a series of documentaries, among which *Ghali-Shoyan* (*Washing Carpets*) was most important, due to its portrayal of a religious ritual known for its theatrical values. After many trips between Paris and Tehran, Farrokh Ghaffari finally settled down in Iran in 1957 and established a movie studio, Iran Nama. Its first production was a feature film, *Jonobe Shahr* (*South of the Town*), in 1956. For a variety of reasons, including improper portraying the image of the police, the film was banned, Ghaffari was denied a license to show the film.[5] After making *South of the Town*, and failing to get it released, Ghaffari devoted most of his time to research and writing about the cinema, and also tried to attain a position in government cinematic bodies. In 1964, he made another film, one that Iranian film critics like Parviz Davai believe to be one of the first important films of the new wave of Iranian cinema.[6] *Shabe Qossi* (*The Night of the Hunchback*), which in terms of form and content was a free and modern adaptation of a story from *One Thousand and One Nights*, soon became one of Iran's most respected films. This provocative work, rooted in the culture and traditions of the society it portrayed, masterfully depicted the various characters and behavior patterns of different Iranian social classes.

In *The Night of the Hunchback*, a hunchback actor who is a member of a Comedia group that performs at private wedding functions in private houses gets a piece of bone stuck in his throat during a meal. The rest of the group thinks he has choked to death, and they all distance themselves from his corpse, each thinking that they may have been responsible for his death. Fear of the police and interrogation grips the small community, revealing each character's true personality. The film appears to be about crime and the police, but it is in fact about the psychology of the society it represents. Investigating the psychological and social behavior of a small community, a microcosm of the greater Iranian society, *The Night of the Hunchback* depicts the life and behavior of an entire society haunted by constant fear of the police. Under the shadow of this fear, people's inner characters come to the fore in the film. Massoud Mehrabi wrote of *The Night of the Hunchback*:

> In 1964 Iranian filmmakers were still busy making low-grade films that deceived their audience, earning enormous wealth but not taking any progressive steps for the cinema itself. The only bright spot this year was *The Night of the Hunchback*, directed by Farrokh Ghaffari. This film was the most important film of the year, and the years to come in Iranian cinema.

The clarity of Ghaffari's modern version of *One Thousand and One Nights* allowed the audience to understand the quality of the life in different classes of society, and the dark and light sides of human behavior.[7]

We can summarize the theme of this film in one word: fear. By taking the camera inside the house and turning it on each individual, using extreme shadow and darkness, and low angle camera shots, Ghaffari portrayed the impact of fear on each character.[8] In an environment dominated by Iranian Film Farsis and imported American and Indian films, *The Night of the Hunchback,* with its realistic portrait of people and their society, showed Iranian filmmakers it was possible to step outside of the restrictions of commercial cinema.

Even though *The Night of the Hunchback* was not successful at the box office — a direct result of the limited tastes of an audience influenced by domestic and imported commercial films— it succeeded in creating ripples in the small community of Iranian cinema. Most critics and filmmakers welcomed the film as a pioneering example of the kind of work they wanted their country's cinema to produce. As Hajir Daryoosh, a film critic writing in the 1964 edition of *Majaleh Honar va Cinema* (*Art and Cinema Magazine*) noted, the film was a good beginning for a new style of Iranian cinema. Daryoosh saw the new movement growing in Iranian cinema as one that could be considered a repudiation of Film Farsi, a new style of cinema with the potential to "be a portrayal of Iranian culture and Iranian people."[9]

The next Iranian filmmaker to shape the creation of the new wave would be Abrahim Golestan, with his film *Khasht va Ayineh* (*Mud-brick and Mirror*), made in 1965.

Abrahim Golestan: Kasht va Ayineh (Mud-brick and Mirror)

Abrahim Golestan was an Iranian novelist who learned about films largely by viewing foreign films, especially the films of Italian neorealism. He spent most of his career making documentaries, all the while accumulating the experience and skill that would influence his feature films.

In 1956 Golestan established the Golestan Film Studio, in which he made most of his documentaries, and in 1962 he began his first feature film, *Chera Darya Tofani Shod?* (*Why Did the Sea Become Stormy?*), which remained unfinished. In 1965 he began — and this time completed — his second feature film, *Mud-brick and Mirror,* in which he had an indelible presence as scriptwriter, director and producer. This film has since become one of the most talked about films in Iranian cinema, and many critics believe that it should be considered the first true Iranian new wave film.

In *Mud-brick and Mirror*, an unknown woman leaves her newborn baby in a taxi and vanishes. The taxi driver, Hasham, a middle-aged man without a wife or children, must enlist the help of his lover, a woman who works in a nightclub, because the police will not accept the baby until Hasham can prove it is not his. Hasham has no choice but to ask his lover to care for the child. The woman (who is unnamed in the movie) has always wanted a baby, accepts the child, though Hasham refuses to let the baby into his life. Here the audience can see how the woman opens herself up, showing her inner desires, while the man resists, keeping his true self hidden, living in isolation. The woman is burning to have a lover and a true relationship. The man, though he is clearly searching for the same, resists his own will and rejects the idea of accepting the baby and starting a permanent relationship with the woman. Because she is caring for the baby, Hasham's lover has to move in with him. This baby becomes a reason for these two, man and woman, to enter a new stage of life, to test each other and their relationship. Both lonely and without hope, wanting affection and love but not knowing how to find it. Finally the woman, defeated, has to hand the baby to the police and resume her life of loneliness, as the man is not ready to break his isolation and move forward towards a new life.

Mud-brick and Mirror, with a very simple story that was completely different from anything found in commercial Iranian films, displayed a refined cinematic technique that exhibited the knowledge and experience of the director. The film, like *The Night of the Hunchback*, was warmly welcomed by critics but failed at the box office. There is no doubt that this film exhibited some of the characteristics of Italian neorealist films. Like many Italian films, for example as *The Bicycle Thieves* or *Umberto D*,[10] *Mud-brick and Mirror* used a mixture of professional actors and real people. The honest faces of everyday, real people, working in harmony with the on-scene locations in which the film was set and shot, gave the movie a distinctly different flavor that was new to the Iranian cinema. Most of *Mud-brick and Mirror* was filmed outside of the studio in locations such as the bazaar, Justice Court, and city squares. Using skills acquired from making documentaries, Golestan captured the true sense of the places and the people existing within them without resorting to fabricated naturalism. Also, as with many of the neorealist films, *Mud-brick and Mirror* had a very simple story. A baby is left in a taxi and the taxi driver is forced to take care of it for a while. Using this simple storyline and plot, Golestan was able to portray the characters and their behavior in an effective manner. The film has long sequences of dialogue, but through the simplicity of the story and by closely examining the true feelings of the characters and realistically portraying their internal existence, Golestan takes the audience into the characters' inner world, keeping the dialogue from becoming boring. Mohsen Seif echoed this idea:

> The whole story of the film takes place in a closed, restricted time and place which is shown by long shots. The dialogues, especially between man and woman, are many and long, but because of the quality of being close to poetry, the powerful language does not create disinterest or boredom. Apart from this, the masterly visual structure and the precision used in the composition of every frame makes Mud-brick and Mirror successful in connecting with its audience, and in transferring its message to them.[11]

Mud-brick and Mirror is a psychologically realistic film, which is in many regards in line with what Zavattini has called the manifestation of neorealism in cinema:

> There must be no gap between life and what is on the screen.... I want to meet the real protagonist of everyday life.... Neorealism has perceived that the most irreplaceable experience comes from things happening under our eyes, from natural necessity.[12]

If fear was the theme of The Night of the Hunchback, loneliness through existential isolation was the theme of Mud-brick and Mirror. This loneliness, and ultimately the pessimism it induces, is shown through the eyes of both the man and woman, allowing us to see their different perspectives. In the eyes of the man there is no escape from isolation, while for the woman there is still a chance and hope for escape. The man is like a piece of brick and the woman like a mirror, and when the two come together they ultimately destroy each other. While the mirror exists, so does the reflection of the brick within it; when the mirror is broken the picture of the brick ceases to exist.

The third artist who was instrumental in the creation of the new wave of Iranian cinema was Ferydoon Rahnema. He participated in this movement mostly through intellectual debates about cinema, and also through his influence as a member of government cinematic bodies, where he assisted young filmmakers inspired to participate in the new movement.

Ferydoon Rahnema: Siavush dar Takht-e Jamshid (Siavush in Persepolis)

Rahnema studied film at the University of Paris, where he wrote a thesis titled Realism and Film in 1957.[13] He was also a poet, writing most of his poetry in French rather than Persian. When he started to make his own films the influence of poetry on his productions was apparent. Moreover, it is not just the language of Rahnema's films that is poetic, their structure and style also share a deliberate poetic quality.

Rahnema is considered one of the founding patrons of the *Cinemayeh Azad* (Free Cinema),[14] a movement followed by many young filmmakers who created artistic, low budget films on 8 mm stock. Many filmmakers of the new wave began their careers as participants in this movement, joining the new wave after early success with 8 mm films.

The first film made by Rahnema was the documentary *Takht-e Jamshid* (*Persepolis*) which was made in 1961; it was a poetic film about the great palace of the Persian Achaemenian Empire that was destroyed by Alexander the Great. Of *Persepolis*, Hamid Sho-aei wrote:

> In this film we see how a great empire is established, and how it is destroyed. War caused the creation of such great empires and also was the cause of their destruction. We (Iranians) who built the great empire of Achaemenian with many consecutive wars, and extended the Iranian borders to Greece, Egypt, and other lands, behaved like a lion that wanted to crush the rest of the world with his claws. All of a sudden, however, we too became so weak that others came and did the same to us. In *Persepolis*, Rahnema's camera, after depicting war and peace, shows us the ruins of gates, columns, and steps for a long period of time.[15]

Unlike other documentaries that tried to produce postcard-like pictures of palace ruins, Rahnema disrupted the accepted historical and archeological perspective of this site. He delved into its history to represent an empire unable to stand against the wave of time. In Rahnema's view, though the past was glorious, what remains of that past lies in ruin. The most important message in Rahmena's film is that it is useless to console ourselves with our glorious past.

Rahnema returned to Persepolis once more in 1967, this time using it in the feature film *Siavush dar Takht-e Jamshid* (*Siavush in Persepolis*). The plot of the film was based on two sources, one being the epic poem *Shahnameh*, and the other the ruins of the palace itself. The film depicts the conflict of Ahriman and Ahura Mazda, the gods of darkness and light, who are symbolized through a war between Iran and Turan, according to Iranian mythology. In the film, the martyrdom of Siavush[16] becomes a symbol of Iran herself, and can be considered to signify purity, justice, and light.

Siavush escapes the court of his father, the King of Iran. He does maintain his innocence by avoiding the corruption of his father's court. He then seeks refuge at the court of Turan, Iran's enemy. However, in

Turan Siavush finds no escape; as in the court of Iran, the devil dominates Turan. Siavush is imprisoned, and eventually the people of Turan kill him. His blood is shed upon the ground: According to legend, a plant sprouted from his blood—called "the Blood of Siavush," the more it was cut, the taller it grew.

Siavush in Persepolis, which has a theatrical structure and was influenced by the performance style of religious rituals, is unlike any other Iranian film on the same subject, particularly in terms of its context and historical perspective. The film received mixed reviews from critics, some praising it for its originality and portrayal of the essence of Iranian culture, history, and thought, while others criticized it as an intellectual product that could not connect and transfer its messages to an ordinary audience. One of the critics who praised the film was Nasib Nasibi, who wrote:

> The technical skill of Rahnema is evident in this film in his ability to mix mythology with reality, without using the common flashbacks of today's cinema. Rahnema uses an Eastern, mystical, directorial technique that has been taken from our heritage. One of the important aspects of this film is, therefore, a clash of mythology and reality, as it mixes past and present through the character of Siavush. The technical superiority of *Siavush in Persepolis* lies in the fact that the beauty and the history of Persepolis does not remove us from the film. This is because Persepolis acts only as a connection with the construction and destruction of the film's central character…. *Siavush in Persepolis* is an expression of an Iranian mind aware of the problems of the culture and history in his country.[17]

Siavush in Persepolis explores the idea of immutable destiny. Siavush seems to be unable to escape the destiny that has always awaited him, and thus it is not important whether he is living in the court of his father or in the court of Turan. He has to be a martyr for history to be written. It seems as though Siavush, and people like him, come into this world to bear the pain of a purposeful destiny, while others come instead to oppress, or to be oppressed. This theme is felt throughout the film, portrayed beautifully by Rahnema through each frame.

In spite of many debates and much controversy surrounding the film in Iran, when it was screened in Paris it was welcomed warmly by audiences and critics alike. The film won an award at the Locarno Festival in Switzerland for its advancement of cinematic art. The success of the film outside Iran allowed Rahnema to make his second feature film, *Pesar-e Iran az Modarash bi Khabar ast* (*The Son of Iran Does Not Know His Mother*) in 1976. This film was in some ways related to Rahnema's previous two films; the three films form an Oedipus-like trilogy in which fate or destiny is the main theme.

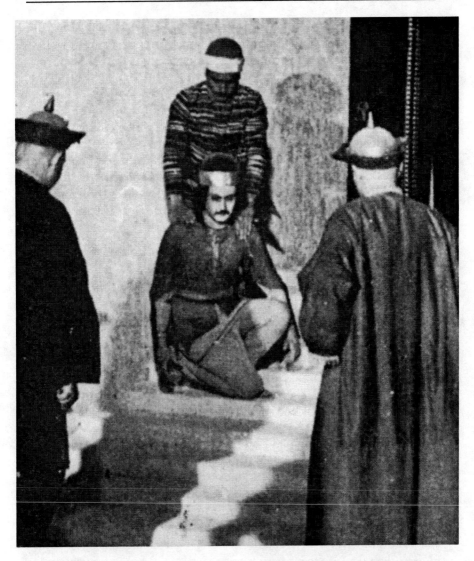

Jiyan, Moghadasi and Sozani in *The Son of Iran Does Not Know His Mother* (*Pesar-e Iran az Modarash bi Khabar ast*), directed by Frydoon Rahnema in 1976.

In *The Son of Iran*, a theatre director wants to stage a play about Iran during the Parthian period (256–224 BC). This period in Iran's history followed its defeat by the Greeks in 330 BC. The Parthian government was a mixture of Iranian and Greek representatives, generating a homogenous cultural identity. In other words, Iran was losing her identity through the influence of an alien culture, and this was one aspect of the film's narrative. The other side was the story of the director himself, who experienced the same problems of identity in modern Iran. Unlike most of his friends and the people around him, the director wants to rebel against the Western culture that was attracting many Iranians during the 1970s. Here again we see two cultures confronting each other. The director was trying to discover and preserve his own identity while those around him forgot themselves, their identity dissolving in an evolving culture heavily influenced by the West, a changing culture not truly Iranian. In this film we can see that Rahnema is again portraying the ideas central in his first two movies—a search for an identity that has been lost, and the constant sorrow or nostalgia, that overtakes the characters through their unsuccessful attempts to remain true to, or to discover, a sense of who they are.

Rahnema believes that by recognizing the past we can understand the present, and better know what awaits us in the future. He shows that some people ignore the reality that surrounds them, and by not understanding the present they are denying their past. The movie's beautifully filmed sequence of scenes in the museum portrays a reconnection with the history of civilization, the history of art, and the history of Iran. As the young director searches through the museum, he slowly travels through the thousands of years of history surrounding him, at the same time filling the historical atmosphere with his heart, blood and skin, bringing together the past and the present. The camera shows the viewpoint of the director in this scene, and in essence becomes the character; it seems to want to smell every object, to touch it, to put one piece beside another. Then we see the director exit the museum and step into a noisy world of hardship, iron, and machines. He goes to a newspaper stand and buys a newspaper, the headline reading "The Son of Iran does Not Know Who His Mother Is." This headline "falls like a hammer on our head and tells us how we are unaware of what we are, unable to think and live as Iranians."[18]

In all three films Rahnema followed the theme of a search for national and cultural identity.[19] We should not forget that Rahnema made these films while Iran was quickly becoming westernized. The modernization—or westernization—of the country, with the help of money coming from oil production, left nothing intact. Western dress, western music, western foods, and finally western thought were prominently apparent in most of Tehran's streets.[20] Rahnema saw this new invasion and recorded it with his camera. His use of the past to portray what was happening today was, in part, a choice made to avoid censorship. He knew that the censorship board would not allow him to depict the cultural invasion by the West and the loss of Iranian identity in his films, as the government of the time was promoting and supporting such change, so he used the past in these films in order to reflect what was happening in the present. He skillfully linked the past to the present in this film through the device of the theatre director who is staging a play about the past. Rahnema expressed his love for Iranian culture in an interview:

> We need a cinema in this country which is built on our culture, philosophy and our traditions, we must have a cinema which is able to take what it needs from our literary and cultural sources. A glance at the literature of this country shows us what rich sources we have to portray.[21]

A national cinema based on Iranian history, culture and traditions is exactly what Farrokh Ghaffari, Abrahim Golestan and Ferydoon Rahnema himself were looking for. They wanted a cinema that could use its resources and techniques to portray the values of the society in which they lived. This ideal national cinema, dealing with issues like who we are, where we live and how we live as Iranians, would be a mirror of Iranian society, even though its techniques used and the equipment required to capture the images of Iran on film were from elsewhere.

The interest in the culture and literature of Iran shown by the filmmakers who took the first steps in creation of a new Iranian cinema, their documentary experience, and a familiarity with world literature and film, helped Iranian cinema take the first step toward a realistic style, and that realism was requisite in the creation of a truly national cinema. Ghaffari, Golestan, and Rahnema started their careers making documentaries and knew how to use the camera to capture real faces and real moments in life. With films like *The Night of the Hunchback*, *Mud-brick and Mirror* and *Siavush in Persepolis*, they introduced Iranian society to a different approach to moviemaking, and fostered the development of a new Iranian cinema.

III
The New Cinema
Before the Revolution

The year 1969 is considered a landmark year for the New Iranian Cinema. After the years of experimentation by filmmakers like Ghaffari and Golestan, in 1969 three filmmakers would release films that had a profound effect on the development of the new Iranian cinema. Audiences were introduced to a type of movie divergent from the commercial Film Farsi through Dariush Mehrjui's *Gav* (*The Cow*), Masoud Kimiai's *Qasar*, and Naser Taqvai's *Aramesh dar Hozor-e Digaran* (*Peace in the Presence of Others*). Though they shared the desire to create a different, more artistic form of cinema in Iran, the filmmakers and the films were ideologically and artistically different. The new genre established by these films, finding form from the seeds of Ghaffari, Golestan and Rahnema, has attracted both critical and popular attention, and the films and their influence greatly contributed to the creation of a truly Iranian national cinema.

The Cow was the first film to point towards an important new direction in Iranian cinema. *Qasar* is considered to be somewhere between the new genre and the product of Iran's commercial film industry. Although *Peace in the Presence of Others* was made in 1969, it wasn't until 1970 that it was shown at the Shiraz Arts Festival — and was banned immediately afterwards, and not shown to the public until 1972. Unfortunately, when it was released to the public it had been so heavily censored that the main structure of the film was lost, the result being unrecognizable and difficult to understand. Consequently, this film did not have the same impact of *The Cow* and *Qasar* on the new movement. However, it definitely had a great impact on those who saw the film during its original screening. These three films marked the birth of a new genre in Iranian cinema, which later came to be known as the New Wave. This movement flourished and continues to survive today despite various difficulties, and now holds a respected place in world cinema. When *Tameh Gilas* (*Taste of Cherry*), directed by Abbas Kiarostami in 1997, received the Golden Palm at the Cannes Film Festival, it was clear affirmation of the continuing influence of these earlier films.

Dariush Mehrjui: Gav (The Cow)

Dariush Mehrjui first studied film at UCLA, in 1961, but he left the course, dissatisfied with the heavy influence of Hollywood on the class as a whole, and on the structure that students were being taught to use in movies.[1] He went on to study philosophy at the same university, and in 1966 returned to Iran to pursue his interest in cinema. His intention was to make films with a different attitude, look, and purpose than those already being produced in Iran. His first attempt was *Almas-e Siose* (*Diamond 33*), which was made in 1967 and released in 1968. This was a ridiculous imitation of the James Bond films, and was so badly made that instead of creating the kind of suspense and tension that defines the genre, the farcical result made the audience laugh. A taxi driver fell in love with a European woman, who later was revealed to be a very dangerous spy. Mehrjui himself spoke about this first unsuccessful experience in cinema: "This film was only an attempt for me to join the professional cinema at that time."[2] If we accept this we cannot criticize *Diamond 33* further, as the film exhibited none of the talent of the filmmaker behind it. But when, in 1969, Mehrjui picked up the story of *The Cow*, he chose well; the result was a film that is recognized as one of the best examples of Iranian cinema. With *The Cow*, Mehrjui proved he wanted to make films that had a serious purpose. *The Cow* was based on a story written by Sa'adi, then one of the most famous Iranian playwrights and novelists. The story had already been made into a stage production and most of the dramatic elements in the film already existed, and this, along with Sa'adi's popularity, contributed to the movie's success.

Mash Hassan, from the village of Bail, owns the only cow in the village; the cow is not only the source of his income, but is also the life of the whole village. The cow is so important to Mash Hassan that he takes care of it as if it were the most precious thing in his life. One night while Mash Hassan is away in the city, a few people from the nearby town of Blori attack the village, and the next morning the cow is found dead in its stable. Grief dominates the whole village and the people do not know how they can tell Mash Hassan when he returns. Finally, they decide that they should bury the cow in the square and tell Mash Hassan that the cow had escaped. When Mash Hassan returns, he cannot believe what the people tell him. He goes to the stable, and when he returns, Mash Hassan believes that he *is* the cow. All the efforts of the people to heal Mash Hassan, who is now living in the stable and eating straw like the cow, are unsuccessful, and finally they have to tie him up and take him to the city for treatment. But on the way to the city Mash Hassan tears the ropes like a mad cow and escapes, only to drop from the mountain into the valley below.

The film portrays a number of ideas and themes to the audience through Mash Hassan's metamorphosis into a cow.[3] The economic dependence of the village relies entirely upon Mash Hassan's cow, and this perhaps is symbolic of Iran as a country, which was and still is totally dependent on the production of oil. If the production of oil for any reason stopped, Iran's economy would collapse. This is one of the subtextual meaning of Sa'adi's story itself, though the film perhaps uses the symbol more effectively. In the film the cow is a symbol of life for the village as well. When the cow is alive, there is life in the village, and with her death grief captivates the people and they no longer know what to do with themselves. The cow is a symbol of the social being of the village, it is the dignity and the grace of the village and its people, it is the foundation of their existence, and without it they are lost. The film also shows how religion and religious beliefs have been turned into superstitions; these superstitions dominate everything in the village, including the characters' behavior, their actions, and their reactions. Through the metamorphosis of Mash Hassan, the film explores the psychology of human consciousness—the metamorphosis reveals the psychology of this small community, which has been created and shaped by the economic, religious, and social factors. The people of the next village, those who kill the cow, are portrayed as mysterious, and can be interpreted as more than just hostile and jealous neighbors: they could represent another country hostile to Iran, or they could be mysterious forces from within the village itself. The important thing is that they have been portrayed in such a way that we see that the people of Mash Hassan's village stand helpless against their threat. The other village is like a shadow that gradually comes and engulfs the life of the villagers, who instead of standing against the threat try to hide or run away. We feel a mysterious and dreadful force living among the people of the village, which creates a building sense of anticipation and tension among the audience. It seems laughter and hope do not exist in this society, that fear and tears are what they are used to living with. All these elements contribute to the movie's structure, creating a kind of surrealism

Ezatollah Entezami in *The Cow* (*Gav*), directed by Dariush Mehrjui in 1969.

that is rooted in metaphysics and mythology, imparting a highly mystical atmosphere throughout the film.

The Cow was released in 1969, and unlike most of the earlier films of the new wave, it was not only well received by critics, but also by Iranian audiences. This in turn did much to fuel the progression of the new Iranian cinema.

The film begins with silhouette pictures of Mash Hassan and the cow, showing from the beginning their mutual dependency. At the same time, the sound of bells creates an atmosphere of fear. The camera then moves along the village, showing the mud houses and the villagers, who seem, through the manner of the photography used, as if their faces have been engraved on the walls of mud. From the beginning, each image tells a story of fear and dreadful anticipation. During the scene when Mash Hassan returns from the city, we see how he goes to the pond and fills a bucket and then goes to the stable, when one of the villagers tells him that his cow has escaped. Instead of showing an exaggerated reaction or asking for more information, we see only the bucket of water drop from Mash Hassan's hands and the water form a trail on the thirsty dust. This kind of picture visualizes — instead of narrating — Mash Hassan's reactions and emotions. This visualization is employed in many parts of the film through its use of symbols. In this manner the original literary story has been changed into a visual story. Parviz Noori wrote of some of *The Cow*'s cinematic qualities, and its place in Iranian cinema, in a review:

> The beginning scene of the film shows pictures of the broken faces of the villagers, and Mash Hassan who, like always, is washing his cow by the river (which is presented as a kind of sexual union between the pair). The composition of Mehrjui's pictures are exact and expressed to show the central theme of the film. Although there is a kind of abstraction in the aesthetic of the film the director is very sensitive when portraying the film's environment and inhabitants.[4]

Similar views on the film were expressed by foreign critics who saw *The Cow* at different festivals, including the Film Festival of Chicago in 1971, and the Festival of Venice (1971), praising the film as a simple heartbreaking tragedy. Tom Milne wrote in *The Observer*:

> *The Cow* at first glance is a naturalistic picture of village life, hostility, tradition, and all those common issues surrounding the primitivism of the life of these people. A sense of impending tragedy dominates the whole film, especially when the hero of the film sits on the roof of the stable in mourning, and looks at the night's sky and stares at it until he comes down and becomes the cow. This satanic possession is so dark and so frightening.[5]

The theme of the film and its narrative is hard to explain without considering the angles from which the Iranian audience perceived it. The metamorphosis involves many factors, and features social, religious, economic and psychological elements. *The Cow* is a film of multiple voices or multiple visions, and as the Iranian critic H. Kavosi has stated, if we perceive the film based upon the relationship between the cow and Mash Hassan, the social and economic perspectives come to resemble those of *The Bicycle Thieves* of De Sica, which portrays how the dependency of man on his tools determines his existence.

With *The Cow* Dariush Mehrjui opened a new window for the Iranian cinema by not only presenting a story from Iranian literature, but also through his use of technique and narrative. Scenes, shot, composition, camera movement, lighting and performance all function in harmony with each other, giving Mehrjui's creation a cinematic voice that speaks more than the literary language of the story.

After the success of the film inside and outside Iran, Dariush Mehrjui's activity in cinema became continuous, finding, in a sense, a cinematic style for itself. *Aghayi Haloo* (*Mr. Simpleton*, 1971), *Postchi* (*The Postman*, 1972), and *Dayereh Mina* (*The Circle*, 1976) are three films that show the evolution of Dariush Mehrjui's cinematic narrative. In these films Mehrjui investigated the inner contradictions and conflicts that people experience within themselves and with others. In *The Postman*, Mehrjui returned to the theme of metamorphosis, this time of people in a city environment. Mehrjui has never distanced himself from philosophy in his films. All his characters have problems, philosophically, both with themselves and with others. They cannot understand themselves, something necessary if they are to be understood by others. Because they are unable to confront the realities of their lives they are pushed more and more toward isolation and the comfort of their own minds, but even there they cannot come to terms with themselves, and these contradictions create a kind of philosophical disappointment that, sadly, dominates the characters' lives. Through close-ups we can see this sadness in the depths of the eyes of Dariush Mehrjui's characters, and the dust that blankets them, within as well as without.

The Islamic revolution of 1979 stopped the cinematic and philosophical evolution of Dariush Mehrjui. For a few years confusion and misunderstanding regarding the place of cinema within the revolution were prominent. The new regime had no cultural policies, and filmmakers like Mehrjui either had to stop working or to emigrate. Mehrjui chose the second, though he soon realized that he couldn't live or work away from his homeland, and he returned to Iran. After a few years he succeeded in making *Ajareh-Neshinha* (*The Tenants*), in 1987. This is regarded as his first important and serious film after the revolution, even though it was a comedy. This was followed by *Shirak* in 1989, and *Hamoon* in 1990.

In general, if we want to categorize Dariush Mehrjui's films as pre- and post-revolution, it might be said that in his films before the Islamic revolution social and psychological concerns dominated, whereas the films made after the revolution dealt primarily with philosophy. This evolution, moving from the social and psychological to the philosophical aspects of the characters, was made because of the revolution and the resulting censorship, which did not allow filmmakers to deal with social issues in any obvious way. This pushed Mehrjui and artists like him toward an isolation that ultimately bound them more to philosophy and questions about being and the nature of existence, affording them sanctuary from the stifling political environment. In this regard, *Hamoon* most effectively presents Mehrjui's philosophical concerns. Despite much controversy among critics, this film was well received by the people, and is the most important film that Mehrjui made after the revolution.

As noted, changes in Iran after the Islamic revolution compelled intellectuals and artists like Mehrjui to use philosophical modes of expression rather than risk crossing the ill-defined boundaries of what the new regime considered acceptable. After the revolution, social life was restricted. Mehrjui addressed a number of issues in films like *Hamoon* besides larger questions about life and the nature of existence: the closure of cafes and restaurants, some of the primary meeting places for artists and intellectuals, and the abolition of artistic meetings; the impact of a slow and depressed economy; the psychological effects of a long war with Iraq that took the lives of many Iranians (and consequently drove the country to a state of mourning); and the harsh censorship that severely restricted filmmakers. In the film, Hamid, the main character, is in a critical economic, social, and psychological situation. He is forced to turn inward, to an introspective soul-searching journey that takes him from his youth, ultimately, to his death. He experiences death in this spiritual journey, and his character, in the movie, eventually does die. Illusion and reality wrestle in this film, and Hamid goes more and more into the depths of his life, in search of answers to his questions. In his mental, philosophical turbulence he turns inside out, sounding the depths of his being, and at the end he and the audience are left with the tension of unanswerable questions. This film can be read as being about the Iranian intellectuals displaced by the Islamic revolution, their values and way of life in contradiction with the values propagated within the revolution itself. For Hamid and intellectuals like him the question is whether the years of revolution were a

Khosroo Shakibai in *Hamoon*, directed by Dariush Mehrjui in 1990.

dream, or a reality that they experienced in a dream-like state. F. Nasir Muslim writes:

> Hamoon represents thousands of intellectuals who are in conflict with themselves and in this everlasting conflict are asking who they are, what they want, where is the solution, and hundreds of other like questions. The souls of these individuals are sad, their minds are turbulent, and they are all captives of impatience. They suffer, they escape, they yell and they rebel. In dreams they are looking for the meaning of their existence and they hang between tradition and the progress of time. They neither have the ability to go nor to stay. They are uncertain and they are exhausted.[6]

Although he made *The Cow* in a village and the film dealt mainly with the psychological and social aspects of its characters, Mehrjui gradually brought his camera into the cities and chose mostly middle-class men and women who still were struggling to reconcile tradition and the new values of an urban lifestyle. After the revolution, Mehrjui gradually left middle-class citizens and moved toward the elite men and women of the society, who were not only in conflict with social and cultural aspects of the revolution, but also with their own status. This progression clearly shows Mehrjui's artistic and intellectual development as a filmmaker.

Masoud Kimiai: Qasar

Although some Iranian critics, including H. Kavosi,[7] believe that the film *Qasar* was made in the tradition of Iranian commercial cinema, many others, including N. Daryabandari,[8] believe that *Qasar* is a good example of a movie that drove and influenced an improvement in the quality of commercial films. This is a continuation of the argument that some of the filmmakers of the new wave had an impact on commercial cinema, bringing a quality to Iranian film that would otherwise not have existed. *Qasar* and Kimiai should not be placed completely or unconditionally in the new wave movement, nor should they be recognized as only Film Farsi. This film and this filmmaker properly belong somewhere between these two forms of cinema, and helped to bring more people into the cinema while improving the artistic taste, awareness, and appreciation of Iranian audiences.

Masoud Kimiai, like Dariush Mehrjui, started his filmmaking career with an unsuccessful effort, *Biganeh Biya* (*Come Stranger*) in 1968. With his second film, *Qasar*, and many other commendable films produced later, Kimiai has found for himself a solid place in Iranian cinema.

Kimiai made *Qasar* in the pivotal year of 1969. During this year attention given to higher quality cinema led to the growth of what would be recognized as a new, national cinema within Iran, as demonstrated by the critical notice generated by the release of films like *The Cow* and *Qasar*. The latter film improved popular commercial cinema and for the first time Iranian audiences accepted more artistic and intellectual films, making the new movement successful on a popular level. Although *Qasar* was made in the tradition of Film Farsi, using the same character archetypes of violence and street life that dominated commercial cinema, the difference was that Kimiai's view, and the technique of presentation in the film, made *Qasar* superior to the standard Film Farsi genre. In fact the manipulation of recognized archetypal characters shows both Kimiai's talent and his sense of timing for bringing more people into the cinema, thus introducing them to a film that had superior cinematic qualities. The combining of the two types of cinema and the introduction of the movement to a broader new audience could be considered as the greatest achievement of Kimiai.

The story of *Qasar* takes place in a suburb south of a town that is struggling between tradition and modernism. This community is struggling on the one hand to keep its traditional values, such as family closeness and religious practice, while on the other hand it cannot resist modern influences, especially the modern order of life observed by the local police (as opposed to the town elders who once maintained authority). Farman and Qasar are two brothers who have accepted this new order and put away their knives; however, Qasar, the younger brother, still harbors some of the anarchic, rebellious attitudes of his peers. In this context the knife is the traditional weapon for vigilantes (as per Iranian archetypes), and is recognized within Iranian tradition as a symbol of aggression and crime. The peace and order generated by the new way of life are suddenly disturbed when Qasar and Farman's sister is raped by one of the suburb's vigilantes.

In this film, Kimiai is portraying a number of themes, the first being the confrontation of tradition and modernism. Through this he portrays moralistic or traditional characters alongside those who do not have any respect for morality. This was manifested by filmmakers at a time when this kind of confrontation could clearly be seen in Iranian society itself. In Iran, the sixties was a decade in which the society was forced to turn its back on what it was and step from an old but traditionally accepted frame into a modern world, without time to digest the transition. Consequently, the society and the people of Iran were confused and confronted one another, a fight that ended, in many cases, in death. *Qasar* created a new type of hero in Iranian cinema, a kind of anti-hero.[9] The Iranian anti-hero (contrary to the heroes of the Film Farsi, like Fardin in *The Treasure of Gharoon*) had a nihilistic attitude toward life, and acted like an anarchist who wanted to stand alone against power, force, law and tradition. Consequently, these anti-heroes could not win their battles and were crushed, though their confrontation and their fight, defiantly ending with death, became a sort of legend that the audience could respect and enjoy. *Qasar* no doubt contributed most to the development of this new kind of anti-hero, which later became one of the most dominant character types in Iranian cinema.

The third point Kimiai clearly made in this film was through the use of Iranian tradition and ritual, which were fading in the face of modernism. By reviving these traditions and rituals in the movie, Kimiai gave his film a folkloric quality.

Qasar begins and ends with death, so it could be said that it is a tragedy from beginning to end. The film has an epic quality, reinforced by the use of nature to propel the narrative. Qasar, the main character of the film, has all the qualities of an epic hero, the most important of these being his willingness to confront death in order to defend his principles. This is a well-known issue in Iranian history, religion and culture. *Shuhadat*, or martyrdom, is the core motive for not only historical Iranian heroes, but also modern Iranians, driving them toward a tragic destiny. Qasar stands and fights, though he knows that the final result will be his death. He kills and ultimately is killed; this confrontation with destiny would have been familiar to Iranian audiences. Siavush, a mythical hero, was martyred because he rebelled against what he could not hope to defeat. But deep down, these heroes knew that their death would be their victory. The theme of *Qasar* is martyrdom, which can be distinguished from revenge because martyrdom entails the implicit knowledge of one's own impending death.

The film begins with a brilliant scene at a hospital, showing the shocked and worried faces of the people within. Fatima, the daughter of a loving family, has committed suicide by poisoning herself. For Farman, her brother, who still believes in the religious and traditional values of the society, the news of the suicide is doubly shocking, because suicide is outlawed by Islam. When the family is informed that she committed suicide because she was raped, the moral implications of her manner of death fade in the light of what has become an unbearable tragedy. Fatima was raped by Mansor from the Ab-Mangol family and because of this she killed herself. Her two brothers, Farman and Qasar, now adopt the heavy burden of revenge. Because Qasar is working in another city, Farman is bound to carry out the revenge alone. However, Farman has performed the ritual pilgrimage to Mecca, and promised God not to pick up a knife again. Weaponless, he goes to exact revenge for his sister's rape and death. Bare-handed, Farman begins to fight with the brothers of the Ab-Mangol family. The brothers have no moral aversion to striking someone from behind, and this is exactly what they do, killing Farman. Now the family has to face two deaths. In fact, the film really begins at this point. The younger brother, Qasar, arrives, and unlike Farman, Qasar has not fully removed himself from a life of fighting. He is young and quick to take up a knife, as his emotions overcome his judgement. When he fights the Ab-Mangol brothers, Qasar shows more cleverness and cunning than Farman, and kills three of the brothers, hunting them down one at a time. The first murder takes place in the public baths. The tension and fear of this scene is heightened by the way it is edited; we see the naked bodies of people who are taking showers, the sharp blades of employees who have to shave the patrons of the bath house, and the water which washes blood into the drain. Qasar does his job while Karim (one of the brothers) is under the shower. The camera is positioned over the shower and it is mostly Karim's hands that we can see, clawing the tiles of the bath as he is being stabbed by Qasar.

This first fight gives Qasar the smell of blood and propels him toward his second hunt. Qasar finds Rahim in a slaughterhouse, and the audience can see the blades that slaughter animals, and the blood that is left behind. Qasar slaughters Rahim among the corpses of lambs, and we can see Rahim's blood, rather than the lambs,' pouring onto the floor. After this, there is one more death expected by the audience, that of Mansor, the brother who actually raped Qasar's sister. But here, Kimiai cleverly enriches the suspense through a subplot in order to heighten the atmosphere for the final tragic scene of the film. Before his sister's rape, Qasar had promised to take an old woman working in his house to the holy city of Mashad to perform her religious pilgrimage. Qasar knows that he will not return alive from his encounter with Mansor, so he first fulfills his promise to the old woman. Taking the old woman to the holy city is also an excuse for Qasar to purify himself before his final task. He might want to ask for forgiveness for what he has done and what he is going to do. The scene is shot in the shrine, with Qasar sitting outside waiting for the woman, but the flight of doves around the building connects Qasar with the shrine, conveying a sense of innocence despite deaths for which he is, or will soon be, responsible. After this purification, all is ready for the final encounter. Qasar returns to find Mansor in an abandoned train depot, where the wreckage of trains creates a sense of death and decay. We see the sharp blades of knives in motion and both characters receiving wounds. Mansor drops on the dust and dies while Qasar, bleeding and struggling, takes himself inside an abandoned train car. This is in the tradition of the epic, where the hero, or the antihero, must die alone to complete the tragedy. This is the end of Qasar's story, but not the end of the film. Due to government strictures, the filmmaker was compelled to take certain measures when portraying someone who takes justice into his own hands and does not recognize the power of the police. Consequently, all of sudden, a policeman arrives from nowhere and shoots Qasar, imposing order and demonstrating the power of the justice system. However, the audience recognizes that Qasar had done his job, and the story was over well before the police arrived.

As we said, *Qasar* is a quality film. For the first time a movie portrayed the character types audiences who favored commercial films wanted to see, coupled with a high standard of production and performance. *Qasar* made better use of the elements found in commercial films, but which were always produced badly in Film Farsi. It was a notable film because, for the first time, the Iranian audience could see and feel something that was traditionally close to them, although it could be claimed that the movie had modeled itself on Western films in terms of production and technique. In the film, the tradition of being moral is presented and praised, but at the same time is questioned in a society that no longer respects these traditions. The film raises the question of whether anyone can live correctly in a society that is no longer good, or whether anyone can ignore the new order. *Qasar* questions the new way of life presented by the capitalist system, which threatens the moral and social foundations of a traditional society. Farman has sworn not to take a knife in his hands, but when confronted, for this reason his fate is to die. In *Qasar* Kimiai is able to raise serious questions within a commercial film, keeping the interest of the audience without using the song and dance of Film Farsi. In this way, Kimiai was able to create a new style for Iran's cinema, bridging artistic and commercial film. No doubt, this was the most suitable approach to bring Iranian audiences into the movie theaters and introduce them to a more intellectual and artistically orientated style of film.

After making *Qasar* and finding a respectable position in Iranian cinema, Kimiai attracted producers who were interested in this new style, and made a series of films which were built around the concept of the antihero: *Reza Motori* (1970), *Dash Akol* (1971), *Baluch* (1972), *Khak* (The Earth, 1973), *Gavaznha* (The Deer, 1975), *Qazal* (1975), and finally *Safare Sangh* (Journey of the Stone, 1978). Even though these films are sometimes quite different, all follow the same themes that Kimiai had presented in *Qasar*. Resistance and fighting, even at the price of death and destruction, dominate these films. Kimiai's anti-heroes are sometimes people who rebel because of family honor and traditional beliefs (*Qasar* and *Baluch*), and sometimes they are people standing against power and the system because of social and political values (*The Deer*). All of them are able to defeat their enemies through solid determination and their own death, putting an everlasting spell (politically) on their enemies through their nihilistic martyrdom.

After the Islamic revolution, Kimiai continued to make films. These were *Khat-e Ghermez* (*The Red Line*, 1982), *Tigh va Abrisham* (*Blade and Silk*, 1986), *Sorb* (*The Lead*, 1989), *Dandan-e Mar* (*Snake Fang*, 1990), *Gruh-ban* (*The Sergeant*, 1991), and *Sultan* (1997). Even though these films, like most of his pre–Islamic revolution films, display some artistic values, none of them is as challenging as those made before the revolution. Perhaps this is partly the result of harsh censorship established after the revolution that did not allow Kimiai and other filmmakers to portray rebellious, anarchic anti-heroes because they were in sharp contrast to the Islamic values of the new regime. We know that most of these anti-heroes also embody a kind of anti-moralistic attitude. Living alone, having casual affairs with women, and drinking and smoking were among those habits cinematic anti-heroes could not possess after the revolution, by government dictate. No character could stand against the religious order of the society, and without this important element, Kimiai was unable to make the bitter, tragic films of his pre-revolution period. Kimiai had to compromise his earlier style in order to keep making movies, and he started making films that were all only shadows of the previous ones.

Naser Taqvai and Peace in the Presence of Others

Naser Taqvai was a novelist from the south of Iran (Port of Abadan) who wrote and published his short stories in literary journals. With this experience he migrated to the capital in 1967 and began working as a technical assistant in the Golestan Studio. It was there that Taqvai became familiar with the production of documentary films, making a few educational documentaries and, in the process, learning filmmaking techniques as well as developing an interest in the real images and situations of the Iranian people, which later became one of the main strains of his feature films. Even in his short documentary *Taxi Meters* (1967), which he made for the Roads and Traffic Department to introduce the new phenomenon of taxi meters to Iran's taxi drivers, Taqvai showed his ability, going beyond

Said Raad in *The Red Line* (*Khat-e Ghermez*), directed by Masoud Kimiai in 1982.

the educational purpose of the film and with every shot showing the problems these taxi meters were causing drivers and their passengers, turning this film into a picture that depicted the problems of real people.

After making these educational documentaries, Taqvai moved to another style of documentary, which mainly dealt with the cultural aspects of life. In these pieces he showed the traditions and rituals of the Iranian people, but Taqvai went beyond merely photographing traditions, instead making films about the function of tradition in relation to society. Two of these documentaries which have been widely shown and discussed are *Bad-e Jiin* (1969) and *Arbai'in* (1970).

Bad-e Jiin is about the ritual of *Zar*, which has been practiced in the south of Iran for many years. This ritual, which originally was brought to the Persian Gulf by African slaves, became combined with local traditions and beliefs and evolved into the dramatic ritual of Zar, used to cure an imaginary disease caused by the winds. This "disease" was mainly associated with poverty and its psychological and social side effects. According to belief, there is a variety of dangerous winds that come from the sea and possess those who are vulnerable, making them sick. The cure is to conduct a ritual managed by a shaman (called *Babazar* or *Mamazar*). In the ritual, the sound of drums and the smoking of a special plant which has intoxicating effects, as well as the presentation of gifts to the shaman, cast out the wind and the patients recover. Of course, in many cases this does not happen, and those affected by the malady actually become mentally and psychologically disabled by it.

The film begins with background pictures of a stormy sea and the voice of the narrator saying "Zar is a type of wind, and the winds are evil and mysterious forces who wander the sky of the south like Genies, like ghosts, and like illusions. To escape from their everlasting wandering, these winds are always poised to possess the poor of the south." Then the narrator speaks of a city which has been closed by the people and turned into a cemetery. The camera travels over graves and broken doors and windows until it reaches the house in which the patients of this disease are suffering. The sound of drums is heard as a woman goes from house to house inviting the afflicted to attend the performance of the ritual. An old man is sitting in a corner of the house shaking his body in harmony with the sounds of the drums. White windows, which are beautiful and simple, and the locks upon each door, signify and symbolize the mentality of this old man. Through the presentation and editing of the images Taqvai shows the ruined souls of the people within the ruins of the city. This is a documentary where one can easily see the domination of image over narration. M. Jafari, a film critic, wrote of Taqvai's documentaries:

> *Arbai'in, Mashhad Ardehal, Bad-e Jiin*, and *Nakhl* are among Naser Taqvai's documentaries that could compete with any of his current feature films. In particular *Bad-e Jiin*, in which Naser Taqvai is keen to show the psychological and inner world of the people through images and words. Despite most of the domestic documentaries which are made in the Ministry of Culture and Art, with their emphasis on the construction of buildings and the years the buildings were made — Naser Taqvai in his documentaries was able to go deep into his characters' soul, something many Iranian filmmakers before him were unable to achieve.[10]

Taqvai, with this background in literature and documentaries, stepped into the world of feature films and made his first feature, *Aramesh dar Hozor-e Digaran* (*Peace in the Presence of Others*), in 1970. This film is considered one of the first examples of new Iranian cinema by many film critics, including H. Bani-Hashemi, who wrote that the film was "a brave search for opening a broad intellectual horizon in Iranian cinema."[11]

The screenplay was written by Taqvai and was based on a novel by Golam-Hussien Sa'adi.[12] Sa'adi was mentioned before, in the discussion of *The Cow*, the first film of the new wave; this novelist was an important presence in the formation of the new wave, showing how Iranian literature of the 1970s had a particular influence on the formation of a new direction in Iranian cinema.

The story is about the life of a retired colonel who had gone to a village to farm chickens so that he can spend the rest of his life in peace. The colonel has two grown daughters from his first wife, who had died years before, and these two daughters live and work in Tehran as nurses. The colonel marries a woman the same age as his daughters and lives with her in the village, but after a while he gets bored with village life and decides to return to the city, where he can be closer to his daughters. However, when he returns to the city, he finds out that life is not the same as it was when he left. Many things have changed, including his daughters, who have grown up working and now live a carefree existence. The colonel, who once was able to run and manage a barracks, now is not able to even control his own family. Here we can clearly see the conflict between two styles of life and two mentalities, between two systems of social life. This conflict exists within the colonel himself and between the colonel and his new environment, including his daughters. It infects the family so deeply that it ends with the elder daughter committing suicide and the younger daughter marrying a very unsuitable man. Finally, the colonel himself is admitted to a mental institution. At the end the only thing left for him is the pure love of his young wife, whose role is more that of a mother to him than a wife. Naser Taqvai explains:

> There was something mysterious in this story which drove me to select it. Mystery not as it has been seen in detective films, but mystery or atmosphere which could be perceived, like a destiny which cannot be explained but only felt. Fortunately this atmosphere — I mean that mystery which has been communicated within the film — is captured. When I used to write novels myself, I always tried to create such an atmosphere. In the film one can feel that there is always something unknown. It is the same in the original story. It seems as though people are carrying a secret which they hide from each other.[13]

One can easily perceive that the atmosphere of the film is dominated by a secret or a mystery. Although we can see this secret reflected in every character within the film, it is felt most in the connection between the colonel and his wife, and to understand this secret one must examine every scene and every character.

We begin with the colonel himself. In one of the first sequences of the film his character is revealed to the audience, to a degree. It is morning. The colonel goes into a café and starts to drink vodka. Intoxication helps him revisit the past and lets him live with his glorious memories of that time. He starts walking in the street alongside a row of trees that, to him and to the audience, look like a line of soldiers, which the colonel salutes. The sound of a military band along with close-ups of the colonel's steps portray the feeling of a man made into a phantom, a shadow of what he used to be, through melancholy and alcohol, a man who is not able to understand or adapt to his new situation. This includes not understanding his daughters, instead considering them as soldiers who have to obey his orders. The unanswered question throughout the film is: Why has the colonel turned into this mentally ill person who drinks excessively and is plagued by nightmares? What is he trying to forget through alcohol, and what is the cause of his continual nightmares? There is no question that this is the secret that drives the film, permeating its entire atmosphere and every characterization. One interpretation is that the answers can be found in the colonel's profession. There are very unclear hints in the film that he used to work as a security officer in the secret police, this within a regime notorious for some of the most brutal and violent secret police in the world, responsible for jailing, torturing, and killing many intellectuals and opposing citizens. This might be helpful in understanding the colonel's secret and why, after retirement, he escaped to a village and tried to busy himself by working on a chicken farm and marrying a young woman outside his class, and also why he drinks so much and is plagued by nightmares. Throughout the film the relationship between the colonel and his young wife gives the impression that the two share an understanding of something of which they do not want to speak. Is it possible that the colonel has revealed to her the cause of his nightmares? And is this perhaps the reason that we see the young wife taking care of the colonel more like a mother taking care of her son? To know the colonel we should go a step further and discuss his daughters and why they started to live a carefree existence. It is obvious that the daughters have grown up in a barracks rather than a house. When they find the opportunity to step outside the barracks, they do so in an extreme and rebellious way. The only links the colonel still had to his old life were through his daughters, and when these are broken, the shock sends him to a mental institution. Even in this dark, hopeless, helpless environment the filmmaker does not completely eliminate hope, and he opens a small window at the end of the film through which we can see the light behind. This is seen in the last sequence: the colonel is in a hospital bed, and shattered glasses, which might have been broken by the drunken colonel, cover the floor. But when we see him for the last time, he opens his eyes, sees his young wife sitting beside him, and he asks her for a glass of water, not alcohol. This could be interpreted as a change in the colonel — not in terms of recovering or getting back to his life, but as his release into death. For the colonel, death is freedom, and through asking for a glass of water the colonel's life is symbolically ended. This connection is found in an earlier scene in the colonel's house: the maid is going to slaughter a chicken for a party, but first gives it water to drink. Giving water to animals before slaughtering them is a long tradition in Iran and the audience is given a very clear sign of the end of the colonel's life when he asks for the same thing. Although the filmmaker does not depict the colonel's death, the colonel is no doubt taking his last breath and is released, not from death, but from the horrible life which was like a torture chamber for him.

In any discussion of *Peace in the Presence of Others,* several factors should be considered, including Taqvai's background as a novelist, which gave him the ability to add his own literary quality to Sa'adi's story; the fact that the story itself provides such magical atmosphere; and the impact or the effect of Golestan's *Mud-brick and Mirror,* with its neo-realistic style, on Taqvai, who himself worked on that film as a crew member. These factors, as well as Taqvai's background in documentaries dealing mainly with the psychological aspects of characters, helped make *Peace in the Presence of Others* one of the most important political and psychological films of Iranian cinema. Taqvai stated that:

> *Peace in the Presence of Others* is the only real political film of our cinema.... In his novel Sa'adi does not show clearly that the colonel was working in the secret service, but one could see this in my film. This colonel, after retirement, has gone to a town to seek peace. Now he has returned to his house in Tehran where his two daughters are living, and he feels that it has become a brothel. The daughters are the product of the discipline that he himself imposed on society. I could not portray these things any more directly than I did in the film at that time.[14]

Peace in the Presence of Others was screened for the first time in 1970 at the Shiraz Arts Festival, and despite being very well received by the audience and critics, was immediately banned. Showing an army (or secret service) colonel who was an alcoholic and who could not control his family, and who has constant nightmares, at a time when a commander of an army was respected like a king was a dangerous undertaking for any director. The army was the most important institution in the country and was consuming most of Iran's budget, and criticizing the army was like criticizing the king himself. Consequently the film was banned immediately, though it had a lasting effect on the small number of audience members who saw it at the festival. Almost all of the reviews that were written about the film bespoke the promise of the coming of a brilliant ilmmaker to the Iranian cinema. This was a film that in both content and technique was far ahead of even the best Iranian films of the time, such as *The Cow* or

Qasar. K. Pour-Ahmad wrote, *Peace in the Presence of Others* is an extraordinary work, even a masterpiece. Taqvai means to show the corrupted and boring life of a group of people from our society and to leach out the corruption and ugliness. Taqvai is the first in our national cinema to portray such original and such provocative content, and is able to compete at the level of international films.[15]

After *Peace in the Presence of Others*, which earned him a very good reputation, Naser Taqvai gave up making documentaries and started to make only feature films and television series, with one exception, the short film *Rahaie (Freedom)*, which he made in 1971. *Sadeq Kurdeh* (1972), *Nafrin (Curse*, 1973), and the television series *Daie-Jan Napoleon* (1973) were among Taqvai's works made before the Islamic revolution. Although feature films like *Sadeq Kurdeh* and *Nafrin* could not compete with *Peace in the Presence of Others* and were mostly directed toward a commercial audience, we can see even in these films the mark of a filmmaker who understands the language of cinema and makes films that are definitely different from the usual products of commercial cinema. The television series of *Daie-Jan Napoleon* has been recognized as one of the most well-made television series during the period before the Islamic revolution, and was also one of the most successful.

Naser Taqvai, like many other filmmakers, had little opportunity to work for a few years after the Islamic revolution. In 1982 he started to make the television series *Kochak-e Jangali*, but after shooting only a few episodes Taqvai was replaced by another director who was endorsed by the new establishment. Despite this failure, and despite constant rejection of his scripts by government authorities, he finally succeeded in making his first post-revolution film in 1987. *Nakhoda Khorshid (Captain Khorshid)* was one of Naser Taqvai's dreams, as he himself has said. Aside from Taqvai's beautiful documentaries and *Peace in the Presence of Others*, *Captain Khorshid* is Taqvai's best-made film, and one of the best Iranian films. In this instance, Taqvai used all of his experience and knowledge to make a beautiful — and very Iranian — film from a story written by Ernest Hemingway. In fact, *Captain Khorshid* was based on two stories that were very similar to each other. In part the movie was based on a real Captain Khorshid, who lived in the south of Iran. Taqvai knew about him and his life, as he himself was from that part of Iran. Captain Khorshid's profession was the illegal transportation of Iranians who wanted to find a job in the Emirates States of the Persian Gulf. During one of his trips, the wooden boat was caught in a storm and he lost his way. Because of this, and a lack of food and water, the passengers revolted; in spite of this he finally succeeded in taking the boat to Kuwait, but unfortunately it was spotted by

Parvaneh Maasomi (above) and Dariush Arjmand (below) in *Captain Khorshid* (*Nakhoda Khorshid*), directed by Naser Taqvai in 1987.

the coast guard, which shot and sank the boat. The second story, which Taqvai used and mixed with the first, was from "To Have and Have Not" (1937), by Ernest Hemingway. In Hemingway's story, Harry Morgan is a lonely man who works on his boat smuggling liquor, illegal immigrants, and Cuban revolutionaries even though he has only one hand. The isolation and bitterness that surrounded Harry Morgan made him a very tough,

Hejazi and Pour-Samimi in *Captain Khorshid*.

cold, and pessimistic man. Taqvai mixed these two stories together and wrote his own script, which has something of each story but as a whole is not like either. *Captain Khorshid* is an example of a film adaptation that used two stories, one domestic and another universal, to create a film with a strong national character.

The theme of the film is the struggle to survive, and the idea that one should stand and fight, even at the price of death. This fight could be against the rolling waves of the sea, against a group of people who want to abuse one's rights, or against a political and social system. This is what Taqvai presents in *Captain Khorshid*, and the theme has something to do with the filmmaker himself — he always wanted to make quality films, but the powerful authorities would not allow him to do so. His best film, *Peace in the Presence of Others*, was disliked by the Minister of Culture and Art of the old regime (the Pahlavi dynasty) and was banned, and his TV series *Kochak Janglai*, upon which he spent years and years preparing the text and production, was taken from him by people who were connected within the new regime (the Islamic Republic) and wanted to make it themselves. We can see the reflection of this life in Captain Khorshid's character. G. Rabihavi wrote that "In my belief Naser Taqvai, after years of silence, with *Captain Khorshid* shows that he is still one of the best Iranian filmmakers. We can say that his latest film is also one of his best, because in this film he clearly has employed the cinema to serve the cinema, and not to serve anybody or anything else."[16]

Taqvai's most important contribution was to introduce and to use various indigenous cultural aspects of Iran in his films, because in commercial Iranian cinema different parts of the country were continually misused and presented improperly. Taqvai's films were the first to present the culture and traditions of the South of Iran, allowing people in other parts of the country to understand that culture and its people, and to get an impression of the other cultures that existed in various parts of the country. As well as being a good filmmaker, Taqvai pioneered the introduction of Iran's different cultures through its national cinema. In other words, Taqvai was a filmmaker searching for an encompassing domestic language for the Iranian cinema.

Bahram Bayzai: Ragbar (Downpour)

Bahram Bayzai started his literary and artistic career in the theatre and made his first feature film, *Ragbar (Downpour)*, in 1971. By this time he was already a well-known figure in Iranian theatre and had published a number of important works, including *Namayesh dar Iran* (*Theatre in Iran*, 1963), *Namayesh dar Japan* (*Theatre in Japan*, 1964), and *Namayesh dar China* (*Theatre in China*, 1969). Bayzai was interested in traditional forms of Iranian theatre as well as the theatre of the East. Having no formal education, he learned about theatre and cinema by observing and analyzing films and theatrical productions. He wrote a few scripts for short and feature films, all except one denied approval by the Ministry of Culture and Art as they were "cultural and too sophisticated"![17] In 1970 an organization for children and youth, Kanoon-e Parvaresh-e Fakri Kodakan va Nojavanan (K.P.F.K.N.), invited him to make *Amo-Sibilo*, which was based on a short story by F. Hadayatpour. This short film, only 29 minutes long, attracted the attention of audiences and film critics when it was screened at the International Festival of Children in 1970. *Amo-Sibilo* was about an old man and the group of children he watched playing soccer in a vacant lot attached to his house. He is upset about the noise they are making, but after constant protests that produce no results, he finally capitulates, becoming used to the noise. However, when the children break the window of his room, the old man becomes angry and punctures their ball, violently driving the children away from his home. After a while, when the children no longer come to play, he gradually comes to feel a loss, sensing an emptiness in his life, so he buys a ball and lets the children play once more. He stays to watch them — the ball drops at his feet and he kicks it, again breaking the glass in his window.

Amo-Sibilo shows an old man's loneliness and need for others, using the simple language necessary for children's films. Along with very clear pictures full of meaning and a manner of editing that served the theme of the film, the natural acting from the children, which could hardly be found in Iranian cinema at that time, showed that *Amo-Sibilo* was directed by someone with a great deal of potential. *Amo-Sibilo* paved the way for Bayzai's film career. The following year, 1971, he made his first feature film, *Downpour* which is one of the best Iranian films, earning a place alongside *The Cow*, *Qasar*, and *Peace in the Presence of Others*. The film had a very solid script and an excellent cinematic technique, and in terms of acting, no other Iranian film of the time could compare.

A young teacher named Mr. Hakmati is transferred to a suburb south of Tehran. Viewers are introduced to the social and psychological structure of this small community through their reaction to the arrival of a strange man in their midst. Among the people in the town is a dressmaker who feels that she is above her neighbors and claims that she used to work in the north of the city for upper-class clients; a butcher who, when in love, has a heart sharper than his knife; and finally, a young girl, Atefeh, who is working for the dressmaker, her little brother in the new teacher's class. Soon rumors form in the school that the new teacher is in love with Atefeh, and Mr. Hakmati is forced to go and see Atefeh to explain, to tell her that the rumor is untrue. Strangely, during the meeting he cannot tell her anything except that he *is* in love with her. The butcher, who is also in love

Maasomi (left) and Fanizadeh in *Downpour* (*Ragbar*), directed by Bahram Bayzai in 1971.

with Atefeh, comes forward and stands against the teacher. Atefeh is indeed in love with the teacher, but at the same time she cannot ignore the butcher and all he has done to support her and her family. Just as the teacher is about to be accepted by the community, an order arrives transferring him to another suburb. Despite being in love with him, the girl decides to stay for the sake of her young brother, and Mr. Hakmati, who came to the neighborhood as a stranger, leaves as the same stranger.

Other than Golestan's *Mud-brick and Mirror,* which portrayed the role of women not as shadows but as equal to the men in the film, *Downpour* was the first Iranian new wave film to give a new dimension to the role of women. Atefeh is a deep, strong woman who supports her brother and sick mother by working in a dress factory. She knows that she is loved by both the butcher and the teacher, but she also manages to control and conceal her own feelings. The director seems to be portraying love ambiguously, as a subterranean presence within the woman's eyes. With the characters and the film, Bayzai rejected common cliches; the woman rejects marriage to the wealthy butcher and also rejects the teacher's requests to leave with him. She stands, she is determined to resist, perhaps to gain something hidden from the audience's understanding. At the end, the audience is left wondering what Atefeh is really looking for, and what really connects her to the place and to its atmosphere when she had both wealth and love open to her. Although the teacher is supposed to be the mysterious character of the film, a stranger about who little is revealed, the true mystery of the film is what Atefeh is hiding in her mind and heart.

When the teacher arrives his belongings, including a precious old mirror, are carried by a man wearing dark glasses. It is clear that the man's job involves more than carrying other people's possessions. At the end of the film, the same man again takes the teacher's belongings and goes away. We never learn who actually issued an order to transfer the teacher to the town, and who called for him to leave. It seems that a mysterious force, perhaps a social system, brings the man to this town so that we, the audience, can know the woman. The teacher's character remains undeveloped and mysterious. It seems apparent that the filmmaker was not interested in providing answers to some of the film's questions, leaving the audience in doubt about the situation and giving the film both a symbolic and political dimension. One possible interpretation of the man with dark glasses is that he is a member of the secret police, and the teacher represents the intellectuals who were sent into exile. This interpretation overlooks the quality of a film that goes beyond the political, and deals with complex metaphysical and metaphorical ideas that give the movie a religious subtext.

It has been argued that most of Bayzai's films and characters represent the search for one's identity. This cannot be said of *Downpour*, as there is no attempt by any character to achieve self-knowledge or to understand the meaning of their existence. The film instead explores the question of what it means to be accepted and to accept.

The tone of *Downpour* is bitter, a tone common to most of Bayzai's films. The characters carry a mythical and historical bitterness into a modern environment. If there is laughter in Bayzai's films, it is mostly based on ridicule. Occasionally, Bayzai generates true laughter in his films, often when the characters are either drunk or hysterical. In *Downpour* the teacher and the butcher, two rivals, get together and get drunk; they start to punch each other, to laugh together, and end up crying together. H. Azadivar writes:

> The hero of *Downpour*, Mr. Hakmati, is not a type but an archetype that has always existed in Iranian history. He too, like Amo-Sibilo, was a stranger. He was Iranian but he was not fit for Iran; a young man with a secret past, a few photos of his ancestors (like Amo-Sibilo), a full-body mirror, a candelabra he has inherited from his mother, and a few religious icons. He is a simple man with no ambition who wants to live, who wants to be useful, who wants to but does not belong to his environment. Whatever he does, he remains a stranger. Something, a mystical force, or stronger hands do not allow him. Something apparently traditional and cultural, some unwritten law, always presents obstacles for him, and the same secret force, in mythical disguise, comes and takes him away.[18]

Downpour was a good beginning for Bayzai and an important step for the new wave in Iranian cinema. The filmmaker explored inner and outer realities and dreams, showed unmasked and masked faces, broken pictures through broken mirrors or multiple faces through cracks in mirrors, and modern and mythical characters using the simple story of the love of a teacher and a girl who works in a dress factory. *Downpour* was also well received outside Iran. John Russell Taylor, in *The London Times*, described it as "a beautiful film ... with a very human and sympathetic view."[19]

After *Downpour*, Bayzai began to make a series of films which took him deep into realms of metaphysical and mythological representation, becoming more interested in these ideas and also attracted by attention it generated among film critics, but at the same time losing his relationship with the audience. *Gharibe va Meh* (*The Stranger and the Fog*, 1973) was one of Bayzai's least successful films, as its theme was a repetition of ideas Bayzai realistically and richly portrayed in *Downpour*. The same theme was lost and confused; the movie alienated the audience with its separation from social realities. This also made the film unnecessarily un–Iran-

Shojazadeh (right) and Maasomi in *The Stranger and the Fog* (*Gharibe va Meh*), directed by Bahram Bayzai in 1973.

ian. It is obvious that *The Stranger and the Fog* was greatly influenced by Japanese films, in particular *The Seven Samurai* by Akira Kurosawa. The basic storyline of the film is the same as that of *Downpour*: A stranger comes and wants to stay but cannot, or is refused, and is forced to leave still a stranger. Even though a few critics have called the film "complicated," the complication of the film is not in content or technique, but in its collage of all sorts of unreal elements that have no connection whatsoever with the Iranian audience or with Iranian culture.

Bayzai was able to make two more films before the Islamic revolution, both significant in Iranian cinema — *Kalagh* (*The Crow*, 1977), and *Cherikeh Tara* (*The Ballad of Tara*, 1979). As mentioned before, the Islamic revolution halted most activity in the Iranian film industry — there were several years of confusion, pressure, and disappointment, when no place could be envisaged for filmmakers like Bayzai. After years of success making movies, Bayzai turned again to the theatre and wrote and directed a play, *Margeh Yazdegard* (*The Death of Yazdegard*) in 1979, which he succeeded in turning into a film in 1981, marking his return to the cinema. Other films made after the revolution were *Bashu, Gharibeh Kuchak* (*Bashu, the Little Stranger*, 1986), *Shayed Vaghti Digar* (*Maybe Some Other Time*, 1988), and *Mosaferan* (*The Travellers*, 1992), among which *Bashu* has the reputation of being Bayzai's best post-revolution film. Many Iranian film critics, including D. Moslimi, considered this film not only Bayzai's best, but one of the best Iranian movies made after the Islamic revolution. Moslimi writes, "*Bashu* is the most effective of Bahram Bayzai's works in connecting with his audience. This quality of connection is the result of a few factors. One is its immediate social reality of the emigration (displacement) caused by the war, the second a representation of the main source of the war, and thirdly, an honest visual presentation and a realistic interpretation of the war."[20]

In *Bashu*, a city in the south of Iran is in the midst of being destroyed by the bombs of Iraqi forces; a driver weaves his truck among the bombs, trying to save himself. He stops for a moment to check his tires and a dark-skinned ten-year-old boy, who had hidden himself in a bush, throws himself into the truck and hides. The next day the boy opens his eyes to see that the truck is moving along the roads in the green fields of northern Iran, an area quite different from the dry and hot south. The boy hears workers discharging explosives to make a tunnel. This reminds him of the bombs of the war, and he throws himself out of the truck and hides on a farm. After a while, a village woman named Nai finds the boy hungry and shaking. She tries to talk to him, but he cannot understand her because they speak two different languages. The boy is from the south and mainly speaks Arabic, the woman is from the north and speaks Ghilakee. The boy follows the woman, and during the night he goes into her house to escape his fear. Nai attempts to ascertain who the boy is and what he is doing there using gestures and signs. The boy starts to tell how he had lost his family in the war, but of course she doesn't understand him. The arrival of the little stranger in that village causes curiosity and suspicion because his skin color is not like their own and he speaks a different tongue. The children of the village begin to bother him and Nai is forced to come to his defense. Gradually, the boy finds a place for himself in her house as her husband has left the village for the city to find work. The boy gradually learns enough of the local language to be able to communicate with Nai. Her husband returns to the village and these two "men," the boy and the husband, come face to face as rivals, as there is room enough in the household for only one of them. In a conflict between Nai and her husband the boy comes to her defense, wielding a stick; the husband, impressed, agrees to accept the boy into their home. The boy drops the stick and asks to shake

Soosan Taslimi in *Bashu, the Little Stranger* (*Bashu, Gharibeh Kuchak*), directed by Bahram Bayzai in 1986.

the husband's hands, but the man has no right hand. The wife says that the boy can be the right hand of the man. The three of them then go to fight with animals that have attacked the farm.

Bashu, as Moslimi has pointed out, was well received by both critics and audiences, and was Iran's best film of 1985. According to the Australian Film Institute distribution release, the film was "a pure joy in which there are absolutely no false moves."[21]

The background for the film is the eight-year war between Iran and Iraq, a war the effects of which Iranians felt in every aspect of their lives. Thousands of people were killed, and many more were displaced and forced to live in unfamiliar sections of the country. For many of these people, the hardest struggle was to be accepted and to start a new life, and the boy in Bayzai's film provides a very visual and clear symbol of that displacement. He suddenly finds himself in a totally unfamiliar environment, nothing like the one he was raised in. The dry, hot south of Iran is exchanged for a green and rainy environment and the language is different, making him a stranger in his own country. This was also a central theme in *Downpour*, where even though the teacher was from the same country, when he was forced to live in a new community he became a stranger and needed to adapt to the new conditions. This idea can be found in most of

Bayzai's films, as if Bayzai himself is trying to say that *he* is only a stranger in his own country. It could be also interpreted to mean that his country has been captured or occupied by strangers, and that he now feels estranged, as if he no longer belongs. The structure of *Bashu* seems to be a continuation of ideas used in *Downpour*. Unlike *The Stranger and the Fog*, the symbols in *Bashu* work within the film's narrative framework, resulting in a unification of realism and symbolism. The audience has no problem understanding the story, identifying with the people and with the atmosphere of the film. Beautiful images with beautiful composition, excellent editing and acting, the masterly use of two different dialects and languages within the film all make *Bashu* into a harmonious and brilliantly visual film. It shows the tragic consequences of war on those who cannot escape what they have not caused. Although in the film the husband is supposed to have gone to the city to find work, the images tell us that he has actually gone to the war, returning without his hand. Because of censorship the filmmaker was not allowed to show this in an obvious way. *Bashu* does not deal directly with the war and cannot be considered a war film, but it is unquestionably one of the best portrayals of life during that long and devastating conflict.

It is interesting to note that in Bayzai's films, as the place of the woman becomes more important and the woman stronger than the man, male representation becomes weaker and loses its importance. In *Bashu* this progresses to the point that the man in the film only appears in the last sequence. Bayzai's women are mysterious, strong, manipulative; they can easily draw men toward them and make them slaves, torturing them and enjoying torturing them, and finally rejecting them. In fact, Bayzai's women always play a very dangerous game with men which ultimately ends with the men's defeat and humiliation. In *Downpour,* we see the teacher turning his head toward the girl while he was leaving, almost demanding, but the face of the girl shows no reaction or emotion. In *The Stranger and the Fog,* again we see the same situation when the stranger gets into a boat and the woman refuses to go with him. In *The Ballad of Tara* again the woman chooses not to leave with the man. All these women are doing their best to attract and enamor men, and then they cruelly push them away, denying themselves what they need, which is the man. These women are often reflected in old scratched and cracked mirrors, they have long hair, big, black eyes, are dressed in dark and heavy clothing — they are looking for an impossible mythical love while enslaved to the traditions of the family and the society that have been imposed on them, dissatisfied with their present situation and worried about their futures. These are the images of women Bayzai presents to the audience.

Bayzai presented Iranian films with well written and complicated scripts for the first time. He is a master of using the camera not simply as a means of taking pictures, but as a character moving alongside the other characters in the film. He also used both professional actors and ordinary people in his movies. He is perhaps one of the few Iranian filmmakers to spend a lot of time designing every single shot, and he is the only Iranian filmmaker to successfully present both realistic and mythological images side by side in a film.

Sohrab Shahid Saless: Tabiat-e Bijan (Still Life)

Sohrab Shahid Saless first studied cinema in Vienna and then moved to Paris, where he received his degree in film direction from the Conservatory of Cinema in 1968. Although he first made a few short films including *Agar* (*If*, 1971) and *Siyah ve Sefid* (*Black and White*, 1972), it was the feature film *Yek Etefagh-e Sadeh* (*A Simple Event*) that made him famous not only in Iran, but in Europe as well. The film was first shown in 1973 at the Tehran International Film Festival and won Shahid Saless the directing award. It then was selected to be shown at three important film festivals, the Vienna Film Festival, the Bergamo Film Festival, and finally the Berlin Film Festival, at which the film won the jury award in 1973.

A Simple Event presents the simple and boring life of a boy who is living with his parents and helping his father in his fishing business. The most important element in this film is its simplicity in narrative, in photography and composition of the scenes, and in the acting, which is done by ordinary people rather than professionals. These are elements that have contributed significantly to a poetic and simple post-revolutionary cinema.

A Simple Event takes place in a small port by the Caspian Sea and shows the daily life of a ten-year-old schoolboy living with his parents, who generally do not have a comfortable life. The father feeds the family by fishing illegally, and instead of concentrating on his studies the boy has to work shoulder to shoulder with his father to sustain the household. The boy goes to school unprepared for his classes, while also helping his father to collect fish and then taking the fish to the bazaar and selling them. He gives the money to his father — who is usually drunk in a café — and then goes home to a sick mother, usually having dinner and then going to bed, living in the everlasting circle of activity which he repeats every day, almost without using any words. This circle of life, a life with no dialogue and no prospects, shows the stagnation of life in the family and especially in the boy. The only unusual event for the boy is the death of his sick mother, which we immediately see leaves him unchanged; the boy simply continues life within the same circle, his mother no longer present.

The picture presented is cold, sad and depressing, and the film uses a documentary style, shot outside of studios, on location with real people. This makes the bitterness of the film more real for the audience, as they feel they are watching a real documentary and not a cinematic version of life produced inside a studio. *A Simple Event*, despite its title, was not a simple event in Iranian cinema, as many filmmakers at the time were busy trying only to copy the techniques of well-made and successful Hollywood and Indian films. N. Servizio, after seeing the film in the Festival of Vienna, wrote:

> *A Simple Event*, as can be understood from its title, presents a glimpse of a simple life in which no extraordinary event takes place. All elements have been chosen from very ordinary events of life — but these simple elements have a rich human insight which recalls fresh memory of the best films of Italian Neo-Realist cinema, in particular *The Bicycle Thieves* of De Sica.[22]

After *A Simple Event*, Shahid Saless made *Tabiat-e Bijan* (*Still Life*) in 1974; it attracted the attention and praise of film critics at many film festivals. This film won the Silver Bear at the Berlin Festival in 1974, and also the Critics' Award. *Still Life* also took first place on a list compiled by Iranian films critics in 1977 and for years held its acknowledged place as the best Iranian film made prior to the Islamic revolution. It is interesting to note that on the same list critics selected *A Simple Event* as second, and third place went to *The Cow*, directed by Dariush Mehrjui.[23] This standard shows the high place of *Still Life* in Iranian cinema.

Still Life (it is also known as *Dead Nature*) is made in the same tradition as *A Simple Event*: It is a simple picture of a static life. A signal operator lives with his wife in a government house attached to the railway. They have one son who has left to perform his military service, who once in a while comes to visit them. He stays a night and the next day he leaves, and again the woman and man resume their life of routine. It seems that there is nothing outside of their own life for them, and the passage of time means little beyond the endless cycle of sunrise and sunset. A very uneventful life which sometimes seems poetic suddenly changes when railway inspectors arrive. They inspect the buildings, they ask a few questions, and then they leave. A few days later, a letter arrives, notifying the old man of his retirement and that he must leave in order to be replaced by another,

Mohammad Zamani (right) in *A Simple Event* (*Yek Etefagh-e Sadeh*), directed by Sohrab Shahid Saless in 1973.

younger signal operator. This means the end of an existence the couple has shared for years, yet they can go nowhere else as they have become a part of the place, a part of an atmosphere that can't be found elsewhere. J. Akrami writes:

> Sohrab Shahid Saless, by making *Still Life*, makes not only his second feature film but essentially makes his own cinema. In this film he portrays the unique values that he attempted to show for the first time in *A Simple Event*. These two films in a way give a new identity to Iranian cinema. I am not sure what title we can give to this kind of cinema, the titles have become repetitive and cannot convey a true sense of this cinema. For instance, it is not accurate enough to call Shahid Saless's work realistic, naturalistic, or cinema verité, or any other such titles. Even as tools for comparison these terms are useless. His films are only "life," with all of its originality, reality, with all of its details. If we are supposed to give a name or title to Shahid Saless's cinema, we should call it *life's cinema*.[24]

The film beautifully (or should we say bitterly) shows the uneventful life of the old couple in simple scenes, like the woman's attempt to thread a needle, or the closing of the road by the old signal operator for the train to come and pass. In this film, as in his first, Shahid Saless uses an economy of dialogue that comes from the nature of the story, and of the people, who do not need to speak to each other. Silence is the language of the film. Ordinary people without make-up, a camera that moves from scene to scene and face to face in a simple way, not hesitating to linger at length on an object or a scene, a dark and cold tone that shows the sadness of life of people who remind us in many ways of Chekhov's characters— all are cinematic tools in the hands of Shahid Saless, used to portray not the text of his characters' lives, but the subtext. This film, as Shahid Saless himself has described it, is "the way of life of people and their unconditional surrender in life."[25] When the film was shown in 1998 in New York, Leslie Camhi wrote:

> Stark and beautifully photographed, Shahid Saless's *A Still Life* (Dead Nature), follows an aging worker in rural Iran who shuffles between a railway crossing he guards and the hut he shares with his wife. A hypnotic pace pervades the imperturbable rhythm of their lives until disaster strikes. The film marked a turning point in Iranian cinema, away from Hollywood models.[26]

After the success of *Still Life* in the Festival of Berlin, Shahid Saless migrated to Germany and began making films there. Among these are *Expatriate* (1975), and *The Daily Memoir of a Lover* (1977). Although these films were made in the same tradition and portray the mental and pictorial world of Shahid Saless's previous works, they have no connection with Iran (neither stories nor characters are Iranian in these films). Still, Shahid Saless, with *A Simple Event* and *Still Life*, would greatly influence the new Iranian cinema in the years after the revolution. Shahid Saless's films were works of depth, simplicity, poetry and sadness, qualities later to be found in films like *Where Is My Friend's Home?* and *The Taste of Cherry* by Abbas Kiarostami, and *Nar-0 Nay* by S. Ebrahimifar, as well as other good films of the post-revolution cinema. Although the films of Shahid Saless portray the cultural identity of one nation, they are universal at the same time. On the one hand his work is nihilistic, having roots in Sadeq Hadayat's works,[27] and on the other hand it reminds us of the attitude of characters in Chekhov's and Beckett's plays in terms of the philosophy of their lives. Their appeal is global; audiences the world over can feel and understand Shahid Saless's characters and the way they surrender to their existence.

Other Films and Filmmakers

Apart from the films and the filmmakers already discussed, were many others participated in the formation of the Iranian new wave cinema before the revolution. A few contributed to the movement with many films, others with only one. To separate these films and filmmakers from those already discussed is not to devalue their artistic importance to Iranian cinema, but only a handful of filmmakers actually created a particular style and had an effect both on other filmmakers and their audience. Those works of the artists who we've examined at length also showed more unity as a whole. Their evolving techniques and interests may have taken them down numerous paths, but their movies retain a certain style that is unique to each filmmaker's body of work.

Though they did not make the same contributions to the development of the new wave, several others warrant some discussion. Among these is Ali Hatami, one of the most important Iranian filmmakers using historical characters and events as the basis for his work. Ali Hatami was a playwright and theatre director whose first film, *Hassan Kachal* (1970), was an adaptation of one of his own plays. From the beginning Hatami showed a very strong interest in folklore and history, an interest he maintained until his death in 1996. Hatami was one of a few Iranian filmmakers relatively unaffected by the Islamic revolution. The cultural and political consequences of the revolution had little impact on his style and ideas and he continued to make films utilizing the same pattern even after the revolution. His historical representations, however, become more elaborate over time, as the advancement of cinematic technique after the revolution led to the creation of more elaborate and historically accurate settings and visual effects. Among his films made before the revolution, *Sotehdelan* (1977) attracted the most critical attention. He also made a very popular television series at the same time, gaining him both fame and notoriety as the only Iranian filmmaker making historical films. After the Islamic revolution, he kept making similar films and television series, among them *Haji Washington* (1982), *Kamalolmolk* (1984), *Jafar-Khan az Farang Bargashteh* (*Jafar-Khan Is Back from Europe*, 1984–89), *Mother* (*Madar*, 1990), *Dalshodeghan* (1992), and *Johan Pahlevan Takhtie* (*World Champion Takhtie*), which remained unfinished due to his death in 1996. Hatami also made a big television series called *Hezardastan*, which ran in 1988. As many of Hatami's films were based on historical characters and historical events, attention to the past and cultural traditions were his main preoccupation. However, whether an accurate representation of history is presented within these pictures is certainly questionable. Hatami's approach to history, and the way he portrays the events and characters, have generated a heated argument between filmmakers and historians. In *Satar-Khan to Kamalolmolk* Hatami treats the past like a museum, displaying it more as an antique whose only value is its age. The Qajar period (1787–1925), which Hatami is primarily interested in, is regarded as one of the most unfortunate, dreadful, and dark periods in Iran's history, a time in which the country almost vanished from the map through the actions of the kings of this dynasty.[28] However, Hatami portrays this period as if he was creating images for post cards. Colorful and elegant, shot against beautiful landscapes, Hatami's historical characters appear and talk as though they are poets and philosophers. Beautiful and exaggerated settings appear beside gorgeous costumes that are clean and ironed, and one would never imagine that Tehran at that time was a poor city with dusty roads. Apart from the unrealistic presentation of characters and historical events, the films themselves lack any clear-cut plot and were filled by minor characters and subplots that come and go without rhyme or reason, confusing rather than enriching the main narrative. The most famous character Hatami created was Naserdin-Shah. He was portrayed as an innocent Hamlet, forced into a situation against his will and interests. Naserdin-Shah, in Hatami's films, is not portrayed as a brutal king, a womanizer who was ready to do anything to entertain himself. Hatami's handsome king, who was not in life handsome at all, talks like a learned scholar and walks like a trained ballet dancer, and of course does not hesitate to express his sorrow for Iran and lament that no one can help her. Whatever the historical facts, a filmmaker is not bound to history, and he does not need to portray history as it truly was. A filmmaker can make his own history, but this should be done openly, rather than under the guise of authenticity. History is not a museum. Hatami's films, including *Soltan-e Sahabqran* and *Kamalolmolk*, are museums populated with historical marionettes created only

Shahla Mirbakhtyar in *Hezardastan*, directed by Ali Hatami in 1988.

to show grandiose costumes and settings. Regardless of the historical merit of his films, it should be noted that Hatami was highly skilled in the techniques of scene composition and set and costume design. Before Hatami, art direction was nearly nonexistent in Iranian cinema and he was largely responsible for its introduction.

While Hatami was successful making films after the revolution, four important filmmakers were unable to continue working under the new government, and their connection with Iranian cinema was interrupted: These were Khosroo Haritash, Bahman Farmanara, Parviz Kimiavi, and Nosrat Karimi. Bahman Farmanara and Parviz Kimiavi left Iran during the Islamic revolution, Khosroo Haritash died soon after. Nosrat Karimi was arrested and not allowed to work in cinema once he was released from jail.

Khosroo Haritash came to Iran after graduating from UCLA and made four films before his death in 1981. *Adamak* (1971), and *Berehne ta Zohr ba Soraat* (1976) portray the reactions of a filmmaker to the social situation that began developing in the 1960's and climaxed in the 1970's with the Islamic revolution. The westernization of Iran created a social and cultural gap between two generations, and Haritash's films explored this gap and the confrontation between the two generations. Haritash's films showed this confrontation largely from a Western perspective rather than exploring the causes of what was an Iranian cultural crisis in the context of the culture itself. His third film *Saraydar* (Concierge) broke new ground in terms of both atmosphere and technique. This film, made in 1975, told a realistic story and used the dramatic form of plays within plays in its narrative structure. The film depicted the distance between rich and poor widening every day through the capitalization of society, the pouring of oil dollars into the country, and the distribution of this wealth without regard for social justice.

Rahman, a concierge, is forced to rob his own company to solve his financial problems. He wants to compete with his neighbor, who earns more than he does through sycophantic opportunism. Rahman robs the safe, but he is not aware that his son, who is interested in filmmaking, secretly filmed the event. When the film is shown the robbery by the father is revealed, thus creating a family rift. In this film Haritash shows the whole event from two points of view — that of a third person, a "director," and from the son's camera. These two viewpoints are mixed together in a new cinematic technique, showing the deep gap between classes of the societies, within a single class itself, and the different views of two generations. Unlike the director's previous films, *Concierge* is realistic, and each character is recognizable to the audience. The film was also connected to the movement of Azad (free) Cinema in Iran, which was created by a group of young amateur filmmakers who were trying to make films using the super 8 format.

One film that was the subject of protest and controversy before the Islamic revolution finally led to its maker being arrested and jailed for "insulting Islamic values."[29] This was *Mohalel*, made by Nosrat Karimi in 1971. *Mohalel* was based on one of the Islamic laws relating to divorce. According to this religious law, if a man divorces his wife three times (one after the other) he cannot remarry her unless the woman marries another (this is called *Mohalel*, or Solvent) and divorces him to then again marry her first husband. This religious law and historical tradition in *Mohalel* is used as a comedic device in order to criticize the law itself. However, the movie's comic side is featured more prominently than its social criticism.

The film is about a religious businessman who believes that if a woman betrays her husband by having an affair with another man she should be divorced, whereas if the daughter is going to make love with a man outside marriage, she should be killed. When the businessman returns home from work and sees the silhouette of his daughter making love with the neighbor's boy, the man decides to kill his daughter, but his wife sacrifices herself and tells the man that the daughter was innocent and she was the one

Faramarz Sedighi in *Berehne ta Zohr ba Soraat* directed by Khosroo Haritash in 1976.

Kangarani (right) and Mohammadi in *Concierge* (*Saraydar*), directed by Khosroo Haritash in 1975.

making love with the neighbor. The angry businessman divorces his wife three times, making it almost impossible for them to ever be reunited again.[30] After a while, it is revealed to the businessman that his wife was in fact innocent and he decides to remarry her. But according to the Islamic law, he has to find a man who will temporarily become her husband and then divorce her if they are to remarry. He finally succeeds in finding someone who is willing to do this in return for payment, but this new man turns out to have had a twenty-year infatuation with the businessman's wife, which he has been unable to pursue. When he marries the woman he is not willing, as per the arrangement, to divorce his new wife and a conflict between the businessman and the new husband begins. Comically, the businessman by his own hand brings his rival into his former wife's life, gives him money, and lets him make love to her. This comic situation, from the businessman's viewpoint, could be considered tragic. This neorealistic film was one of the best comedies produced in Iran before the revolution. A misconception arose that the filmmaker intended to ridicule the law for comedic purposes, rather than to criticize it. According to Jamal Shir-Mohammadi, "Nosrat Karimi had a common ground with the Pahlavi regime in that he was in opposition to the Islamic religion. We must say that none of those intellectual films sharing the task of attacking religion were as successful as Nosrat Karimi and his film *Mohalel*."[31]

However, the filmmaker himself rejected this interpretation, claiming that his only intention was to criticise the negative consequences of the particular law and to highlight the superstitions surrounding it, rather than criticizing religious law itself. As Karimi stated in an interview,

> In *Mohalel*, the story is formed in this way — the zealotry and fanaticism of the businessman is ridiculed, as the best solution to the problem is brought up by a young girl who has not been affected by the poisonous traditions of society. In a meeting arranged to solve the problem, without knowing its depth, the girl says "daddy, kiss mum and finish it." This translates to "make peace and do not make it more complicated than it needs to be." The girl's statement makes the others laugh, even though it was the best and easiest solution to the problem. But the character in my film cannot accept or understand her suggestion because of his fanatic superstitions.[32]

The themes of *Mohalel* and other films of Karimi, including *Doroshkehchi* (1971), are mostly based upon superstitions and traditions, which are in contradiction to new social values. *Mohalel* and the rest of Karimi's films are about the confrontation of modernism and tradition, although most of these traditions and superstitions had been banned for a long time and were no longer major issues for Iranians. In any case, this film led to Karimi being arrested after the Islamic revolution and he was unable to make any more movies.

Parviz Kimiavi left the country during the revolution and was not able to return until 1992.[33] Kimiavi established his importance in the new Iranian cinema when he made *Mogolha* (*The Mongols*) in 1973. Before making *The Mongols*, he had made two other good films, including the documentary *Ya Zamen Ahu* (1971), which is considered one of Iran's best documentaries. It was about the seventh Imam (leader) of the Shi'i sect of Islam, Imam Raza. The other film, a semi-documentary entitled *P mesleh Pelikan* (*P for Pelican*, 1972) shows the solitary life of an old man living on the edge of a desert. His solitude is suddenly broken by the arrival of a migrating pelican that has lost its way and has ended up in an unfamiliar and hostile environment. For a short time, the pelican brings a childlike happiness to the old man. The success of this short film prompted the filmmaker to leave documentaries and make *The Mongols*, his first feature film.

A television director is assigned to go to Zahedan (a very poor state in the east, south of Iran's border with Pakistan) to oversee the installation of a television relay station. The installation will allow television to reach into remote areas and to gradually usurp the people's traditional ways of filling their time. Despite working in television, the director knows that bringing it to the area could be a devastating cultural invasion. At the same time, he wants to make a film about the cinema itself. His wife is writing a thesis about the invasion of Iran by Mongols in the eleventh century, which almost completely destroyed the country. In his fantasies, the director mixes these elements (the coming of television and making a film about the cinema on one hand, and the invasion of the Mongols on the other) to show the same invasion in a new form. In one sequence, we see the arrival of the television antenna on one side of the village and the arrival of the Mongols on the other side. A clear message for the audience.

The Mongols was perhaps one of the first Iranian films to pay attention to the subject of globalization and cultural invasions through the mass media, and in particular by television and satellites. It shows how indigenous cultures could be affected by such globalization. The film was made with talent and accuracy, and shown in Iran at a time in which the national culture and its values were under attack through Westernization. If the unrest within Iranian society that led to the making of a film like *The Mongols* had been taken seriously by the country's policy makers at the time, perhaps there would have been no need for the Islamic revolution.

The style of the film moves beautifully between documentary and drama, and the camera is able to record this, and show the confrontation of past and present, new and old. It is clear, however, that the director, who graduated from the Louis Lumière School of Cinematography (1964) and IDHEC (1967) in Paris, was heavily influenced by the work of Jean-Luc Godard. We even see the name of Godard on a sign in the film, and we also hear the music from Godard's *Pierrot le fou*. The film's style and the filmmaker's technique and skill create an atmosphere such that the audience feels they are watching a documentary, not a drama, thus allowing them to better connect to the characters and their situation. On the other hand, this documentary style interrupts the continuity of the film in some parts, purposefully creating a sense of alienation in order to pose questions for the audience. This technique hinders the movie's ability to completely capture an audience. David Wilson writes:

> The film immediately presents itself as a discussion about the cinema itself. A television director is paging through a book which is about the pioneers of cinema and we see gradually that their photographic inventions enter his own life. At the same time the director's wife is writing a thesis about the invasion of the Mongols in Iran. The television antenna which has been planted in the desert in place of trees, the celluloid films which have been buried under the sand, and the village people who are sitting and watching an educational program and asking "why do we need television to teach us to plant trees while we ourselves already know how?." With the arrival of television the domestic storytellers retire. This film from the viewpoint of images is too inventive. The message of the film is that Iranian cinema is well alive and we can say that it is moving in between the border of two worlds.[34]

Apart from these filmmakers who had a share in the development of the new Iranian cinema, there were other movies that are associated with the movement. *Showhar-e Ahoo-Khanom* (*The Husband of Ahoo-Khanom*), *Cheshmeh* (*Spring*), *Sobeh Rooz-e Chahrom* (*The Morning of the Fourth Day*), *Topoli*, and finally *Shazdeh Ehtejab* (*Prince Ehtejab*). These films were works of filmmakers who either did not make any more movies or who were unable to make better films, due mainly to the revolution. *The Husband of Ahoo-Khanom* was made in 1968 by Davood Mula-Qolipour, and has always been considered as a good, simple, realistic film. It is an adaptation of a famous novel written by Ali Mohammad Afghani which portrayed the situation of women in Iran's patriarchic society. In the novel and the film we see that the woman is a weak creature stripped of most social rights, whose main duties are to run the family, to make children, and to cook and clean the house. This theme is portrayed in a simple yet effective way, and the movie is considered one of the first and most exceptional films made before the revolution to show the true face of Iranian women. Most commercial films made at that time presented unrealistic images of women, which consequently helped in keeping women unaware of their rights. The women characters in commercial films were usually seduced by men and forced into prostitution or to work in bars, always dependent on a man who controls and abuses them. These women seldom make any attempt to escape their situation and can only dream that they will find a good man who will come and save them. Even though freedom and a good life was the apparent goal of these women, this too was employed as an excuse to show their weaknesses. *The Husband of Ahoo-Khanom* for the first time presented the Iranian woman as someone trying to run the family with everything they can, especially in terms of their passion for the family and family values, instead of drinking and dancing in cabarets and being bashed by men. *The Husband of Ahoo-Khanom* portrayed Iranian women as they were, and not as they were seen in works patterned after American or Indian cinema.

In 1972 two good films, *Downpour* (Bahram Bayzai), and *The Postman* (Dariush Mehrjui), were released, there are two other films of that year that had something of the commercial cinema, and something of the new cinema. These two films connected with both elite and ordinary audience members, an important step in the evolution of the new wave. *Topoli*, made by Reza Mirlohi, and *The Morning of the Fourth Day* by Kamran Shirdal, used the familiar techniques of attractive stories and a mixture of heroes and anti-heroes. *Topoli* was a successful adaptation of John Steinbeck's *Of Mice and Men*, with great acting by Homayoon and Aqili, a beautiful atmosphere and good editing, and it succeeded in gaining the attention of both audiences and critics. *The Morning of the Fourth Day* by Kamran Shirdal was made mostly in the tradition of anti-heroic films like *Khoda Hafez Rafiq (Goodbye Friend)* by A. Naderi. The main character, Amir, accidentally kills someone, and finds himself in a situation where escape is the only option available. For three days he runs, asking for help from various people, until finally on the morning of the fourth day he is killed in a confrontation with the police, who have been informed of his location by his fiancée. In a sense Amir is fleeing the lack of justice in society, and this creates an atmosphere in which his death, in a way, is a form of freedom. The most controversial film of the year 1972 was *Cheshmeh* (Spring) by Arbi Avanesian. It left audiences wondering what they had seen and the critics attacking each other.

Spring is the story of a life spent wandering between love and family. Jalizban is a man who falls in love with the wife of his friend, a love he does not reveal. At the same time, the woman has a young lover and vis-

Pour-Hussieni and Nojomi (standing) in *Spring* (*Cheshmeh*), directed by Arbi Avanesian in 1972.

Mashayikhi (standing) and Arman in *Spring*.

Homayoon (right) and Aqili in *Topoli*, directed by Reza Mirlohi in 1973.

its him secretly in an abandoned house. When this secret is revealed to
Jalizban, he commits suicide. The adulterous woman also commits suicide and her husband buries her in the abandoned house, and the young
lover runs away. The woman is the center of three different kinds of relationships with three different men. She has a kind of father/daughter
understanding with her husband; in other words this relationship is a
respectful one. She has a very deep and spiritual relationship with her husband's friend Jalizban, and a physical (sexual) relationship with her young
lover. It is obvious that the woman needs all three relationships, and
tragedy strikes because she cannot have all of them at the same time.

Arbi Avanesian was one of the best directors of the Iranian theatre,
and directed controversial performances such as *Pajoheshi Amigh dar...*
by A. Nalbandian (1968), *Cherry Orchard* by Chekhov (1972), and *My Foot,
My Tutor* by Peter Handke (1972). Avanesian studied cinema in England,
but when he returned to Iran he directed plays instead of movies. *Spring*
was his only feature film, first screened at the Tehran Film Festival, and
then the Venice Film Festival in 1972, when critics wrote such controversial reviews that other films were overshadowed. Some film critics
identified the film as a useless intellectual gesture, while others called it a
pure cinematic experience that tried to achieve pure cinematic expression.
Avanesian employed a technique that can be found in Sergei Paradjanov's
films, in particular in *The Color of Pomegranate*.[35] In *Spring*, we can clearly
see the same ideology and technique that Paradjanov employed in *The
Color of Pomegranate*, though Avanesian was not copying Paradjanov's
film; but he had used the same aesthetic in theatre for years, and he relied
upon his own impressions of Armenian culture when developing the story.

In *Spring*, the camera is stationary, and lingers on every scene in an
attempt to show, as the director has stated, "those untouchable movements."[36] To complement this technique, there is little dialogue within
the film, and when there is dialogue it is not like that found in other films.
There is a kind of silence, even when a character speaks. The dialogue is
comprised of words, and this creates a space that allows the audience to
take in the film's images. Again, this recalls Paradganov, who are explained
that "you are asking me why the characters in my films do not speak. It is
true, someone imagines that they are deaf and mute, in painting people
look at each other but do not talk to each other."[37] In a painting, there is
no apparent movement and no dialogue, but if someone concentrates on
the painted image, studying the composition, objects, people and colors,
he can understand not only the atmosphere but the people and their relationships. In *Spring*, Avanesian used the techniques of painting to create
art in the medium of cinema.

As mentioned, this film created a rift among critics, who formed two opposing fronts. Abbas Javanmard called it "rubbish,"[38] whereas Hoshang Taheri claimed that it was "one of the most beautiful and deepest cinematic creations, which with a simple but poetic and glorious language portrayed the story of love and shame between a Christian woman and young man that ultimately ends in their death,"[39] reactions representative of the two camps.

Jamshid Mashayikhi in *Prince Ehtejab* (*Shazdeh Ehtejab*), directed by Bahman Farmanara in 1974.

Shazdeh Ehtejab (*Prince Ehtejab*) made by Bahman Farmanara in 1974, portrays the end of an era of aristocracy. It tells the story of a prince who has a title with a glorious past, but without any money or power as accompaniment. The prince is a sick man (physically and mentally) living only with the memory of glorious days, while continuing a record of committing crimes. The film was based on the novel *Prince Ehtejab* by Hoshang Golshirie, who was a famous avant-garde novelist. The film shows, again, how Iranian literature has always been source material for good films. Farmanara succeeds in turning words into pictures, and with its acting, music, and composition *Prince Ehtejab* ably portrays the decay and death of a family once on the top rung of society but now infected with disease and melancholy, a family breathing its last breath. Jamshid Akrami observed, "*Prince Ehtejab* is a concise story of a time which no longer exists, a story of the dawn of an aristocratic family in an era which has been ended. It is an honest reflection of a corrupt inheritance."[40]

The new Iranian cinema before the Islamic revolution of 1979 was a movement created in response to a very fundamental need: the need for a *national cinema*, able to reflect the culture and the civilization of the nation that it was created within and screened for. Commercial films (Film Farsi) did not reflect such nationality, as they were unrealistic and illusionary pictures of people, relationships, and society, easily consumable stories meant to bring more people into the theaters and to make money. Opposition to such films, and a commitment to society and to art by a few filmmakers, paved the way for a movement that was able to find an established and important place despite facing financial, social, and political problems and opposition. The movement was finally integrated into Iranian cinema, though producers and the government remained slow to offer support. One of the main reasons behind its slow progression was censorship by a government that did not allow criticism of its role in society by filmmakers. Although the government policymakers who were in charge of culture were not happy with commercial films and were aware of their corruption, they did not or could not help the filmmakers of the new movement. The government knew that most of the filmmakers of the new cinema had leftist ideologies that were threatening to the dictatorship of the regime. For this reason, the government did not help the new movement, and private producers did not want to risk their money on films that were high-risk ventures. Consequently, the main problem for the filmmakers of this new movement was finding producers to fund their work. This is why the new movement could not make successive films, and why long gaps exist between films. These limitations may have seriously hindered the progress and artistic development of some new wave directors. However, there were exceptions: A few filmmakers received patronage from the government because they were not known as leftist, or because their films were considered to be purely artistic, devoid of anything critical of the government. Two filmmakers, Arbi Avanesian and Parviz Kimiavi, were able to make their films through the support of Iran National Television, but these were exceptions and in general the government made no effort to help the new cinema stand on its own two feet.

The progress of the new Iranian cinema involved several different factors, but attention to the culture and civilization of the country, in particular Iranian literature, was very important because it provided good sources for cinematic productions. *The Night of the Hunchback* was based upon *One Thousand and One Nights*, *Mud-brick and Mirror* was adapted from a novel of the same title, *Siavush in Persepolis* was taken from *The Book of Kings*, *Peace in the Presence of Others* and *The Cow* were taken from stories by Sa'adi, and *Prince Ehtejab* was based on a novel of the same title. Filmmakers' discovery of Iran's rich literary heritage and their incorporation of traditional material into their work was an important development for the new movement in cinema. Experience making documentaries by most of the new wave filmmakers meant that they had the experience needed to create a simple cinematic form rich with symbolism and meaning.

In general, before the revolution, the new Iranian cinema has a bitter look, because most of its characters are anti-heroes, alone in a world that offers them no hope of justice. This character type's appearance and prominence was related to the social and political situation in Iran during the 1960s and 1970s, a time when the country was ruled by a dictatorial regime, and artists and intellectuals were arrested and denied their basic artistic rights. In a time when no one hoped for a brighter future, and disappointment and nihilism were becoming common traits among Iranian intellectuals and artists, these lonely anti-heroes, destined for death and failure, issued a cry of protest and represented the only opportunity for these artists to express their ideas and their passions. As these anti-heroes were mostly from the lower classes of society and had no apparent political stance or ideology, they weren't likely to be subject to censorship, and Iranian filmmakers used them to speak about the justice denied themselves, and to all Iranian people. The new Iranian cinema was thus formed around rebellious characters who were in conflict with a political order and society that denied them their basic rights. At the same time, similar characters were employed to show the conflict between different segments of society, different economic systems, and different social and moral values. Some people were making money easily, while some were struggling to bring food home to their families. The movies also show the decline of the villages and small cities, emptied of their vitality as more and more people move to big cities in search of a better life, further marginalizing those who remain behind. These contradictions, their social and economic consequences, and the nihilistic attitude of many intellectuals were incorporated into the new films, creating a new pre-revolution cinema about characters running from their own feelings of hopelessness, paralysis, abandonment and betrayal. This was a cinema of rebellion and defeat, a cinema of betrayal and revenge, a cinema of illusion and reality, and a cinema of anti-hero and the anti-narrative.

IV
The New Cinema
after the Revolution

Although the political, social, and religious uprising in Iran which caused the collapse of the Pahlavi regime and the establishment of the Islamic Republic in 1979 began in 1978, the turmoil in both the Film Farsi and Iranian new wave existed long before this time. In fact, early signs of this turmoil appeared in 1971, and every year gained momentum. Independent of the social and political disruption that generated and accompanied the revolution, the disturbance in Iranian cinema faded for one or two years, only to reappear after the revolution with the same problems as before.

The confusion and depression in the pre-revolution cinema were the result of two important factors—censorship and financial restrictions. Both commercial and art cinema struggled with these elements and consequently became progressively weaker each year, so that many filmmakers predicted that Iranian film production would stop completely. In the 1970s, Indian and American films captured eighty percent of the Iranian market. Nationally produced films could not compete in attracting audiences. It was cheaper to import and dub them into Persian than to produce a film inside the country. According to one well-known Iranian producer, Ali Abbasi, the cost of buying the royalties of a martial arts film produced in Hong Kong was $1,000 in 1975, and an Indian melodrama, $1,500. The cost of dubbing films into Persian was another $1,000.[1] The total cost of importing a film was $2,000 to $2,500, while producing an Iranian film, commercial or artistic, was about $80,000 to $100,000. The box office take for the imported films was generally much higher. These figures clearly show that Iranian film producers were forced by circumstance to become, instead, mere importers. In 1972 Iran cinema produced ninety domestic

100

films, among them good ones such as *Downpour, The Morning of the Fourth Day, Topli, Sadeq Kordeh,* and *The Postman.* This number was reduced to 38 in 1977, with only one good film among them, *Sotehdelan* by Ali Hatami. This dramatic reduction in the quantity and quality of cinema production shows the extent of the disruption in Iranian cinema during this period. Besides the influx of cheap, imported Indian and American films and the high cost and financial risks of domestic film production, other social and economic factors contributed to the deteriorating environment.

Iran was changing rapidly into a bourgeois capitalistic society, though she remained dependent on the petrodollars pouring into the country. This money usually ended up in the pockets not of the average worker, but of those who had connections within the establishment, meaning that the money could not be spent on the cultural or social development of the country.[2] Many companies were importing goods into the country and making large profits, and the development of housing in Iran brought short-term profits to many Iranian investors. Hopes of a quick return on their money attracted many independent producers to invest in places other than the high-risk cinema industry, as the boom economy offered much more tempting opportunities. These economic developments led to inflation, and the public was soon unable to afford the ever increasing costs of leisure activities like going to the movies. The salaries demanded by the superstars of Film Farsi were so high that they often accounted for half the budget of the film, further aggravating the unhealthy condition of Iranian cinema at the time.

These problems gradually paralyzed Iran's filmmaking industry in the years preceding the revolution. The only support it could rely on came from government organizations such as National Television and Kanoon-e Parvaresh-e Fakri Kodakan va Nojavanan (K.P.F.K.N.), which sometimes produced films, and from film importers who were forced by law to produce one Iranian film in return for importing their foreign films. This law forcing importers to produce domestic films caused more damage than good in terms of quality. These importer-producers did not care about the quality of domestic films they financed, they only wanted to produce them as cheaply and quickly as possible, and get back to the profitable business of importing films. It was in this atmosphere that directors like Reza Safaie made films in only two weeks. Aside from the economic turbulence in Iranian cinema at the time, there was social and artistic unrest caused by harsh censorship. Economic deprivation and government censorship were equally responsible for the increasingly dire straits in which Iranian filmmakers found themselves.

A cinema can be called a "national phenomenon" only if it truly reflects the culture of that nation on the screen, and embraces the full diversity of views and the many different aspects of the life of the nation. This is the only way any truly national cinema can be developed and survive. If cinema embraces only one particular style or depends upon the support of one segment of society, it risks serious difficulty should that target audience become dissatisfied or more interested in other media forms (such as television, video, or the Internet). A diverse and representative national cinema can easily, with flexibility and innovation, produce films able to attract audiences to theaters. Censorship did not allow the development of an Iranian cinema that could reflect all aspects of society and be a mirror of the variety of life and experience within the nation. Censorship forced Iranian filmmakers to employ only particular stories and characters, and audiences eventually lost interest. Iranian movies usually presented a few young, brave men wandering the streets, helping poor and vulnerable people, drinking and singing and dancing in cabarets, with no justification given for their extravagant lifestyle or explanation of where their money was coming from (*The Treasure of Gharoon*). It also commonly featured young women who had run away from their homes, with or without reason, and were forced to work in brothels and cabarets and usually ended up being saved by those brave young men (*Dancer*). These stories and these character types were, in a way, supported and encouraged by the tight censorship, as any film attempting to break this mold and show characters with real equivalents in society — like a public servant or an army officer — met with severe opposition from censors. According to censors, films could not show such figures as alcoholics, gamblers or adulterers. A woman who was a teacher or a lecturer could not be portrayed in anything other than in a morally acceptable fashion.[3] With such severe restrictions, the only characters left to portray were prostitutes and hooligans, and this is why most of the Film Farsis featured these two character types. Aman Manteqi, one of the most famous directors of Film Farsi, said:

> In cinema we cannot portray any person who belongs to any organization. I mean we cannot portray the real life characters, my own life, the real life of a teacher, an army officer, a detective, or even one who is a member of the influential unions. In fifteen years of making films, I have made sixty long and short films by now, and still I am not allowed to portray my own life on film. The only people who do not have a union are prostitutes and hooligans, people who have no social defenders, and this is why our films are mostly about these people.[4]

Both types of Iranian cinema, the Film Farsi and the New Wave, had to combat these problems. This struggle continued until the Islamic revolution of 1979 put an end to any hope of overcoming the situation.

The Islamic revolution, obviously, was a religious revolution. The attitude of the Islamic authorities toward the cinema was clear even before the revolution. They considered movies as a corrupting influence and were opposed to it. They believed that the cinema was influencing the youth to turn away from religious ideals and practices.[5]

Religious people rarely went to see either Iranian films or American or Indian movies. Establishing theaters in religious cities like Qom became an insoluble problem for the government — soon after a theater was constructed, it would be attacked and burnt to the ground. During the revolution the theaters, along with banks, were the most obvious targets for the Islamic protestors who burnt and destroyed such institutions and buildings.[6] Even after the revolution many theaters were confiscated and turned into storage facilities or religious halls, and only a few were able to continue to show films. Before and during the revolution the cinema was seen as a symbol of corruption and Western cultural invasion. Of course, the type of films shown before the revolution, and especially billboards outside the cinemas, contributed to the religious opposition. Films of the time usually involved a couple of scenes showing a woman (often naked) singing, dancing, and drinking alcohol. These films were often advertised with huge billboards outside the cinemas that exaggerated the tempting naked female form. The religious factions saw these advertisements, and subsequently considered cinema a corrupt institution. The opposition of religious people and the Islamic regime was not to the cinema itself, but to its moral image. These people, and especially those who would later become cultural policymakers of the regime, were equally opposed to the art films as they were to the Film Farsis, but not for the same reasons. The people in power knew that the modern art and literature before the Islamic revolution was mostly produced by people who had the connection with Marxism in one way or another, and that religion, if not rejected all together, was criticised in their artistic works.[7]

The Iranian filmmakers, more than any other of the country's artists, predicted very dark days ahead for themselves with the establishment of the Islamic regime. These filmmakers had no idea that the same regime that opposed cinema and encouraged the closure of theaters, ultimately causing film production to stop, would later offer its help and its support to the extent that the same dying, troubled cinema would become not only the most popular form of artistic expression in Iran, but would also gain worldwide acclaim and become an attraction at any major film festival. According to Geoff Brown, "despite its severe Islamic censorship and Taboos ... [Iranian film] attracts a world cult following."[8] Zhang Yimou, the famous Chinese director of brilliant films like *Raise the Red Lantern* and *Not One Less,* says "his inspiration is Iranian cinema."[9]

While the whole country was aflame with revolution, theaters were burnt down one after another and complete chaos dominated the Iranian film industry. Those who had money either fled the country, or broke completely with the industry and established other business—supermarkets and carpet stores, for example. Some filmmakers who were not purveyors of Film Farsi had a close relationship with the royal regime. These artists, a number having high governmental positions, left Iran fearing arrest. Others remained in the country and awaited the consequences of the revolution.

During the tumultuous period of the revolution, a few filmmakers dared to risk their lives and take a camera in their hands in order to record the public demonstrations and the revolution as one of the most important historical events in Iran. The turmoil began in January, 1978, with the departure of the Shah from the country, and ended around 1980 when Iraq invaded Iran and the Islamic regime started to fight not only the Iraqi army, but also the opposition inside the country, especially those political organizations that were armed and ready to fight against the new regime. In a way the period from 1977 to 1980 was liberating for art and literature expression, as the codes of censorship imposed on them by the previous regime were no longer in effect. In this period, writers and artists, because of a lack of government control, were able to write and publish whatever they wanted to, and to perform what they desired without first obtaining permission from the censorship board. However, cinema was an exception. As filmmaking requires investment, and this was not possible in that turbulent time, this short period of artistic growth did not benefit the film industry, though theatre and literature were galloping along at full strength. This temporary democracy existed only because the government was unable to impose its control and power on the people at the time. The new regime was not in a position to pay attention to its censorship boards or to impose any control over cultural and artistic activities, as its attention was focused on conflicts with other political factions hoping to gain control of the country. During this period, few films were made, mostly by artists who were connected to the left. The films were not shown publicly because all of the theaters were soon controlled by the government. Among the films of the period bearing mention were *Koreh-Pazkhaneh* (*Brick Works*), and *Harfbezan Turkman* (*Speak Out, Turkman*), made by Mohammad Reza Moqadasi and Reza Alameh-Zadeh respectively in 1980. Both films presented a leftist view of the plight of disadvantaged minorities and groups in Iran, and tried to show the discrimination against certain groups and the injustices visited upon those working in harsh conditions without insurance or adequate wages. These films were rejected by the new revolutionary regime because of their Marxist elements.

From 1981 the new regime began to gain control over the country and its governmental bodies, but it still had no clear idea about what to do with Iranian cinema. Therefore in such a situation neither the government nor the filmmakers knew what they should or could do to revitalize the film industry. A few unsuccessful attempts were made by filmmakers of both new wave and commercial cinema. The first attempt was made by a few filmmakers, mostly working in the Film Farsi, in March 1978, one month after the revolution had toppled the royalist regime. These filmmakers went to see the interim prime minister to discuss the status of Iranian cinema in the current political climate. The speaker of the group, Mohammad Motevaselani, said, "The aim of that meeting was to find a policy for the future of Iranian cinema. We tried to convince the new government that the cinema in its correct position was completely necessary for the country."[10]

The same group of filmmakers created a union with its first task being to clean up the film industry. The board responsible for the clean-up consisted of Reza Alameh-Zadeh, Said Motalebi, Siroos Alvand, Bahman Mofeed, Hussien Geel, Barbad Taheri and Hussien Haqiqi. These well-known figures in the film industry held differing attitudes towards their task; some of them were the very sort of filmmakers meant to be thrown out of the industry. Following this attempt, which of course was a failure, a few commercial filmmakers started to make films in the tradition of Film Farsi, with some changes. For example, instead of going to a cabaret and drinking vodka, the characters would go to a mosque and pray, and then go and fight with bad guys not over a woman, but for the implementation of Islamic justice! The content and the form of these films exactly matched the old Film Farsis, even down to the dress and appearance of the characters, and the changes were made only to get a licence for the movies to be screened. One of these films was *Barzakhiha*, directed by Eraj Ghaderi in 1981. Surprisingly, it was able to successfully use the Film Farsi style with an Islamic twist, attracting large audiences in the process. In the film, during the revolution a group of criminals escape from prison and attempt to flee the country. But in a village close to the border, they come face to face with a good guy (the stock figure of Film Farsi) who is a man of God and has devoted himself and his life to the people. He stands against them and thwarts their plan. Despite its success at the box office, fueled in part by its use of the superstars and character types of Film Farsi, some of the religious and revolutionary organizations protested and finally succeeded in halting its exhibition. This made it very hard for filmmakers to continue making movies in the tradition of Film Farsi with an Islamic veneer to give them credibility.

A couple of the new wave filmmakers resumed making films as well, but they were not very successful. These filmmakers didn't understand the new situation and the changes and were unable to adapt. *Khat-e Ghermez* (*The Red Line*, 1982), made by Masoud Kimiai, was an attempt to cheat the censors while at the same time not turning his film into a Film Farsi. A secret police officer whose wife does not know about his real profession gets into trouble because of his secrecy, and eventually is killed by his wife in a fight. The filmmaker did not seem to really believe in his own film, and was unsure of himself in the new climate after the revolution; his seeming self censorship resulted in a confusing work that neither enhanced his reputation nor contributed anything meaningful to the Iranian cinema.

In this confusing situation, the cultural policymakers of the new regime gradually realized the value of cinema both as entertainment and propaganda. People close to the establishment voiced concern over the future of cinema in Iran. Mohammed Ali Najafi, who was in charge of the Department of Cinema at the Ministry of Culture and Art from 1979 to 1980, was the first person to try to convince the government to do something about cinema. In an interview he explained how he, with a couple of other people close to the regime, went in March 1978 to the holy city of Qom to visit Imam Khomieni (the leader of the Islamic revolution) and ask his advice on the problems plaguing Iranian cinema. Imam Khomieni (in one of his speeches) said that he was not opposed to the cinema, but he was opposed to the prostitution that cinema was presenting.[11] Mohsen Kalhor, who was Acting Minister of Culture and Higher Education, and responsible for the art and culture section of that ministry from 1980 to 1982, said:

> My first task was to bring all artistic policies and activities in line with Islam. It is interesting to know that the filmmakers were of two groups. The veteran (not intellectual)[12] directors had the problem of using sex in their films, and the intellectual directors had problems with being political (Marxist). During those years many of the political groups invested in some of these films. Maoists invested in two films by Gholam Ali Erfan (*Aghayeh Heroglif* and *Goft Har Senafareshan*) and a film like *Qarantineh* was made with the support of Mojahedin-e Khalq.[13] The film *Tarikh Sazan*, by Haddi Saber, was made by the order of the Toodeh Party.[14] We talked to both groups of filmmakers and tried to convince them that a revolution had taken place in Iran and the main characteristic of that revolution was being Islamic, and they had to work under the regulation of the Islamic Republic.[15]

Along with the filmmakers' efforts to revive Iranian cinema, the government and some of the revolutionary religious organizations, that were attached to or supported by the government began to establish art departments with the goal of training artists to produce works that were in line with the values of the new regime. For this purpose, two film organizations were established: Hozeh Honari Sazeman-e Tablighat-e Islami (The Art Institute of The Islamic Propaganda Organization), and Bonyad-e Cinemaie Farabi (The Farabi Cinema Foundation). These two organizations played a vital role in the development of the new Iranian cinema in different but connected ways. Hozeh Honari provided all necessary facilities and privileges for young revolutionaries who were interested in filmmaking, and allowed them to learn the art of making films. The task of Bonyad-e Farabi was to support and control the professional filmmakers, while at the same time providing necessary support for young artists. Clearly anyone who wanted to make films under the control and guidance of these organizations had to reflect the ideology of the Islamic regime in their films.

Hozeh Honari was created by a few young Moslem revolutionaries, who initially wanted to use various art forms to spread the message of Islam and the new regime. This group soon merged into the Islamic Propaganda Organization with the support of Mohsen Makhmalbaf, despite the fact that he himself believed that no artist should be affiliated with any government. It eventually became the art section of the Propaganda Organization, and became a semi-governmental body with an enormous budget and facilities, along with the power to produce and to present films without being subject to oversight by the board of censorship, which was a part of the Ministry of Culture and Islamic Guidance. The Islamic Propaganda Organization was working under the directorship of one of the most influential ayatollahs, Janati, and was almost a government within a government. The merger of the two institutions provided good financial and political opportunities for young revolutionary artists. This allowed Mohsen Makhmalbaf, who had no experience in filmmaking, to make a series of feature films that failed one after another. Despite their religious content, these films couldn't create an *Islamic Cinema*.[16] However, these films were useful in their own way, if not for the audience, then for those who were making them. They gradually learned the craft of filmmaking, though their films were made at great costs. Young artists working within this organization only knew one method of filmmaking and wouldn't consider other approaches, as they had both the money and power to make films and screen them at their own theaters without being subject to outside control.[17] In 1985 several films were released that showed that their makers had used their freedom and privilege to learn the skills needed to produce quality movies. *Baykot* (*The Boycott*) by Mohsen Makhmalbaf, *Zangha* (*Bells*) by Mohammed Reza Honarmand, *Balami Besoyeh Sahel* (*A Boat Toward the Coast*) by Rassol Mulla-Gholipur were among those films that displayed the skills of their makers. Suddenly, for those filmmakers for whom the creation of an Islamic cinema was the main priority, the artistic side of movie making became their first interest. They looked at the cinema more and more as a form of artistic expression, instead of viewing it strictly through the lenses of religion and ideology. This change of view affected the artists working under the organization so deeply that when Makhmalbaf made *Dastforoosh* (*The Paddler*) in 1987, the Islamic Propaganda Organization itself reacted negatively. The film exhibited a filmmaker's criticism of and objection to the Islamic government for the first time, but it had a cinematic style that was not accepted by the other Islamic artists. The film made the first crack in the solid body of the Islamic organization and caused the institution to go through a rebellious period. Despite some resistance, its members, one after another, finally surrendered themselves to the new wave, which was more artistic, as well as critical of the Iranian social and political situation. This move distanced them from a purely idealistic religious cinema that they were initially hoping to establish. No other organization and its artists made more films that were critical of the regime and the way that it was handling the country, especially concerning social issues. It should be noted that the production of critical movies that criticized the new regime was not unique to those within the Propaganda Organization. Other artists working outside of the organization shared their ideology, but had little opportunity to express their criticism, as they did not have the support of such a powerful organization. The artists working within the Islamic Propaganda Organization enjoyed freedom in choosing subjects, freedom to turn them into artistic representations according to their vision, and an opportunity to show them to the public without having to struggle with the censorship boards and without fear of punishment by the regime, as they themselves were a part of that regime. Having financial resources and having the title of Islamic artist allowed these artists to create films that for the most part contributed something positive to the still developing new Iranian cinema after the revolution. Their critical approach to social issues even made them successful at the box office, as many audience members were eager to see works that reflected their own ideas and attitudes toward the political situation in Iran. This government organization, strangely enough, provided facilities and resources that allowed some young artists to become the best filmmakers of the new cinema. Among them were Mohsen Makhmalbaf and Majid Majidi, whose films have appeared in most major film festivals worldwide; one of them, *Rang-e Khoda* (*Color of Heaven*), was nominated for an Oscar in 1999. At the same time, a second organization, this one a part of the Ministry of Culture and Islamic Guidance was making its own plans for Iranian cinema, and they would prove crucial for the formation of the new movement. This organization was Bonyad-e Farabi.

Before the revolution of 1979, a group of students and graduates from universities were acting in conjunction with a mosque, Hossuienie Ershad. This religious centre was one of the most important gathering places for religious intellectuals who were opposed to the royal regime. Along with their religious activities they were involved in artistic activities, including theatre. Among these students and graduates were a few who studied architecture at the National University, and after the revolution they secured most of the cultural and artistic positions in the country thanks to their ties with leaders of the revolution, and because they were members of the Islamic Party (Hezb-e Jomhori Islami). One of them, Mir Hussein Mosavi, was even promoted to the post of prime minister, and he paved the way for the other members of the group to gain political power. Mohammed Ali Najafi became the director of the cinema section at the Ministry of Culture and Art, Mohammed Behashti and Fakhrodin Anvar took the important and sensitive positions of production and management in national television, and Hojat become the executive director of the City Theatre, the main theatre of the country. Members of this group practically took control of all artistic activities in Iran after the revolution. Mohammed Ali Najafi could not stand the chaotic and oppressive conditions of those revolutionary years and resigned from his position after only one year, deciding instead to make feature films and television series. His liberal attitude and his open-mindedness towards the arts and artists, his belief in freedom of expression, and his opposition to censorship led him to resign. Fakhrodin Anvar and Mohammed Behashti, who at the beginning thought that the theatre would become the first and most popular form of art after the revolution, went to the City Theatre as its managers for a year. When Mohammed Ali Najafi resigned from his post as head of cinema, Anvar and Behashti, after a change in the government and the establishment of a new ministry for culture and art, went to the new ministry to run its cinema section. Anvar became the head of the cinema and Behashti became the executive director of the newly established Bonyad-e Farabi. According to its executive director, the purpose of establishing Bonyad-e Farabi (in 1983), was "control" and to "support" those films and filmmakers who were ready to work in line with the revolution and the Islamic regime.[18]

Contrary to Hozeh Honari, which was training young revolutionary Moslem artists committed to the revolution and to Islam who would then supplant the Film Farsi and the New Wave filmmakers, the newly established Bonyad-e Farabi was ready to provide resources for both groups, old or young, and support their activities and productions on the condition that they accept control of the organization in order to steer their works toward the Islamic values of the new regime. This is why we see young filmmakers like Jafari Jozani beginning to make films, as well as seasoned filmmakers like Masoud Kimiai accepting the "control" and "support" of Bonyad-e Farabi so that they could continue to make films.

The process of working in Bonyad-e Farabi was this: First the plot for the script was submitted and discussed and approved by Bonyad-e Farabi; usually the scriptwriter, director, or both were summoned to discuss the script and asked to make changes and corrections to meet the guidelines of the foundation. This process was repeated through many drafts, until the script was given the green light for production. The changes were not just minor ones, but sometimes included changing the entire structure of a script and turning it into something that bore no resemblance to the original text. After this long process, which sometimes lasted for a few months, and after the approval of the advisors of the foundation, the script would be sent to the section in the Ministry of Culture and Islamic Guidance responsible for issuing a license for the script to be made into a film. This procedure was largely a formality and wasn't difficult for those who had survived the scrutiny of Bonyad-e Farabi. After getting a license for the production of the script, the producer gave a list of names, including all of those who were going to participate in the production of the film, from the director, the actors, and the photographer to the various crew members. Bonyad-e Farabi even had the power of approval over the people to work on the production, and in many cases crossed out names and replaced them with those whom the foundation wanted to work, or be seen to work, in the production. For example, Bonyad-e Farabi had a series of actors, female and male, that they wanted to appear in the films in place of the popular pre-revolution actors. Therefore, Bonyad-e Farabi proposed that the producers (or better, ordered the producers) to use particular actors in films. It was the same story with the directors of photography and even the film directors. If a film survived the process through shooting, Farabi still maintained its control and could order changes even in the composition of scenes, or the way the film was being made. Usually, an agent of the foundation was assigned to a film and was present during all aspects of its production. All of these controls were exercised under a law that required a licence to make a film. This licence was a lawful means for the Ministry of

Culture and Islamic Guidance, of which Bonyad-e Farabi was a part, to control the production of films from script to screen.[19] After the film was made, meaning that the agenda of controlling the production had been accomplished, the foundation started to work on its second agenda, which was to support the films made under its control. To support these films Farabi had four important tools: the Fajr Film Festival; foreign film festivals; classification of films; and classification of the theaters.

The Fajr Film Festival, which later became known as the International Film Festival of Fajr, took place annually in Tehran, and began in 1981. The festival was practically taken over in 1984 by the foundation, where it was used to support the films chosen by the foundation and to damage those films not approved by Farabi. Fakhrodin Anvar, the head of Cinema in the Ministry of Culture and Islamic Guidance, has explained the agenda of the festival:

> From 1985, we have announced that the Fajr Film Festival is a place to validate the whole cinema of the country. In other words, the festival is the record of one year of the Islamic Republic cinema from January to January, and is used as a guidance to correct policies and methods of function, and to make models for the future of the Islamic Republic cinema. The policies implemented by the cinema section of the Ministry of Islamic Culture and Guidance, which were planned in general to be "guidance," "support," and "control," from 1983 had a special cultural target, which was to quickly place the cinema on the road toward the magnificent Islamic Culture and Arts.[20]

According to an unwritten law, drafted by the cinema department, all films which were supposed to be screened during a new season in Iran had to participate in the film festival. If a film for any reason — including not having finished its post production — was unable to participate in the festival, that film would have to wait until it could be shown at the next festival before it could be released in theaters. The Fajr International Film Festival of Tehran was the only film festival in the history of world cinema in which filmmakers were forced to participate. Some films that were not finished, or had technical problems with sound or something else, would be shown at the festival before the imperfections could be fixed in order to avoid a year's delay. Films were either supported at the festival or doomed to be ignored by the Iranian film market. The films supported by Farabi were usually screened in the competition section. These were films that won awards at the festival, having been judged by a jury that was in some way connected with the foundation (and if not, at least one of the members of the jury had the duty of relaying the foundation's views on which film should win to the other members).

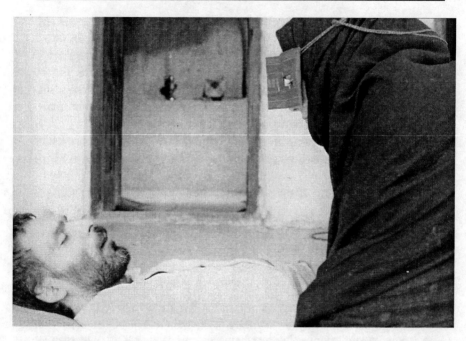

Almassi (left) and Mirbakhtyar in *The Red Wind* (*Bad-e Sorkh*), directed by Jamshid Malekpour in 1990.

The second tool Farabi used to support films was the placement of certain movies in film festivals outside Iran. Every year Farabi, which had an international department, chose a few films and then sent these to film festivals all around the world. For years, Iranian film producers and directors had no right to independently send their films to such festivals, as Farabi mediated all of these transactions. Farabi usually provided the foreign currency to pay for the movies to be subtitled outside Iran in order to be presented at the festivals. (The subtitling of the films is now performed in Iran in a laboratory belonging to the foundation itself). The films were usually accompanied by a representative of the foundation, whose responsibility was to provide necessary publicity for the film, as well as controlling the associated group of artists and filmmakers. The foundation used these tools to make certain filmmakers famous, but Farbi also truncated the potential of filmmakers who did not gain its support. For example, *Bad-e Sorkh* (*The Red Wind*), written and directed by Jamshid Malekpour in 1990, was not made through Farabi's channels; consequently, the film was banned and never screened in Iran.

The third tool for supporting certain films while suppressing others was the classification of movies, which began in 1986. From that year, dur-

Shahla Mirbakhtyar in *The Red Wind*.

ing and after the festival, Iranian films were divided into four categories: A (alef), B (bi), J (jim), and D (dal). Those which were classified as A and B could be shown for longer periods at the better public movie theaters, while those films classified J and D usually were shown for a short time, at theaters in less than optimum locations. Although the department of cinema claimed that this classification was based on the quality of the films, but it was clearly a tool used to suppress even good movies if they were not in line with the policies of the cinema department, or were disliked by the members of Farabi for whatever reason. Even some of the finest Iranian films were given lower classifications, and denied a wide showing. For example, *Bashu* was classified J, while *Ansoyeh Meh* (*Behind the Mist*) was classified A, because *Bashu* did not reflect the views and policies of the cinema department, whereas *Behind the Mist* was made by Farabi itself.

Finally, the fourth tool was the classification of the theaters. This classification began in 1987, when all theaters were divided into categories based on their locations, the quality of projection equipment, and the size of the audience that the theater could attract. Usually those films classified A, or those supported by the foundation, would be shown in the best movie theatres. This meant better box office receipts for those films.

These were the tools that Farabi used to control the cinema industry as well as to guide and support those films in line with the policy of the government. However, there were other ways in which Farabi implemented its political policies onto the films, even if they had less impact than the previous four. These included categorizing the films during their productions into different groups; after the script was approved the producer had to get a licence to make that script into a film, and the license entitled that film to certain technical support from the government. The film, cameras, and production equipment was imported (usually by the government through Farabi) and a film classified A had access to more film and could use it for multiple takes during production, while projects with low classifications were denied the same advantages. This provided another tool for the foundation to support some filmmakers while suppressing others. Those filmmakers supported by Farabi were able to use as much film as they wished, and consequently could choose from a larger selection of scenes during production, while those left without support had to make their films with a minimum of resources.

With this collection of tools and the complicated process of licensing films, Farabi created one of the most advanced and complicated methods of film censorship ever seen. Farabi and the Cinema Department of the Ministry of Culture and Islamic Guidance were not censoring the films, but controlling the entire film industry and even influencing the artistic decisions made by the producers and directors. Consequently, Farabi was the primary film producing body in Iran, although the films were made using money invested by other people.

The place of the Bonyad-e Farabi of the Ministry of Culture and Islamic Guidance and Hozeh Honari of the Islamic Propaganda Organization, and their effects on Iranian cinema, needs further study. Currently, this might not be possible for political reasons, and the difficulty of accessing documents required for such a study. But Bonyad-e Farabi and the Hozeh Honari were clearly the two most powerful forces in the development of Iranian cinema after the revolution. In this climate, several important filmmakers were able to make movies and successfully release them in theaters after the revolution; these include Amir Naderi, Abbas Kiarostami, and Mohsen Makhmalbaf.

Amir Naderi and The Runner

One of the first successful films of the post-revolutionary cinema in Iran was *Davandeh* (*The Runner*), directed by Amir Naderi in 1985. This film was warmly received both inside and outside the country and shown at more than twenty international film festivals, including the London Film Festival (1985), the Venice Film Festival (1986), the Sydney Film Festival (1986), the Melbourne Film Festival (1986), and the Montreal Film Festival (1986). The film won many awards at these festivals, and later was distributed worldwide on video. It was one of the first productions of the new Iranian cinema after the revolution to open the world's eyes to the potential of Iranian cinema.

Amir Naderi is one of the most talented and exceptional directors of Iranian cinema; he learned the craft of filmmaking first by viewing films, and then by working on movies as a photographer. He made his first film in 1971—*Khoda Hafez Rafiq* (*Goodbye, My Friend*). The film was about three young men who are in the business of robbery. They decide to stage a large robbery at a jewelry shop, hoping to put an end to their lives of poverty. But during the robbery one of them betrays the others, and at the end all three are defeated, and the jewels are left on a train for anyone to find. The story was not new, as similar American films existed. However, there was an element in the film that distinguished it from the rest of the Film Farsi products, and even made a few critics defend it. Parviz Davai named that element the "love and passion" of the filmmaker himself, which made the film different:

> The film has many faults or weaknesses and I do not know what exactly they are, I cannot judge the film in that regard. What I can judge is "love." This is the filmmaker's first film. It has no philosophy or extraordinary artistic innovation, and definitely does not have any real place in the history of cinema. But despite all this I believe *Goodbye, My Friend* is a punch in the face of Film Farsi.[21]

Eskandari, Raad and Bakhshi (right to left, at table) in *Deadlock* (*Tangna*), directed by Amir Naderi in 1973.

Naderi made his second film, *Tangna* (*Deadlock*) in 1973, with the experience he had gained from *Goodbye, My Friend*. Ali, the anti-hero of the film, kills someone unintentionally while playing pool and has to escape. He runs not only from the law, but from the brothers of the victim, who are also after him. The movie begins with a brilliant scene: Tehran at dawn when the sun is rising and the city is clean and quiet, empty of people and cars. But soon the camera takes us to the narrow streets and alleys of the city, underground cafes and gambling houses, brothels and rubbish depots, revealing the real face of the city in contrast to what was first presented. In this city, Amir Naderi's city, the people are living like a colony of worms, interacting and passing among one another in a chaotic compression of personality and environment. They deceive each other and run away. It seems no one is caring and no one is willing to help. This is a theme that Naderi employs in almost all of his films. However, it is hard to disagree with E. Jamshidi, who believes that *Deadlock* is "an exaggerated, or over done film."[22] Naderi portrayed everybody and everything in his film so darkly that one cannot accept it as an hon-

Said Raad in *Deadlock*.

est portrayal of a society or individuals. There is no way to garner anything but a bad impression, psychologically or socially, of the characters
in the film. The bitterness and the nihilistic attitude in the film was connected to the filmmaker himself, and the journey through the underside
of Iranian society he undertook to make his films. When the movie is over,
viewers are left with the question of whether, if life is like Ali's, there can
be any hope for change and recovery, especially since the anti-hero is tortured to death. The audience leaves the movie theater in shock and dis-
belief.

After the failure of *Goodbye, My Friend*, and *Deadlock* at the box office
— mainly because of their sad endings, which the Iranian audience did not
like to see — Naderi, in order to survive in the cinema, turned to a famous
novel, *Tangsir*, written by Sadeq Chobak. *Tangsir* (1974) had the potential
to be made into an action drama that could satisfy the tastes of the Iranian audience and attract them to the movie theaters. However, the themes
of rebellion and the search for justice (this time not using an anti-hero but
a classic hero) was in the same tradition as Naderi's two previous films.
This time the hero, for motives that are legitimate and correct in the eyes

of both God and society, takes up a rifle and, with the assistance of a group of people, stands against an evil force. The film has an epic quality not found in his previous works, and audiences filled the theaters and received the film warmly.

Zar Mohammed, from Tangsir in the south of Iran, decides to take revenge on rich and influential people who have stolen his money. He takes a rifle in his hands and begins to fight them, and he is soon joined by other people who help him in his fight. At the end, when he has punished the forces of injustice, he passes his rifle to a young man (a symbol for the continuation of the struggle) and goes toward the sea and disappears.

Although the film has something of Naderi's style and was not a completely faithful adaptation of the novel, on the whole the film was nothing like Naderi's previous work, and it seems apparent that Naderi's only purpose was to make a highly sellable action film. Naderi was able to do this, while at the same time not resorting to making a Film Farsi. The film has a few beautiful scenes that separate it from the quickly made and easily consumable commercial films. One example is the scene in which Zar Mohammed goes to a barber for a haircut, and emerges truly changed, both physically and mentally a new man. As his hair falls onto the floor Zar Mohammed raises his head and we see him through the mirror; and we realize then that he has changed into a man who will soon enter battle.

After the box office success of Tangsir, Naderi had the opportunity to enlist the support of government organizations in order to make films as he himself preferred to make them, rather than making films according to the wants of private producers. *Sazeh Dahani* (*Harmonica*) was one of the best films that Naderi made before the revolution, in 1974.

Harmonica is indirectly about Naderi himself, and can be considered a precursor to his post-revolution movie *The Runner*, and part of a cycle that ended with *Water, Wind, Dust*. In these films, we see the main character (Amiro) not as a cinematic character, but as the filmmaker himself constantly running to survive, running to learn, running to win, and finally running to escape from his situation. *Harmonica* is the story of Amiro, a boy living with his mother in a village near the Persian Gulf. In this village there is another boy, Abdolah, who gets a harmonica from his father. Abdolah uses his harmonica to enslave the other children of the village, as they love to play the harmonica and will do anything Abdolah asks for the chance. Amiro accepts humiliation and enslavement more than the other children in order to play the instrument, even if only for a second. Amiro puts Abdolah on his shoulders and carries him from place to place, as if he were Abdolah's donkey. With this simple story about abuse within a society plagued by a lack of social justice and by poverty, Naderi portrays well the social context that is the film's subject. The film is made with such realism that the audience might think they are watching a documentary instead of fiction, and this adds to the bitterness of the film. The sense of reality causes the audience to crave revenge. One beautiful scene within the film shows Amiro standing behind a high window; on the window's other side Abdolah sits behind the bars, in his house. Unlike Abdolah, who is sitting comfortably behind the window, Amiro is standing on a couple of sharp stones, trying desperately and painfully to reach the harmonica that Abdolah occasionally puts to his lips.

Abdolah's actions toward Amiro are not meant to satisfy him, but to make him frenzied and tired at the same time. But the humiliation that Amiro has brought upon himself through his weakness for the harmonica finally shakes him at the end. In a moment of rebellion and wild frustration (such as we see in most of Naderi's films), Amiro throws the harmonica into the sea, taking his revenge. Kiumars Pour-Ahmad wrote of the film, "Naderi shows beautifully in this film a kind of violence which matches his own temper and character. This film is a very important step in teaching children (and also adults) to protest and to revolt, far from advertising slogans and other popular moral codes. Through his pictures he teaches these elements as necessities in the education of children in society."[23]

The success of *Harmonica* persuaded Naderi to continue working in the same model, again using children as his central performers in the next film. *Entezar* (*Waiting*) was made in 1974; it was a short film, 47 minutes long. "Running," which we will see later as the most important element in Naderi's films, first appeared here. In the first scene, we see a boy running from the sea, coming from the right and leaving to the left. The film is about the boy and his desire to see the face of a girl from whom he receives a pot of ice every day. The boy lives with his aunt and is sent every day to the girl's house to collect ice. A henna stained hand comes out, takes the pot, fills it with ice, and returns it to the boy. He cannot see the face, only the hand, and gradually the stained hand seizes his imagination with a passion, and every sign or object becomes the hand, and every hand becomes a face. When he finally dares to step inside the house, the henna-stained hand disappears forever, and when for the last time he goes to the house to retrieve ice, an old hand comes out to give him the pot of ice. The boy should not have broken the spell of the henna-stained hand by breaking an unspoken taboo by entering the house to seek the true source of his fantasies.

We can view this film from different perspectives. Naderi wishes to portray the idea that a search is beautiful as long as it remains a search; when the object of desire is found, it loses its attraction. In other words, love is passionate as long as it does not meet the object of its desire. When it does, whatever is loved loses some of its status, becoming like all other ordinary, humanly accessible objects of desire. At the same time the film can be viewed as the maturation of body and mind, and the process of passing through this development — embodied by the young hand that changes into the old hand by the end of the film.

The film is symbolic, but one can sense the connection between the symbols used in the films and certain realities. The ice symbolizes coolness, which can satiate the heat of lust and make lips that are dry with desire wet once again. For the people living in the south of Iran, ice has great significance; a pot of ice water on a hot summer day could be as pleasurable to a man or woman as making love. For this reason — and because Naderi himself was sold ice water when he was a child in the streets, living day by day with what he could earn through this trade — it gradually became an important symbolic elements in this and other films. Naderi also uses mourning rituals to give the disembodied hand a very mystical and significant place in his film. In *Waiting*, Naderi uses a unique style of editing to juxtapose these symbols and create an atmosphere around the central conceptual theme of "the search." He continued to use variations on this theme even until his last film, in 1993, when he left Iran for America, searching for his own utopia.[24]

Before the revolution took place in 1979, Naderi made a feature film that was unlike his other films. (Those films that used the archetype of the anti-hero who had to fight to survive, and in the end would be defeated and killed.) *Marsiyeh* (*Elegy*, 1975) was about a shadow of a man whose big, black, innocent eyes transport us into his internal world.

Seyed Nasrolah, the main character, is released from prison after being held captive for eight years. He attempts to return to his previous life, but he soon realizes that nothing of that life remains and perhaps nothing had existed in the first place for him to return to. In the tradition of Naderi's characters he begins to wander in the city and walks from street to street, alley to alley, and suburb to suburb. Through these wanderings, and through his innocent eyes, we see horrible pictures of the environment and the people. It seems as though there is nothing but ugliness and bitterness. In *Elegy*, we see the first signs of Naderi's style of composition and editing that would later appear in their fully developed form in *The Runner*, known as a "collage of images." The images are presented one after another, and there is no apparent intention to create a unified plot. In fact, they are photographs taken by Naderi with a still camera and then placed within what might be considered a cinematic photo album, with no intention of creating a story that has a beginning, middle and an end.

As everything in Iran was being affected by mass demonstrations and the scent of revolution lingered over every street and suburb, Naderi finally realized one of his dreams — to make a film in the United States, in order to become an international filmmaker; the result was *Sakht-e Iran* (*Made in Iran*).

The character Ali is a young Iranian boxer who goes to America with the dream of becoming famous. Predictably, he is deceived by an American gang that trains and supports boxers before using them in fixed fights in order to make money. Ali makes a name for himself by winning a few fights, but the day comes when he is supposed to throw a fight because the gang has money bet against him. Ali refuses to accept this arrangement and wins the fight despite his orders. He is beaten to death, but before his death manages to kill those responsible for his situation. *Made in Iran* was made in 1979, in the middle of the revolution. The message of the film was anti–American, and most suitable for Iranian people who eventually saw the revolution as an anti–American movement. The film therefore could have been seen as an artistic move in support of the revolution, but it was made in such a trite fashion, using a plot long out of fashion even with Iranian audiences, that it was a failure both in Iran and in the United States, where Naderi dreamed it would open doors and allow him to make films.

The filmmaking career of Naderi after the revolution in fact began with the revolution itself, through the making of the 1978 film *Barandeh* (*The Winner*), which took five years to complete and was never given the opportunity to be shown to the public. One might consider *The Winner* as practice for *The Runner*, which was made a few years later and became one of Naderi's most famous films. The main theme in both films (and even some scenes) is exactly the same. *The Winner* is about a couple of children from the south of Iran who play in the sea; one of their games is to collect the empty bottles floating in the water (these empty bottles were thrown into the sea by the employees of oil cargo ships coming into the Persian Gulf, and the children collected them from the sea and sold them for a small profit). One day, they decide to use the money they have made from selling bottles to buy a watermelon, which they'll then place on an empty barrel of oil. They invent a game in which the winner is whoever reaches the watermelon first. The competition starts, but the "winner" is a man on a bicycle who grabs the watermelon and rides away. In fact, *The Winner* was in a manner practice for making *The Runner*, but before Naderi would make *The Runner* he made two more films, during the revolution:

Josteju Yek (*Search 1*), and *Josteju Doo* (*Search 2*). *Search 1* (1981) is about those people who vanished during the revolution; presumably they were killed, but their bodies were never recovered. Most members of their families were still waiting for them to return, or for their remains to be found. Naderi, with a camera in hand, searches among rubbish, dead lakes, ruins and cemeteries for a sign of the vanished, and throughout the search he captures the most horrible images with his camera to show to Iranian audiences. *Search 2* (1983) is about the war between Iraq and Iran in 1981, a war that lasted for eight years. The film, is not about the battlefields and soldiers, but about innocent people who are caught in between and do not know how to escape. In both films, Naderi mixed documentary style with drama, along with the technique of taking photographs and using them as freeze frames. It seems that Naderi, with these two films, reached his goal, which was the portrayal of waiting, fear, hopelessness and exhaustion, familiar elements in most of his nondocumentary films and the films to follow. Although a few critics, like Hoshang Golmakani,[25] believed that *Search 1* and *Search 2* did not satisfy one's expectations of a Naderi film, in both we see a quality that was unique to Iranian cinema at that time. This was a particular form of dramatic improvisation, which became an integral artistic device in Naderi's feature films *The Runner* and *Water, Wind, Dust*. In these two films, Naderi shot most of the scenes unscripted, with no plan or particular scenario in mind. His experience helped him later to take the camera in his hands without notes for guidance, and move quickly from location to location, filming wherever he sensed a good opportunity at any given moment.

In the 1980s, as the cultural policy makers of Iran became more aware of the cinema and its influential place within society, they decided to use it not only as a propaganda tool to forward the regime's ideological maxims, but also as a cheap form of popular entertainment for the people. About the same time, Amir Naderi made *The Runner* (1985) and created not just a quality film, but also a template for all of Iranian cinema, which at that time was in a state of disarray and lacked any direction. In this regard one might consider *The Runner* to be the most important film of the new Iranian cinema after the revolution; it helped spur the development of a pictorial style of cinema, and used children's characters as metaphorical representations of universal themes. This kind of movie became the main attraction of Iranian cinema, capturing the attention of an international audience. Naderi, with *The Runner*, pioneered such cinema, which was later labeled "cinema of children," rather than for children.

The Runner (1985) was shown at most international film festivals, including the Nantes Film Festival in France in 1985, where it took the award as the best film of the competition section. Hal Hinson writes:

> Amir Naderi's *The Runner* hovers somewhere between poetry and documentary. Its subject is an orphaned Iranian boy named Amiro who lives in an abandoned ship in the port of Abadan, and on one level it deals with the deprived conditions of his life in classic, neo-realist style.... The movie is about an almost savage futility, but there is a kind of exaltation here too, which has less to do with Amiro's fervent attempts to educate himself than with the joyous expressiveness of this young actor's face. His unguarded exuberance hits you with unexpected force. It stays with you.[26]

Amiro is a ten- or twelve-year-old boy who lives alone in an abandoned ship on the coast of the Persian Gulf. To stay alive, he has to run and fight. He collects empty bottles from the sea to sell, and he carries a bucket of ice cold water on his shoulders and sells it to thirsty people to make a few pennies. He works as a shoeshine boy, and does other odd jobs. The film is about Amiro's life, and the reality of this type of life for those who must subsist in such a manner. It is also about Amiro's dreams, which are not as easily portrayed; through metaphor and subtext, the filmmaker subtly relays Amiro's hopes and dreams. The film does not have a storyline in the traditional sense, nor does it have a distinct beginning or end. Those critics who have written that Amiro, at the end of the film, achieves some kind of victory have imposed a structure where none exists (in terms of the formal language of cinema). The film is a collection of photographs taken without order, without any consideration of unifying time or place. For Amiro, life is to run and to reach, but when he arrives he is not satisfied, so he runs again, and reaches, and runs. This context is exactly in line with the film's technique, a collection of randomly arranged snapshots. As noted, Naderi began his work in cinema as a photographer, and as a director he

Majid Niroomand in *The Runner* (*Davandeh*), directed by Amir Naderi in 1985.

approaches *The Runner* with a photographer's mindset. In photography, every element has an important place within the composition; in *The Runner* each element that possesses kinetic energy, whether it's water, fire, an aeroplane, train, or a bicycle, is used to show Amiro's desire to run.[27] He does not want to stay in any environment that will stop him from reaching his goal. He wants to learn the alphabet so that he can write. He wants to go to other lands beyond the sea, of which he has already seen beautiful postcards in magazines. Amiro literally runs to reach this dream, this vision: he runs after ships, he runs after aeroplanes, and he runs after a train that would take him to such places. Amiro knows that he has only his own two feet to take him from place to place, and they become his most precious and important asset. These elements give the film paradoxically tactile and untouchable aspects, and impart a pace that reaches neither a crescendo nor a decrescendo.

Although the film is an artistic product and a product of the imagination, *The Runner* was heavily influenced by Naderi's own life. *The Runner* is, in part, autobiographical: Amir Naderi was eight years old when he lost his parents and began to live in the streets in the port city of Abadan. During this time, he took the type of jobs that most orphans and other poor children of the city would perform in order to survive — selling ice water, shining shoes, collecting empty bottles from the sea, selling lottery tickets, and so on. Amir Naderi left this life of wandering when he was twelve years old for the capital of Iran, Tehran. Once there, he concentrated mainly on jobs that were connected to the cinema or photography. He worked in printing labs and later in cinemas, doing everything from cleaning the venues to working inside the box office. Through all of those years, he was training himself by studying the photos that were published in magazines. He finally learned the art of photography, and, with some difficulty, secured a job in the film industry as a photographer. Passion, enthusiasm, honesty and hard work soon made him a very familiar face within the industry, and he eventually succeeded in making his first film, *Goodbye, My Friend*, with almost no resources. When we examine *The Runner* we see the connection between Amir, the film's director, and Amiro, the film's main character: the first, with a camera in the hands, is running after the second, who himself is running after something to take him away.

The Runner opens with a long shot of the sea and Amiro. In foggy weather, we see Amiro facing the sea, shouting into the mist. The shadow of super tankers that have come from far and unknown lands to be filled with oil can be seen in the background. This very first scene portrays the dream of Amiro — to leave the place where he lives and to experience life in unknown lands. Why Amiro wants to leave is, in fact, the question of the film, and the answer is revealed through the photographs that appear throughout the film. Amiro is alone. Though for a short time Amiro finds a friend, he is again left alone when his friend leaves him in order to join his brother, who is working on a ship. Amiro does not have parents, and in a sense does not have a homeland either. The place where Amiro lives is used to express this idea: he stays in an abandoned, rusty ship, half sunken in the sea, with no windows or electricity. Without a secure job Amiro struggles to feed himself, and even in this he has to fight violently with others who are in a similar condition. One of the film's most effective messages is how poverty robs people of their sympathy for their fellow man, often leading to violence as they struggle to survive. In one scene Amiro is selling ice water when a young man drinks and then runs away without paying. Although Amiro cannot demand his rights from the legal system, he feels that he can justifiably take what he is owed from such a man. Even here, Amiro faces a challenge: the man is riding a bicycle and Amiro is barefoot, but in the end Amiro succeeds in stopping the man and getting a worthless coin from him. Again, we see that for Amiro getting the money was secondary; what matters most is extracting a kind of moral and personal justice from his situation. A sweet smile on his little innocent face says it all.

The film does not follow the straight line of most stories, neither in narration nor image construction. It is obvious that the director did not attempt to develop a unified narrative. He has taken a series of photos, framed them and hung them on a wall, in order to lead the audience through their enigmatic presentation: the director presents the film as a collage. This technique functions alongside the impressionistic atmosphere of the film. Strong emphasis on open air, nature and its elements, such as water, fire and wind, and the combination of warmth, vitality and movement in each scene give the film that impressionistic atmosphere. In a sense, there are no interior scenes in the film: the director has taken interior spaces—like the classroom of the school—and mixed them with the outdoor spaces through editing. When Amiro begins to learn the alphabet in the classroom, we see images of Amiro practising each letter while he is walking and chasing the wild waves of the sea.

The last scene of the film is without doubt one of the most beautiful scenes of Iranian cinema; one might even consider it an independent piece of work, a film within a film, complete in and of itself. In this scene, which uses fire and ice to establish a theme, a piece of ice has been placed on an empty barrel that is close to a huge fire from a burning oil well. In the distance, children run toward the ice, competing to get to it, even as the ice melts beside the fire. The game begins, but rather than running toward the ice the children fight, punching each other in order to gain the upper hand, actually making the run take longer as the ice continues to melt. This sequence is again portraying the brutal struggle and the fight to survive and win, a theme that the film has already presented. At the end, Amiro succeeds in reaching the ice first, though by this time only a small piece remains. While yelling from the depths of his heart, he takes the ice over his head as a sign of victory, while the flames of the fire fill the background of the scene. We can see the piece of ice on his dry lips, and when the rest of the group reach him one after another, Amiro offers the piece of ice to them so that they can satisfy their own thirst. At the same time an aeroplane passes over their heads, reminding us of Amiro's need to keep running even during moments of satisfaction. The beauty of the scene is increased through the use of slow motion and the cutting between fire, ice, and the competing children's faces.

The Runner was screened in 1985 after years of stagnation in Iranian cinema, and became a source of motivation and encouragement for other filmmakers. Despite its success both inside and outside of Iran, an unseen political and artistic movement hurt the film, a reaction to the director's refusal to accept the support and structural guidance of the Farabi Cinema Foundation. This conflict ended with the emigration of the director from Iran, which was something he had been willing to do for many years. Critic Khosroo Dehghan entered the fray when he accused Naderi of having no knowledge of cinema, not once but twice, and recommended that he buy books on the subject and learn how to properly make a movie:

> No, The Runner is not a good film. It has problems even with its basic cinematic alphabet. If we judge domestic and foreign films by one standard, then we can say with greater confidence that The Runner is not a successful film. There is a scene in the film dedicated to learning the alphabet. It would be good for [Naderi] to start here. He must gain determination, and make himself confident. The bookshops across the university in this season are usually open to seven thirty.[28]

This is obviously not a review of a film, but an insult and an attack on Naderi's integrity and morals as an artist. The "knowledgeable" critic knew that Amir Naderi didn't have a formal education and could not compete in this regard, so he rather maliciously brought up that fact in his review instead of analyzing the film itself. The problem with Naderi's film, in the critic's eyes, probably was that he did not make the film under the guidance of the authorities.

The Runner is a beautiful film, though it has its weaknesses. These are largely related to the filmmaking process, rather than the film itself.

The movie was made during the war between Iraq and Iran, and Naderi was unable to shoot in the real location (the port of Abadan); instead he was forced to shoot in different locations and paste the scenes together to recreate the atmosphere of Abadan (which was being bombed by Iraqi airplanes at the time). For this reason, the process of filming of *The Runner* was constantly interrupted as the crew moved from one place to another, extending the time taken to complete the film. It also caused clearly visible discontinuity in the film; in one scene, for instance, the boy's hair is long, and in the next scene it is short, and even his age appears different. There is a scene in the film which seems meant either to please the authorities who decided whether a film would be released, or as sentimental revenge by the filmmaker, aimed at the sailors who were coming to the port of Abadan during Naderi's childhood. In the scene, Amiro is shown fighting with an American who accuses him of stealing his lighter. This scene is hardly in keeping with the atmosphere and overall style of the film, and in a way it contradicts the main subtext of the film, which is Amiro's (or the filmmaker himself) desire to travel to the United States. However, the weakness of this scene is overcome by the strength of the last sequence, that of the fire and ice. Some critics have even compared the film with the works of De Sica and Truffaut. Lisa Albert writes:

> Amir Naderi's *The Runner* is a landmark film and a work of astonishing simplicity and power…. *The Runner* bears comparison with the classics of its genre: De Sica's *Shoeshine*, Bunuel's *Los Olvidados*, Truffaut's *The 400 Blows*…. *The Runner* is wholly distinctive in its form, differing greatly from the standard Western format.[29]

After the international success of *The Runner*, Amir Naderi made *Ab, Bad, Khak* (*Water, Wind, Dust*) in 1989, which one might consider a complete and polished version of *The Runner*. It also comprises the third part of a trilogy that began with *The Winner*, a trilogy with a central theme of running.[30] With no unified plot, *Water, Wind, Dust* was even more radical than *The Runner* in many respects.

The opening scene takes place in the middle of a desert, where a dust storm clouds one's vision. A dark-complexioned boy (Amiro) gets out of a pick-up, and while carrying a small goat in his arms faces the camera and tells how, two years ago, his father had taken him to work in the city. During these two years, he sent money to his family, but then he learned that the lake beside which his family lives has dried up. Now he has returned to see what happened to his family. He begins to look for them, though there is no one left to help him search. Amiro begins his search in the desert, where the blowing wind and dust make his efforts difficult. In

this environment, Naderi leaves the impressionistic pictures of *The Runner* behind, moving into a surrealistic space and creating images reminis-
cent of Luis Buñuel's films (for example, *Un Chien Andalou*) but
transposed into Naderi's own context. Realistic images of the decomposed
body of a cow and of a man digging in search of water soon change into
surrealistic collages, among them a jar of water containing two red fish
dropping to the ground and a watermelon that has been placed on the
burning sands of the desert. But even these surrealistic images seem realistic within the framework of the film when we see its other elements. Soon
Amiro's search for his family changes into the search for water. Amiro is
no longer alone, but joins others who are moving about in the desert helping each other to search for water. Here is a big difference between *The
Runner* and *Water, Wind, Dust*. In *The Runner*, Amiro wants to run and
to win alone. Now he is asking others to stay with him, convincing them
that they must all work together. At the end of the movie, Amiro digs into
the earth with a pick, and we see the water coming out of the earth, set to
the music of Beethoven's Fifth Symphony. The water running on dry land,
covering the dry, dead fish, seems to bring new life to the barren landscape.

We have said that Naderi relied upon the art of improvisation in *The
Runner*, but according to Mani Petgar, Naderi's assistant director, *Water,
Wind, Dust* was almost completely improvised. The director began with
only a single image: a little boy wandering in a big desert. With only this
image, Naderi took the crew and the actors into the desert, and began
hunting for other images that he could shape into a movie.

The use of color in this film is magnificent, as the entire film was shot
in an environment that was full of dust, giving a kind of khaki brown hue
to the background. Naderi brings out other colors, particularly warm colors, in contrast to this background. A red fish is in sharp contrast to the
dried and brown land on which it lays, for example. However, Naderi's
most important technical and artistic achievement in the film is the sound
composition. The sound of wind and dust coupled with the sound of
Amiro's breathing create the music throughout the film, joined at the end
to the sound of water exploding from the earth.

Water, Wind, Dust, like *The Runner*, was well received inside and outside Iran.[31] Bahman Maqsodlou wrote:

> In the development of a cinematic language and a personal aesthetic Amir
> Naderi has been successful. In Iranian cinema this is the first time that a
> filmmaker tries to portray philosophical thoughts through poetic pictures.
> I believe that Naderi is the most important filmmaker who has stepped into
> the industry in recent years. The experience of childhood and youth has
> become an enormous resource, generating a poetic attitude toward life for

him, which he has been able to transfer to us through the images one after another.[32]

"Loosely autobiographical" cinema might be the best description of Naderi's work; most of his characters at some point diverge from the path of Naderi's actual life. Naderi's struggles in his childhood and the difficulties he overcame to become an established filmmaker profoundly influenced his stylistic evolution. It is obvious that he had moved from narrative cinema, found in *Goodbye, My Friend*, *Deadlock* and *Elegy*, to a kind of anti-narrative expressed in *The Runner* and *Water, Wind, Dust*. But through all of these films, we can see the same nihilistic, rebellious, and bad-tempered character, always being punished or paying for what other people have done, people to whom he is somehow connected, willingly or unwillingly. These adult characters can be considered to represent Naderi himself; in his latter films they are replaced by innocent children, again representative of the director when he was a child — showing the innocent child, as remembered and fantasized about when he has become an adult. In his films before the revolution, we see his characters running to escape, to vanish from the sight of others, while in his films after the revolution his characters run in order to be seen and be recognized.

Abbas Kiarostami and Where Is My Friend's Home?

Abbas Kiarostami is easily recognizable today as the most important filmmaker of the new Iranian cinema, having gained not only an international reputation, but also having influenced the whole of modern Iranian cinema. He and his work have been lauded in reviews, and won awards and acclaim at international film festivals. David Sterritt writes:

> The filmmaker most responsible for Iranian cinema's renown is Abbas Kiarostami, who earned praise for gentle dramas like *And Life Goes On* and *Through the Olive Trees* before winning the Cannes Film Festival's coveted Golden Palm Award for *Taste of Cherry*, an exquisitely filmed meditation on life, death, and the search for meaning in a frequently uncaring world.[33]

Confirmation of his breakthrough of Iranian cinema onto the world stage can be found in a review written by Geoff Brown:

> Iran's films are regularly invited to the festivals, win prizes including the Palme d'Or at Cannes, and have become a cult among cinema aficionados. Directors such as Abbas Kiarostami and Mohsen Makhmalbaf have ascended into the world's top league.[34]

Abbas Kiarostami, after graduating with a degree in painting from the College of Fine Arts at Tehran University, started his cinema career by working on the titles for films and commercials. He made his first film, "Nan va Kocheh" ("The Bread and the Alley") in 1970; it was a ten-minute short film about children. The fruit of his labors and his interest in children's subjects and their representation ripened in 1987, with the film *Where Is My Friend's Home?*, one of the masterpieces in children's cinema.

In "The Bread and the Alley," a boy is returning home after buying bread, but on his way a dog stops him by barking. The boy does not dare to pass the dog and sits, waiting perhaps for the dog to move away. Passersby, without paying attention to the boy, move on without offering help. The boy, who sees that he should not expect help from anybody else, eventually finds a solution: he throws a piece of bread to the dog, and while the dog is eating he moves past safely.

The message of the film, like the film itself, is very simple — have confidence and rely on our own ability, rather than others. The film is also about a fear that has important psychological consequences for children, which, when overcome, can benefit them greatly by instilling a strong sense of independence and self-confidence. Apart from the didactic message in the film, we see a filmmaker who is able to catch all of the boy's reactions in a short time, in an effective and economical way. After this film, Kiarostami made more than ten long and short films till 1978; among them *Mosafer* (*Traveller*) in 1972, and *Gozaresh* (*The Report*) in 1978, were well received by critics and audiences, and are recognized as Kiarostami's best films in his pre-revolution career.

Traveller is the story of a young man who loves soccer, and his dream is to attend a soccer match in the main stadium of Iran's capital. He'll do anything, including cheating his own friends, to acquire the money he needs to make the trip. He boards a bus for the overnight trip to the stadium; because of his excitement and anticipation about the game, he stays awake all night — and then falls asleep just before the match, only to awaken in the empty stadium after the contest has ended. Apart from having a beautiful theme, that of disappointment in desire, the film is very intense from a visual perspective. Jamshid Akrami wrote of the movie:

> Abbas Kiarostami, the maker of the successful film *The Bread and the Alley*, showed us that he had a new style at last year's festival of children's films with his work *The Experience*, now shows this style in its complete form with *Traveller*. A fresh, passionate, honest and likable film, *Traveller* is a brilliant example of maintaining unity of plot in a film. Through live characters, passionate events, and complementary Iranian music composed

from the invitation of images, Kiarostami creates a simple, attractive, and intelligent film.[35]

Traveller shows the first signs of combining simplicity of expression with a sophisticated philosophical aesthetic, which in his later films made after the revolution, like *Taste of Cherry* and *The Wind Will Carry Us*, are employed in their best way and in fact create Kiarostami's cinematic style.

Another important film Kiarostami made before the revolution (1978) was *The Report*. Unlike the rest of his films, which were usually produced by a government organization (K.P.F.K.N.), *The Report* was produced by a cinema company, and it might be considered as his first professional film—for the first time the cast was made up of professional actors, rather than the ordinary people used by Kiarostami in his previous films.

The Report truly *is* a report, detailing the realities of life for a taxation office public servant who is accused of bribery, has difficulties with his wife, and at the same time is evicted from his rental house. The film chronicles four days in the life of the couple, and at the same time it portrays an ugly city full of people and cars, all nervous and impatient. The couple take their frustrations out on each other, and the conflict escalates until the man beats his wife and leaves the house, taking their children. When he returns, he finds that the wife has attempted suicide. He takes her to the hospital, and after a while the couple leaves the hospital for home, more exhausted than ever. The film ends, though it seems obvious that their life will not be any different in the future.

The Report shows Kiarostami's passion for exploring a subject or following a character through the streets and suburbs of a city. It is through this chase that Kiarostami portrays the reactions of other people. This dual perspective later becomes a central concept in films like *Taste of Cherry*. The face of the character works as a mirror, reflecting the faces of other people as if, in essence, the character is the camera. The main character in *The Report* is shown from two points of view: One is the camera's viewpoint, which captures the tax officer, and the other is the officer himself, who views the people and life around him. These two combine to create a unified narrative, simple yet meaningful. This is what we have already described as simplicity of expression with a philosophical aesthetic. According to Hoshang Golshirie,

> It seems one of the four walls of a house have been removed in order for us to watch the secret tragedy of life taking place in one of the cage-like rental apartments in Iran. And his success is exactly here.... At the end of the film when this stranger goes to compromise with this hostile world we see not another life but the life of ourselves. Instead of that wall ... we sud-

denly see a mirror, placed so that we can see our own house, our own office, or our own husband or wife.[36]

The Report has a few vital elements commonly found in Kiarostami's films. Among these are realism, created through the documentary style employed by the director, and simplicity, which is achieved through the camera work, the composition of scenes, and especially a very simple and understated acting style used both by the amateur and professional actors. Two other elements of Kiarostami's works should also be mentioned. One is his portrayal of brutality and violence in relationships and in life, something he tends to relay through poetic stylizations rather than direct depictions. The other element is a condensed and concise use of dialogue in the films. We see all of these characteristics in *The Report*, although not as prominently as in Kiarostami's post-revolution films.

Abbas Kiarostami was able to continue making films after the Islamic revolution of 1979, as his body of work before the revolution contained nothing that precluded him from working in the new political and social environment. Uncertainty about the future of Iran's film industry after the revolution did keep him from working immediately after the upheaval, and until 1986 he again concentrated on short, mostly educational films. In 1987 Kiarostami was able to make his first post-revolution feature film, *Where Is My Friend's Home?* (*Khaneyeh Dost Kojast?*), a film which earned international acclaim both for Kiarostami, and for Iranian cinema, which was also gaining world notice because of films like *The Runner* and *Water, Wind, Dust*, by Amir Naderi.

In *Where Is My Friend's Home?*, Mohammed Reza is a primary school student living in a village in northern Iran. He is criticised for not doing his homework by a teacher who threatens to expel him from school should this continue. After arriving home, Ahmad, Mohammed Reza's classmate, finds out that he has taken Mohammed Reza's notebook by mistake. Ahmad knows that if Mohammed does not have his notebook, he won't be able to do his homework and will definitely be expelled from class. Ahmad decides to take the notebook to his classmate, but Ahmad knows only that Mohammed Reza lives in the next village, and he does not have the exact address. Between the two villages lie a hill and a winding road, which Ahmad walks along, carrying the notebook. On the way Ahmad asks people he encounters for help as he continues to seek Mohammed Reza's home, but when nighttime falls, Ahmad's search has been unsuccessful. The following day, when the teacher begins to check their homework, Ahmad places the notebook on his friend's desk. Mohammed Reza opens the notebook and sees that Ahmad has done the work for him; there is even a flower pressed between the pages of the book.

Even though the film is about children, it is not a film just for children. Beautifully photographed, with a poetic style and a theme that extended beyond the children's film, *Where Is My Friend's Home?* transcended cultural barriers and created a humanist movie, portraying the most important problems of life in the simplest form. Fifteen years of experience with the same stylistic elements that Kiarostami used in *The Report* and his other works finally bore him sweet and colorful fruit. If we are to select the best films of Iranian cinema post-revolution, we should include *Where Is My Friend's Home?* along with *The Runner* by Amir Naderi and *Bashu* by Bahram Bayzai.

After a successful screening at the Tehran Film Festival, and a warm welcome by the audience and critics in Iran, the film quickly was accepted by many world film festivals. First it was shown at the Locarno Film Festival (1989), taking home three important awards, including the best film award. The film then played at many other film festivals around the world. Bruce Kirkland, who saw the film at the Toronto Film Festival in 1997, wrote:

> The cinema of simplicity would serve Hollywood well, if only it didn't believe that bigger is always best. Look elsewhere for good examples, such as *Where Is My Friend's Home?* This is a modest 85-minute Iranian movie ... which brings us back to the elegance of simplicity. This story is basic and the film modest, yet its ambitions are as big as the indomitable human spirit.[37]

The theme of the film is the challenges faced when helping others. The theme is portrayed through a very simple and realistic plot, the delivery of a notebook to a classmate. But there is a second theme, presented alongside the first, which is no less important, and that is the portrayal of the world of children inside the "larger" world of adults. This can simply be defined as a lack of attention, and the failure to listen to each other. We hear each other but we do not understand, and this lack of understanding, in broad terms, is one of the key problems plaguing human relationships. The challenge to help and the lack of understanding of those around us creates a unified theme in the movie. If we are going to help each other, we need to listen and to understand each other — otherwise the attempt to help will miss its mark. Whenever Ahmad meets someone in the village, rather than listening to Ahmad and understanding what he is asking, the person begins to explain himself, and speak for himself; the people feel no motivation to listen to Ahmad and understand what he is asking. Ahmad consequently wanders hopelessly through the narrow alleys of the

village, with a look of despair and defeat on his face. The worry evident
on Ahmad's face, and the concern in his eyes, comprise the most important pictorial motif of the film. Ahmad is worried that he will not deliver
the notebook to his classmate; that he will become lost, and be unable to
find his home again; about the falling darkness; and he is worried about
many other things. The audience can sense these concerns turning in
Ahmad's mind and heart. In future films like *Taste of Cherry* and *The Wind
Carries Us*, this sense of concern is gradually replaced by one of alienation,
which will be discussed in due course.

Apart from being a beautiful film, *Where Is My Friend's Home?* had a
major impact on a few filmmakers who would begin to make films in the
same tradition, and gain an international reputation with similar techniques. Among them were Jafar Panahi (*The White Balloon*) and Majid
Majidi (*Color of God*) who made their own films in the tradition of *Where
Is My Friend's Home?* and *The Runner*. Kiarostami's films showed other
filmmakers the potential of such stories, and the beauty of a simple, poetic
style. It was a form of movie in which the filmmaker could discuss social
issues without being hindered by the board of censors, as the characters were
children, who in the eyes of those censors were likely innocent creatures,
free of any political motivation. This was an important consideration, and
can be recognized in films of this type made in Iran in the '80s and '90s.

The success of *Where Is My Friend's Home?* gave Kiarostami the
confidence to expand the context of his films, and his evolving technique
would ultimately lead to the creation of a type of cinema known as the
cinema of alienation, best represented by films like *Taste of Cherry*. However, before making *Taste of Cherry* Kiarostami first made *Mashq-e Shab*
(*Homework*) in 1989, which was an educational documentary about homework and the problems that children have with it. On the one hand, there
is the entire system of education (which seems more sadistic than encouraging) and on the other hand there are the parents, who cannot understand the education system, adding to the children's problems and
multiplying the pain they experience through the process. As the film was
a very sharp criticism of the Iranian education system, it was banned and
never released to the public. *Homework* was a return to the educational
and children's cinema in which Kiarostami was working before the revolution. His next film was *Namaye Nazdik* (*Close-up*), made in 1990.

With *Close-up* Kiarostami showed a new direction for his work, and
a style of cinema never before seen in Iranian film. It was very contemporary; a story from everyday life was turned into a drama-documentary,
using the people who were actually involved. He would use this formula
for two other films, *And Life Goes On*, and *Under the Olive Trees*.

The true story behind *Close-up*, as it was published in newspapers, was that of a young man, Hussein Sabzian, who bore a strong resemblance to Mohsen Makhmalbaf (the famous Iranian director). Sitting on a bus beside an elderly woman, he struck up a conversation, presenting himself as Makhmalbaf. Through this opening he stepped into the lives of the woman's family, forming an especially close bond with a young man who was very interested in cinema. Sabzian, as Makhmalbaf, began rehearsals for a film starring the young man, but the father, who gradually became suspicious, discovered the truth, and consequently the pretender ended up in jail for fraud. Kiarostami picks up the story and making *Close-up* by encouraging the participation of all of the people actually involved in the incident. Ahankha's family, Makhmalbaf, and Kiarostami himself all play themselves.

The film follows two storylines. One is of Sabzian and the family, people who seem to be more naïve than anything else regarding the whole event; the second concerns the director himself, who opportunistically and brutally encourages people to display their own ignorance and humiliation in front of the cameras, to be seen by millions of other people. However, the people chose to participate in part because they would be taking part in a film made by a famous filmmaker and hoped to become famous themselves. In any case, the family was presented with a brutality that one finds hard to understand or explain. This raises a question of whether an artist has the right, even for the sake of art, to cross certain lines concerning the humiliation of people. What would be the consequences if films such as this one were released for the friends and families of the people involved? Is it really worth making such a film? The answer to all of these questions depends largely on the attitude and the angles from which the questions are approached. Although Abbas Kiarostami stated that "the film gives people the chance to know that he (Sabzian) is basically a nice person who has enormous social difficulties,"[38] the entire film displays nothing so much as the opportunism of the filmmaker. Sharookh Davalkoh writes:

> Before Kiarostami, there were filmmakers and many other artists who created works that scratched art's innocent face in an attempt to come as close as possible to reality. It seems that reality has become a common excuse among some artists—they say that their intentions were to grab at reality, but more important is the burning issue of dignity.... We have seen many violent films in the west where one bullet can mean the death of many people, but these filmmakers (like Kiarostami), in an even deeper form, ignore the dignity of humanity. They kill humanity spiritually, so Kiarostami can be accused of two crimes—blurring the lines of reality, and ignoring the dignity of humans.[39]

Although some critics, like Ramin Jahanbglou, believe Kiarostami's work serves a purpose, because having the characters face reality allows them to move past their ordinary daily pains. It's questionable whether Kiarostami actually does this in *Close-up*. All of the film's characters know what has happened and consequently what will happen, and none of them can escape this fact to act naturally as "reality" is played out in the film. *Close-up* is nothing but a game played with reality with the dignity of humans; in a sense, Kiarostami is playing with moviemaking itself, which of course is not bad and can be considered as an achievement in terms of his artistic development. *Close-up* can be viewed as a turning point in Kiarostami's career, not because of its quality as a movie, but because of the techniques he employed, and would use and further develop in his future films. Even the technique itself was an improvised and spontaneous artistic creation, as Kiarostami revealed in an interview — he had no intention or idea of making such a film, and at the time intended to make a different film altogether when he read about Hussein Sabzian's arrest in the newspapers. The next day when he was slated to begin shooting for the other film, he took his camera and began shooting *Close-up*.[40] Therefore, improvisation and hunting for the right moments to use as photos in *Close-up* became in a way its own artistic inspiration. In the film, the camera participates as an actor in every scene, and the audience can clearly recognize this in the film. The combination of these techniques and a sense of interpretative alienation or distance in the movie align Kiarostami with a form of cinema that relies more upon characters and their immediate reactions to any given situation, rather than the traditional commercial school in which everything is meant to move the story ahead or serve the plot.

Just as the sad, unpleasant true story of Hussein Sabzian was the inspiration for *Close-up*, a tragic event became the basis for Kiarostami's next two films. *Va Zendegi Edameh Darad* (*And Life Goes On*, 1992), and *Zir-e Darakhtan-e Zieton* (*Under the Olives Trees*, 1994) were both made based on a terrible earthquake that struck northern Iran in 1991. These two films were made as episodes that complemented each other.

In *And Life Goes On*, Kiarostami and his son, played by others, go to the north days after the earthquake to learn news about Ahmad and Babak, two main actors in *Where Is My Friend's Home?*, whose village is located within the earthquakes area. They cannot find these two actors, but are able to confirm their well-being. Through their journey, the filmmaker shows the will to live among people who have lost everything. The Persian-language was title of the film *Zendegi va Digar Hich* (*Life and Nothing Else*), which was changed upon international distribution to *And*

Life Goes On, so as not to be mistaken with Bertrand Tavernier's film (*Life and Nothing More*) made in 1990.

Even though the film takes places in an earthquake-shattered region, and we see some of the physical and mental results of this tragic natural disaster, people are still attempting to smile in the midst of tragedy. The film is not truly about these surface motifs, but uses the earthquake and the people caught amidst the tragedy to explore the idea of searching, in this instance searching for the deeper meaning of existence and the question of how people endure a tragic existence, yet continue to go on. Is there any purpose or meaning behind an existence plagued by pain and sorrow, absent any seeming hope for happiness and success? Is it really worthwhile to work hard, to build one's life, only to have it to collapse with a ten-second shake of the ground? It becomes natural, in turn to consider God, destiny, and the cause and effect, questions that the filmmaker adroitly raises without attracting the attention of the Iranian censors. The film gives voice to complaints of the people ranging from the simple "this was God's will," to "what has this nation done for God to punish it like this?" and "God does not like to kill his people ... then who has killed them?" These kinds of spiritual contemplation continue throughout the film as life itself goes on: we see a woman watering a pot of flowers, and a couple who have lost their two children trying to install an antenna on the roof of their ruined home in order to see the World Cup soccer games; the camera even passes through the framed doors of a ruined house, the green color of the mountains suddenly filling the entire screen, and the trees begin to dance with the hill's winds as accompanied by the music of Vivaldi.

Two years after *And Life Goes On*, in 1994, Kiarostami again took his camera and returned to the same location of the earthquake to make *Under the Olive Tree*. This could be seen as the sequel to *And Life Goes On*, and is Kiarostami's most optimistic, bright, and passionate film, the theme that of love.

In the beginning of the film, the director introduces himself and explains that he is going to find an actor in a girl's high school to act in his film. A girl named Tahereh is chosen, but she refuses to wear the traditional dress for her role. Another problem arises when the young man who is to play the role of the husband is unable to play his part because of speech problems. The assistant director brings Hussein, a crew member, to play the husband. However, this time it is Tahereh, who does not speak, and she refuses to even say hello to the new actor, Hussein. Later, Hussein explains to the director of the film that he had once proposed to Tahereh, but her parents did not accept his proposal because he did not have a house of his own. Tahereh's parents died during the earthquake, but Tahereh's grandmother survived and continues to oppose the marriage. The next day, Hussein and Tahereh (who now is dressed in the traditional costume) arrive for shooting. Hussein attempts to attract her attention, and talk to her during the time between shooting. However, Tahereh remains silent. Despite slow shooting, because of repeated scenes and mistakes, the scenes with the two are finally finished, and the director takes them to their houses in his car. In the middle of the journey Tahereh gets out and begins to walk home alone. Hussein, with the director telling him to go after her, gets out of the car and chases Tahereh. Hussein expresses his love to Tahereh continually, along the same winding road seen in *Where Is My Friend's Home?* (the road ends at the top of a hill that has a single tree standing on top). Hussein follows her, and both can be seen moving like two white spots in the background of vast green, both getting farther and farther away, until one of the spots gets separated and comes back in the same direction toward the audience/director. It is Hussein who is happily coming back.

In *Under the Olive Trees* Kiarostami reaches new levels of technical expertise and cinematic expression. Kiarostami uses the technique of film within film to portray two different types of loves (one real, another based on the script) between Tahereh and Hussein. He employs the technique to impart a sense of alienation, by cutting the scenes and showing the camera and the crew as part of the scene. In this way, the director is able to show the film (which is not real) and the love between Hussein and Tahereh (which is real) from their own point of view and not the film's point of view. In other words, the love is not real from the film's point of view because the two are supposed to be acting. But in reality they are in love, and the camera is directed by Hussein (not by the director) to record his happiness at the end. The actors after a while take control of the film and become directors of their own lives (and in a way directors of the film), practically ignoring the real director and doing what they want to do. This technique (which can be considered a sign of a growing self-consciousness and/or self-confidence in Kiarostami's work) furthers the director's purpose in making the film, which is not to tell a story according to a script, but to do so based on improvisation and the search for real feelings. To give a broader dimension to this idea, the director uses the different takes of a single scene and asks the actors to repeat that scene to extract different meanings. In an interview, Kiarostami was questioned about his technique in making the film and whether the appearance of the film crew in front of the camera was a Brechtian distanciation device. His reply was:

Mohammad Ali Keshavarz reads to a group of children in *Under the Olive Trees* (*Zir-e Darakhtan-e Zieton*), directed by Abbas Kiarostami in 1994.

> Yes, but I haven't taken it from the theory of Brecht only. I came to that through experience. We are never able to reconstruct truth as it is in the reality of our daily lives, and we are always witnessing things from far away while we are trying to depict them as close as we can to reality. So if we distance the audience from the film and even film from itself, it helps to understand the subject matter better.[41]

Under the Olive Trees is in part a documentary, but the director intrudes slightly upon the action. He provides the impetus for truths to reveal themselves, which happens through creative interaction first between the actors, and then with the director; who is more like a catalyst than an intruder or even a creator. That is why in some parts it feels as if there is no plan for the film at all. Hussein uses the film to get close to the girl that he is in love with; he does not care about the film and only acts out his own real life. It is here that a simple fiction is changed into a complicated drama, as the question becomes whether Tahereh, the real person, not the actor, will say yes or no to Hussein. The director beautifully portrays this, especially in the final sequence of the film when Hussein and Tahereh like two white spots disappear in a vast green field, and then one of these spots gets separated and returns again to the camera with such feeling that we can sense that he has finally gotten a yes from his girl. The scene is one of the most beautiful in Kiarostami's films and is a pure theatrical experience. It is like a painting, the two faces becoming alive, and the figures able to move and run for kilometers without stepping outside the frame. This four-minute scene is a portrait of love in which we feel that Hussein has finally succeeded in getting a *yes* from Tahereh. All the elements within the frame start to move and dance together. Trees, sky, sun and the wind all participate in her acceptance of her love for him to the extent that even we, the audience, feel stepping inside the frame and dancing with them. It is a moment of real joy which rarely is found in Kiarostami's films.

Ta'me Gilass (*Taste of Cherry*, 1997) brought the Golden Palm of the Cannes Film Festival to Kiarostami, made him famous as a director, attracting the attention of critics the world over. Iranian critics actually named him as a filmmaker who had come to restore the kind of cinema which has been lost in the face of commercial and action films. It might be also read as a return to the artistic style of early silent films, with obvious technical advances.

Taste of Cherry begins with Mr. Badii, the main character, driving a four-wheel drive vehicle. He is cruising the hills above Tehran, searching for someone, but who and for what purpose are questions that do not get answered until 20 minutes of the film have passed: he is searching for someone to help him commit suicide, and for this service he is offering money. After finding someone to help, Mr. Badii drives him to a nearby place. He shows the person a big hole and asks him to come back to the same place early the next morning to call to him; if he answers, the person can go to the car and take the money that is on the dashboard and leave, but if he doesn't answer, he is dead and the person must bury him. We don't know who Mr. Badii is or where he is from, or his station in life. He does not even explain why he is committing suicide to anyone whom he picks up from the street to help him. It is only through a conversation with a young man from Afghanistan, a theology student, that we get an idea why he wants to kill himself. When asked why he wants to commit suicide, Mr. Badii says "I know committing suicide is a great sin, but it is a greater sin if a human being is not happy," and he also says that "there are times that man gets tired or exhausted." These are the only clues in the film to why Mr. Badii wants to end his own life. But we shouldn't be misled; the film is not truly about a person's desire to commit suicide. The film is more deeply about the trials undergone by people who are in need (of money), and their efforts to maintain their human dignity and not help the man to kill himself. The men that Mr. Badii picks up from the streets are by no means angels or entirely good people who have never committed any crime, but in that particular moment, and in connection

Ershadi (right) and Kiarostami in *Taste of Cherry* (*Ta'me Gilass*), directed by Abbas Kiarostami in 1997.

to Mr. Badii's situation, they refuse to help him kill himself to earn some money. Instead one offers him a cup of tea, and another tells him a story of a cherry tree, attempting to change Mr. Badii's mind. The last person whom Mr. Badii gets into his car is Bagheri, a middle-aged man. Bagheri works at the Museum of Natural Sciences as a taxidermist for the museum's bird collection. He is desperately in need of money for his child, who has leukemia. (Bagheri is the person to whom the title of the film, *Taste of Cherry*, is related.) In a conversation with Mr. Badii, he tells of how when he was young, he had decided to commit suicide because he couldn't tolerate the problems in his life anymore. He picked up a rope and hung it on a branch of a mulberry tree,[42] but the branch couldn't tolerate his weight, so he climbed up the tree to find a stronger branch from which to hang the rope. But while climbing the tree, his hand touched something soft, which was a mulberry. He picked up the berry and tasted how sweet it was. He then picked another and then another and another. Then a group of children from a school nearby arrived and asked him to shake the tree so they could have some mulberries. The sweet taste of mulberries and the enthusiasm of the children eating the mulberries gradually allowed him to forget that he was going to commit suicide. He even collected some more mulberries to take home to share with his wife. After telling this story to Mr. Badii, the man gives his promise that he will come to the hole the next morning, to bury Mr. Badii if he doesn't answer his call. At night Mr. Badii leaves his house and goes to the hole, where he lies down. From Mr. Badii's point of view we see the sky, the moon, the flash of lightning, and all of those elements which remind us how nature is alive. Rain washes his face and the sun rises gradually; Kiarostami and his crew then come into the picture and the director says that for now filming has finished. This technique of ending the film when the actual story, for the viewer, has just begun, with no clear conclusion about the fate of Mr. Badii (who himself appears in the picture), the director himself labeled as "incomplete cinema" which must be finished by the audience:

> With most films, viewers with different tendencies come out of the theatre with the same experience. I believe a viewer can participate by identifying his own world within a film. Therefore, not everything should be made clear, and there should be holes for the viewer to fill in. Today's cinema has accustomed the viewer to knowing everything, but I like a film that I can complete with my mind. The cinema of the future is a cinema of the viewer and the director. The two will be making the film together.[43]

Devices such as "incomplete cinema" or "the cinema of the viewer and the director" are neither new nor exclusive to Kiarostami. There are brilliant examples of such films in the European art cinema. What is important here is that Kiarostami is reviving it through an Eastern mirror full of mystic images.

Apart from the quality of interaction between the director and the audience that exists in *Taste of Cherry*, we must also consider the selection of the location for the setting. Kiarostami has chosen a location which has the exact atmosphere of the film itself and doesn't need any further decoration. This valley outside the town has on one slope a group of workers who are trying to bring life to the hill by planting trees. On the other side bulldozers and trucks are dumping rubble and the dust is everywhere. This is the same dust that Mr. Badii is desperately looking for someone to bury him under. One of the most beautiful scenes of the film shows Mr. Badii hopelessly standing and staring at a flood of dust that is being poured into a hole. He casts a shadow on the hole, and it seems that he is being buried by the dust; when the dust fills the whole space, we see Mr. Badii standing like a buried statue. Here we see clearly how Kiarostami is using the element of dust symbolically and physically in relation to Mr. Badii's suicide. As fire was the most important element in *The Runner* by Amir Naderi, dust becomes a very important element in *Taste of Cherry*, reminding us of creation itself and how we have come from dust and will return to dust.

Taste of Cherry shows the development of two more important elements in Kiarostami's cinema. The first is Kiarostami's separation from the innocent world of children and the young men of rural towns, moving into the complex world of the urban adults. We also see the loneliness that has existed deep within his characters in most of his previous films changes into alienation. In *Taste of Cherry*, Mr. Badii's problem is not loneliness, but alienation. This change is due to philosophical and social influences that Iranian society and citizens have been subjected to in the post-revolution period, when many people, especially those highly educated, became alienated from their society. It is obvious that Kiarostami has moved away from the simple and accessible cinema of *Where Is My Friend's Home?* dealing mostly with the concept of life, touching the heart, towards the enigmatic and personal cinema of *Taste of Cherry* and *The Wind Will Carry Us*[44] dealing with the concept of death, touching the mind. Will his next films be about the "life after death" to complete this journey? Kiarostami is still steadily moving up the same winding road that we have seen in *Where Is My Friend's Home?*, *Taste of Cherry* and *The Wind Will Carry Us*, whispering "Listen! Listen well! Can you hear the darkness howling? The dark hell-wind scything its way towards us?"[45]

Mohsen Makhmalbaf and Marriage of the Blessed

Mohsen Makhmalbaf is probably the most controversial filmmaker that Iranian cinema has produced since the 1979 revolution. He is controversial both because of his films and what he said and wrote about film and theatre. He is also controversial because of his constantly changing views on social, cultural and religious issues. Abbas Kiarostami has made movies at a slow yet constant pace over the last 30 years, never stopping and always maintaining a singular vision even as he grew as a filmmaker. Even something as powerful as the revolution could not stop him or cause him to change his views about making films. By contrast, Makhmalbaf is a filmmaker who constantly changes his attitudes toward the cinema and life in general, making him difficult to understand. He is one of the few Islamic revolutionary artists to begin from the perspective of ideology and art, but then move to *relativism* in these areas of thought and taste.[46]

Before the revolution, when he was seventeen, he tried to disarm a police officer with a knife in an attempt to organize a militant Islamic group to fight the Royal Pahlavi regime. He failed, and spent four years in prison until the revolution in 1979, when he was freed. As a young Islamic revolutionary, he began working in art and literature and soon became one of the most important figures in cultural activities of the new regime. Despite his lack of knowledge and experience, he and other revolutionary artists began to stage plays and make movies and, more importantly, to attack other artists who didn't share their beliefs and ideologies and were generally labeled communist, royalist or pro–Western in an attempt to wipe them out. Many Iranian artists had to abandon the art scene because of what Makhmalbaf and his fellow revolutionary artists were saying or writing about them in the early years of the revolution, when passion was high and reason had no place.

Because of his connection to the Islamic regime and his membership in the Islamic Propaganda Organization, Makhmalbaf made some early films that today even he himself resists watching. These feature films were badly made, trying to portray religious, revolutionary ideas in a form which was closer to fantasy than reality. They have little merit as films, and are the work of an unskilled filmmaker attempting to understand the cinema, to practise and to learn it.[47] The result was feature films like *Tobeh Nassouh*, *Do Chashmeh Bisou* and *Esteazeh*, which all clearly show the filmmaker's preoccupation with god and the devil and the inner conflict between evil and good. Although these concepts could be good themes, due to Makhmalbaf's dogmatism and lack of skills the works do not effectively address the ideas through the medium of film. One can still understand through these early films the philosophical turbulence that existed within the filmmaker. Otherwise, he would not have expended so much energy and imagination searching for answers to issues that have been dealt in most religions through absolutism, and he as a devoted religious person would not have been permitted to question.

It was only in 1984 with *Baykot* (*The Boycott*) that Makhmalbaf demonstrated that he had finally learned the art of filmmaking. *Baykot* was a bridge that took Makhmalbaf from theological arguments about religion to ideological arguments about social issues, while paying attention to the artistic value of his work as well. With this vital change, Makhmalbaf began the second stage of his career, making films that not only found a respected place within the new Iranian cinema, but also in world cinema. To Makhmalbaf, Werner Herzog said of his work,

> *Once Upon a Time Cinema* is a poem in praise of film (in general) and not just the Iranian cinema ... your film voice is highly interesting and personal. It is your own special voice and quite unlike anything I have seen anywhere else.[48]

Tobeh Nassouh (*Nassouh's Repentance*) was the first film that Makhmalbaf made as writer and director, in 1982. It exactly reflected his religious revolutionary ideas and employed an old and clichéd story, one told many times before in literature and cinema. A man seemingly dies, and during his funeral it is realized that he is still alive. He becomes ashamed of his previous life, and decides to be good to people for the rest of his life. But in practice, he realizes that this is not an easy job. This is a theme that had been used with success years before the revolution in Iranian cinema, in *Shab Neshini dar Jahanam* (*A Party in Hell*, 1957). But in Makhmalbaf's version, weak technique, stereotypical characters, and exaggerated dialogue and acting, along with generally poor theatrical presentation, made the film a failure. Next he made *Do Chashmeh Bisou* (*Two Sightless Eyes*), in 1983, and like his first film it had a religious plot dealing with morality, aiming to portray the resistance of man's dignity against the devil's temptations. To overcome the evil forces within themselves, five men exile themselves to an abandoned island, not knowing that the devil can be present everywhere and at every time. Four of them concede and are defeated, giving in to the devil. However the fifth man, by devoting himself completely to God, comes out victorious. Despite showing better technique than his previous film, *Two Sightless Eyes* did not succeed with audiences because it was filmed in a very limited space and it used exaggerated theatrical elements, emphasizing dialogue rather than images.

At the same time Makhmalbaf wrote two more scripts, *Marg-e Digari* and *Zangha,* which were turned into films by other directors in the Islamic Propaganda Organization; both can be placed in the same category as the films we have already discussed. These films try to portray religious and morality themes from a revolutionary point of view with an artistic form that is neither convincing nor attractive. Therefore, before making *The Boycott* in 1985, Makhmalbaf had five films to his credit as director or scriptwriter, and yet showed little promise that he would become a good filmmaker. But *The Boycott* destroyed this image and showed a filmmaker who knew the language of the cinema and knew how to use vital elements such as movement, composition, montage, and acting in his films.

A young man named Masomi, a member of a Marxist guerilla organization fighting against the Pahlavi regime, is arrested and jailed. This provides him an opportunity to think over his past life and his ideology. Over time, he gradually becomes uncertain, and according to his fellow Marxists, he becomes disillusioned and unable to carry on the struggle. His comrades try to restore his faith in Marxism, but they fail. When in the final scene he is in front of the firing squad, and before the bullets penetrate his chest, rain starts to pour down. He looks at the sky, and we see symbolically that he has found God and is saved.

The Boycott is a politically motivated melodrama about Marxism and the rejection of the ideology, and about those people who believed in and fought for it in Iran for years. Makhmalbaf unjustly ignores the struggles of the Marxists against the dictatorship, presenting a false picture of the period before the Islamic revolution in order to publicize his own religious ideas and to endorse the newly established Islamic regime. As he himself was a prisoner of the Pahlavi regime and spent four years in prison with many of these same Marxists, he should have known that many of them were tortured and executed without losing faith or selling themselves to the regime. It is obvious that among groups with different ideologies, there are always people who are openminded and willing to accept others and some who are not.

Some critics acknowledge the film only as another example of opportunism by the filmmaker. He unjustifiably misrepresented history in order to please the authorities and those people who had the upper hand after the Islamic revolution. However, the director himself refused to accept these criticisms, and believed he had made a film about philosophy rather than politics:

> Above all else the film is about philosophy. In the depths of the film there is a philosophical thought or idea. It is about who can carry the fight to the end and it is about the fact that, if there is no belief in God and the resurrection, then all the fighting is useless. In any case, I see the film first as a philosophical film and then as a political film which basically and necessarily is sentimental and action packed.[49]

Although it tries to show the fermentation or disillusionment of the people in political organizations, and the confused mentality of these people in relation to Marxist ideology, the film, despite Makhmalbaf's claim of being philosophical, is more a political slogan decorated with a few passionate scenes meant to have the most effect on audiences which, in those years, often consumed such propaganda. Despite its shortcomings, the movie transferred Makhmalbaf from an unsuccessful period to one that was fruitful both for him and for Iranian cinema, beginning with *Dastforoosh* (*The Peddler*) made in 1987.

The Peddler is a film with three episodes. The first episode, "Bach-e Khoshbakht" ("The Lucky Child"), is about the life of a poor couple with three disabled children living in a shanty house outside of the city. The woman gives birth to her fourth child in the hospital and is told that if the child is not fed well, he will be disabled like the other three. So the couple decides to give the child away to someone who could feed him well.

Morteza Zarabi in *The Peddler*.

First, the mother leaves the child in a mosque so that a man of God will take him and take good care of him, but she soon realizes that no one but beggars will pick up the child, so as to use him for begging. In the end, the couple decide to leave him in the courtyard of a rich family hopeful the baby will be saved from the poverty and disease that await him if he were to stay with his parents. The second episode, "Tavalod-e yek Pirezan" ("The Birth of an Old Woman"), is about a mentally disabled young man who is taking care of his mute old mother. One day when he goes to get her pension money he is hit by a car and is taken to hospital. After a while, he leaves the hospital and returns home to resume caring for his mother, not knowing that she died in his absence. Finally, the third episode, "Dast-foroosh" ("The Peddler"), is about a gang that is making money through

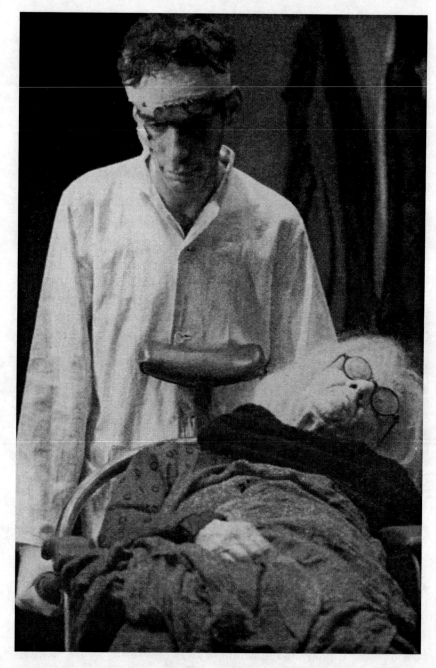

Zarabi (standing) and Basiri in *The Peddler* (*Dastforoosh*), directed by Mohsen Makhmalbaf in 1987.

smuggling and robbery. One of the members of the group witnesses the murder of his friend, but the gang kidnaps him. Unsuccessful in his attempts to escape, he is killed in the end.

We can see how Makhmalbaf with this film distances himself from his previous films in terms of the concepts with which he is dealing with. Firstly, in this film it is not evil appearing in different guises and forcing people to do the wrong thing; for the first time, he presents people as agents of history, not just passive victims. The characters control their own bad behavior, and behave as they do this consciously and willingly in order to profit and gain power. In other words, Makhmalbaf this time makes a film about where he lives and the people who live around him. Secondly, in this film he does not criticize the secret police of the previous regime, or the Marxists. These two groups were frequent targets for Iranian filmmakers after the revolution, just as the Indians and Communists were at times in Hollywood films. In *The Peddler,* the target of criticism is not "pagans," but a system and people who apparently believe in God and build their lives through association with the religion in one way or another. Now Makhmalbaf is criticising the situation not before the revolution, but after the revolution, and not through fantasy, but realism. He is talking openly about an unjust social system in which the majority is suffering and the minority is prospering. This is the most important change Makhmalbaf made in *The Peddler.* Besides this change of ideology the cinematic values of the film bear discussion as well. The concept of the film was controversial and unexpected, but the beauty of the cinematography was unexpected as well. The mixture of realism and surrealism in the film creates images that ultimately help to convey the content of the film in a way that connects with the audience. A good example can be found in the second episode, when the young man who is taking care of his old mother is introduced to viewers. We see him in a window with a scarf (such as women wear in Iran), cleaning up the house. This picture alone shows his absurd metamorphosis into a female housekeeper, due to living in isolation with his mother, far from the harsh reality of life on the other side of the window.

The film had a huge impact on audiences, which were divided into two different camps. The first camp had disliked his previous films and after seeing *The Peddler* was shocked, but ultimately pleased, by this new movie. The second camp had liked Makhmalbaf as an Islamic revolutionary artist and was displeased and even angry upon viewing his latest film, and ultimately accused him of ignoring Islamic and revolutionary values. Hoshang Hesami, of the first camp, wrote:

Yes I was surprised, I was shocked, I was overjoyed because *The Peddler*—
I wish it had the beautiful and symbolic name of "The Birth of an Old
Woman"—is enviable. It is an event which can be interpreted as a turning point. This is a birthday party not only for the filmmaker, who has
progressed so well from *The Boycott* to *The Peddler*, but also for Iranian
cinema. No, we should not doubt that Makhmalbaf has the quality of a
great filmmaker, and ignoring him and his work for whatever reason is
useless.[50]

An example of the counter view came from Jamal Shir-Mohammedi,
who wrote:

He is the first person to criticize the Islamic Republic openly. Makhmalbaf, by having political immunity coming from above and the trust of the
organization (Islamic Propaganda Organization), wrote the script of *The
Peddler* in secret and made it into a film. The attention to *The Peddler* is
not because it has a powerful cinematic structure or a good content, but
because of a crack that this film made in the camp of artists who believed
in revolution. Makhmalbaf has average artistic talent but has an extraordinary talent for creating a false atmosphere and using the social and political circumstances. His fame comes more from his ability to make noise
than his ability to make films.[51]

Undoubtedly arguments such as these were made because Makhmalbaf was a filmmaker who radically defended the revolution and the regime.
With this film, he suddenly put himself in opposition to this position and
openly began to criticize social and political issues that no one else dared
to tackle in a time when criticism was answered with punishment. This
was the most important cinematic event of 1988, and a turning point in
Iranian cinema. It paved the way for other filmmakers to address social
and political issues of the time.

The reactions to and the praise for *The Peddler* drove Makhmalbaf
deeper into the exploration of critical issues, and he began to portray them
as openly as was allowed. His next two films were more salt in the wounds
of those who believed Makhmalbaf was abandoning his revolution-era
ideology and turning his back on the regime. His former colleagues were
probably correct, as both films showed dark images of the Iranian society
after the revolution.

Although *Baicykelran* (*The Cyclist*, 1989) like *The Peddler* was received
very well by the people, it is *Arusi-e Khuban* (*Marriage of the Blessed*, 1991)
that should be recognized as Makhmalbaf's most important film. The film
began a new chapter for Makhmalbaf and for Iranian cinema. It not only
portrayed the consequences of the eight years of war which were imposed on
Iran by Iraq, it was also about the revolution, the regime, and the society.

Haji, the main character, is a young photographer working on the front lines during the war between Iran and Iraq. He suffers a nervous breakdown due to an explosion, and is transferred to a rehabilitation center to recover. His fiancée is the daughter of a rich businessman; her father is opposed to the marriage of his daughter and the young revolutionary fighter and photographer. After leaving the rehabilitation center, Haji takes a job at a newspaper, photographing addicts and the homeless, but the newspaper refuses to print the pictures. His fiancée insists that he marry her, and he does. During the wedding, his father in-law ridicules him, as do his colleagues, due to his radical attitude and his nervousness. He breaks down once more and is taken to the rehabilitation center. He escapes and calls his wife, and asks her to forgive him because he is going to rejoin the army and fight at the frontline. Although it is not set out clearly, the audience can feel that this time Haji is going to the frontline to be killed so that he can be free from the bitterness of reality.

Marriage of the Blessed was a shock for those people who did not want to admit that the war had bad consequences. Although for Iranians the war was about defending the country, the defense came at a price that had to be paid. The problem was that one group of people were paying the price, while another group of people were benefiting from the war. So the physical and mental pain felt by Haji was not caused by the explosion of bombs, but by the lack of justice he found when he left the front and came to the city. He saw that he could no longer blame America or the Marxists for what he was witnessing. This time, he realized that the system itself was to blame for the injustice spreading everywhere — the same system that was created by Haji and people like himself through the sacrifice of everything they had.

Despite the weakness of his earlier films, Makhmalbaf's visual style in *Marriage of the Blessed* effectively conveyed his intended meaning. The selection of camera angles and lenses, sharp lighting, the movement of the camera and the pace of editing were techniques that well portrayed Haji's mental and nervous breakdown and his disillusionment about Iranian society. A. Haji-Mashadi wrote:

> *Marriage of the Blessed* is an important film from many points of view. One is the content of the film, which in an indirect and different way deals with the issues of war. Even though in *Marriage of the Blessed* the reflection of the issues related to war is different when compared to films like *Ensan va Aslahe (Man and Arm)*, *Rozaneh (Small Hole)*, *Ofoq (Horizon)*, and *Dide-hban (Scout)*, the deep depiction of the war and its consequences on the sensitive and vulnerable mind of a young fighter presents the pathology of war on a small scale. In fact, *Marriage of the Blessed* creates a new pic-

ture of a young volunteer who has been injured. It is the exact representation of his actions and reactions (willing or unwilling) to a turbulent society, which is a strange combination of devotion, passion, sacrifice, greed,
selfishness, capitalism, dishonesty, etc.[52]

There were critics who again saw the film as a direct criticism of the
war, and denounced the film as meant to show the failure and the useless-
ness of the Islamic revolution and the resistance of the people. Wielding
this interpretation, they tried to attack the filmmaker and create problems
for him with criticism that was surely motivated by politics. Despite what
these critics were saying, the film was a confirmation of the sacrifices of
people like Haji, made to prevent Saddam Hussein from doing what he
later did to Kuwait. The main point of Makhmalbaf's criticism and protest
in the film was that people like Haji sacrificed themselves for those who
had nothing to do with the war beyond benefiting from it. Makhmalbaf's
criticism in *Marriage of the Blessed* was a just criticism of an unjust system and an ignorant society.

The new period of filmmaking for Makhmalbaf that began with *The
Peddler* reached a climax with *Marriage of the Blessed* and then continued
with *Nobat-e Asheghi* (*Time of Love*) and *Shabhay-e Zayandeh Rud* (*Nights
on Zayandeh Rud*), both banned, and ended there. The period when the
main theme of his films was the people's disillusionment toward the revolution, the holy war, social justice and the hoped-for goals that they had
after the revolution, which proved impossible to reach because of the corruption of others.

Time of Love (1991) is about love, a subject whose public presentation became taboo in the strict religious environment that followed the
revolution. By choosing a love story, the filmmaker challenges some religious and ideological issues, although not as openly as he did in *Marriage
of the Blessed. Time of Love* is a film with three episodes, like *The Peddler*.
In the first episode, the woman (Gozal) is the wife of a black-haired man
and she has an affair with a blonde-haired man. In the second episode,
Gozal is the wife of the blonde-haired man and has an affair with the black-
haired man. Finally, the third episode repeats the pattern of the first. Unlike
in the first two episodes, in which one of the men kills the other once the
affair is revealed, in the last episode the men offer the woman to each other.
It is then discovered that the only person who truly loves the woman is a
deaf old man, who in fact revealed the affair in the first place. Abdol Karim
Soroosh, the Iranian philosopher, felt that with this dialectical style, the
filmmaker is trying to say, "anyone who gets the power will do the same
as the one who preceded him."[53]

In *Nights on Zayandeh Rud* (1991), again are faced with a story the ending of which in particular made critics speak out loudly against the filmmaker, denouncing the work as another anti-revolution and anti-war film, considered a slight by Makhmalbaf's former ideological brethren. The film depicts a young man who volunteers for the army and later attempts suicide.

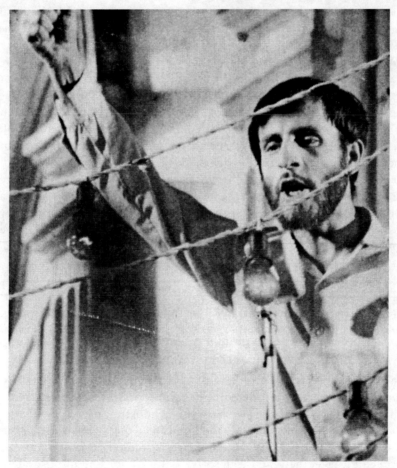

Mahmood Bigham in *Marriage of the Blessed* (*Arusi-e Khuban*), directed by Mohsen Makhmalbaf in 1991.

He is even rejected by the girl he plans to marry. There is no question that the theme of the film is the disappointment felt by Makhmalbaf and people like him because the achievements and idealistic changes they hoped to accomplish when the revolution began never materialized.

The criticism and protests that agreed Makhmalbaf's releases of *Time of Love* and *Nights* forced him to this stage of his filmmaking, and begin working on stories that were less critical of social and religious issues and more preoccupied with the cinema itself. This third stage started with *Nasseredin Shah Actor-e Cinema* (*Once Upon a Time Cinema*, 1992), continued with *Honarpisheh* (*The Actor*, 1993), and ended with *Salaam Cinema* (*Hello Cinema*, 1995). The main characteristic of all three films is the attention paid to the cinema itself — the same cinema that Makhmalbaf had always had a problem with, even before the revolution when he was passing the *Harram*[54] movie theaters with his hands on his ears to block out the sounds of the films being broadcast outside theaters to attract more viewers; or when he himself as a writer and director started to make films and failed; or even when he succeeded in making good films but became the target of the same establishment that helped him become a filmmaker. In the end, it seems he had no choice but to return to the cinema itself, seeking refuge in his search for the artistic secrets that first repelled him and then attracted him. Although in all three films there are beautiful scenes, none was able to capture the development of the cinema nor the filmmaker's relationship with the medium. They mostly come across as a collection of interesting scenes from Iranian films, though of course they are vehicles for the critical views of the filmmaker himself. Among these three films *Hello Cinema* is most important, although it is also the weakest film in terms of artistry.

Hello Cinema was made in 1995 and at first glance one can see the influence of *Close-up* (1990) directed by Kiarostami, especially in the focus on a current event, the use of alienation, and the director's appearance in the film. One of Makhmalbaf's problems as a filmmaker is that an event or a person quickly impresses him, and just as quickly he abandons it. *Hello Cinema* is an example of this quick mood change. That is perhaps why, after making a few profound films, Makhmalbaf returned again to chanting slogans, a style he used in his early works. *Hello Cinema* starts with Makhmalbaf publishing an advertisement in newspapers to audition actors for his new film. Suddenly thousands of young girls and boys from all corners of the country come and gather in front of the studio. To pass through the gate, they endure all sorts of humiliation and insults. Again this parallels *Close-up*, and raises the question of whether an artist has the right to humiliate people in the name of "art." In one scene, Makhmalbaf asks the hopeful actors to cry for the Iranian cinema, and they do so. Makhmalbaf should have asked them to cry for a society that has nothing to offer them but the fleeting hope of a part in a film, and no other way to reach any goals in their lives. This film reminds us of the status of football in a country like Brazil, as the Iranian film industry has found itself in a similar situation; in Brazil, many young people have no hope of work and no chance of a better future, and the only escape they can imagine is through football stardom. In Iran, the movies are for many the only hope of escape. *Hello Cinema* fails to address either this issue or the problems within the Iranian cinema, and instead feels like another highly artificial work by Makhmalbaf.

Makhmalbaf's third stage of filmmaking ended with *Hello Cinema*, and the fourth period, known as the poetic cinema of Makhmalbaf, began. It started with *Noon va Goldon* (*The Bread and the Vase*, 1996) and continued with *Gabbe* (1996) and *Sokoot* (*Silence*, 1998).

Gabbe is a cinema of pure imagery that anyone in the world could enjoy, and this from a director who once said: "A movie that is not a flick to everyone is not cinema."[55] He also once said, "the most important characteristic of cinema after the revolution is its involvement with politics and if this cinema does not shake the oppressors it is useless and the filmmaker must be a man of no commitment."[56] Despite these callous ideas, *Gabbe* is a beautiful movie.

Gabbe is a colorful portrayal of life that is pure fantasy, and the idea is not new; the same themes can be seen in *Nar-o-Nai* (1989) directed by Said Ebrahimifar. However, the best quality of the film is its connection with the national art of making rugs and carpets. The beauty of these pieces mesmerize some people, but when one knows how painfully they are made the sense of beauty is replaced by a sense of sorrow and shame.

Gabbe is a poetic and symbolic film about the love between a boy and a girl from a nomadic tribe. The tribe survives by rearing cattle, and during the winter they have to migrate to the warmer parts of the country in search of green pastures. The story of their love is narrated by both, in their elderly years, during an annual migration. Through the love story we are introduced to the art of making "gabbe," which is a thick kind of carpet made by the women of the tribe. "Gabbe" has no particular design or pattern, instead presenting mostly the impressions and dreams of its makers. The film starts with the picture of one of these carpets, which shows a boy and girl riding a white horse. In the film, this gabbe becomes a symbol of a girl named Gabbe. Or perhaps the girl (Gabbe) becomes the symbol for the carpet ("gabbe"), a carpet woven with blue, a color that is the symbol of love.

The girl and boy fall in love, but the girl's father agrees to their marriage on the condition that they can only get married when the girl's uncle returns from the city. When the uncle returns, the father adds a further condition, that the uncle, who is now middle-aged, must marry first. When the uncle marries, Gabbe has to wait again as her mother, who is now pregnant, must give birth before she is allowed to get married. And when the mother gives birth, she still has to wait because her younger sister falls from a cliff and dies. These stories of birth, marriage and death are narrated by both the young Gabbe and the old Gabbe, and her husband, as the tribe makes its annual migration, moving in a very visual and poetic way, engulfing the audience in a dream-like reality. In winter, the young boy and girl become impatient. The boy is riding a white horse and following Gabbe and the tribe, and encourages Gabbe to escape from the tribe and join him. He does this by howling like a wolf. When Gabbe sees a sheep give birth and the lamb start to stand on his own, she decides to escape and join the boy. This means marriage and independence for Gabbe. She puts the blue gabbe which she herself has woven on her shoulder and escapes, riding on the white horse that the boy has prepared for her. The father follows them with a rifle, and we hear the sound of two bullets. We see the father returning with the gabbe. The eyes of the people in the tribe say that the father has killed both of them, but suddenly Gabbe appears in the same scene and says that her father did not kill them and only pretended to do so, shooting into the air. The father only wanted to scare his other daughters and keep them from doing the same as Gabbe.

In *Gabbe*, the colors are the most important element of the film and perhaps are the film itself. The characters come to life through the reflection of the colors. Blue is the color of love, and green is the color of life. All these colors, as in nature, mix with each other and make other colors which also portray something in the life of these two young lovers. The cinematic imagery that Makhmalbaf presents with *Gabbe* is itself a poetic language, and the images need nothing to enhance them. One of the most beautiful scenes of the film is when the boy expresses his anger and dissatisfaction with Gabbe because she will not flee with him, and we see him under an apple tree beating the gabbe with his staff. Godfrey Cheshire writes:

> An exultantly lyrical vision of nomadic life in southeastern Iran, Mohsen Makhmalbaf's *Gabbe* adds yet another jewel to the crown of recent Iranian cinema.... Mahmood Kalari's fine cinematography adds immeasurably to a film that, like other Iranian works, amazes with the revelation of the technical sophistication that can be achieved on limited means. Indeed, the picture suggests how such feats depend on the kind of poetic sureness

that Makhmalbaf displays here, adding to his reputation as a filmmaker of remarkable daring and sensitivity.[57]

Like most of Makhmalbaf's films, *Gabbe* is complex, and despite its simple story it has its own contradictions and exaggerations. This, however, is not necessarily a weakness in the films of Makhmalbaf, as the filmmaker himself is contradictory and forever changing in relation to the issues that he is dealing with. One could say that his creativity is generated by his contradictory character and his turbulent personality. The direction his works will take in the future is, consequently, impossible to predict.

V

Rising from the Fire of the Revolution: The Resurgence of the New Wave

Thus far we have traced the development of the new Iranian cinema in connection with the social and political forces within the Iranian society by analyzing those films which were part of this development. However, a very important question has been left unanswered until the end: How did the Iranian cinema after the Islamic revolution of 1979 turn from a crumbling institution into a truly national cinema respected around the world, despite being under heavy political and religious pressure and subject to harsh censorship? What elements were working inside and outside the industry helping it to succeed, in spite of its official designation as "corrupt" during the revolution, attracting such antipathy that many theaters were burned to the ground?[1] Could cinema flourish while the country was suffering from a seriously ailing economy, a consequence of the revolution and the eight-year war with Iraq?

As mentioned before, the foundation of the "humanist," "meditative" and "poetic" cinema of Iran was laid before the revolution by filmmakers like Golestan, Ghaffari, Taqvai, Naderi, Bayzai, Kimiai, Mehrjui, Shahid Saless and many others. This form of cinema only needed a suitable time and a ready environment for its parts to come together and to flourish as a dominant art form after the revolution.

The conditions necessary for this to happen did not exist before the revolution because of the political and economic structure of the country. The Iranian cinema was dominated by producers who for the most part had no knowledge of the art of filmmaking; they were businessmen who invested their money in the cinema largely to make profit.[2] They did not understand anything about the need for or importance of a national cinema, and were not interested in fostering development of films that reflected Iranian identity.

The filmmakers of the new wave had trouble finding producers, and when they did, these producers exerted a great deal of control over the film. The government's imposition of censorship that more severely hampered the art cinema than the commercial cinema was a second obstacle for the artistic growth and popularization of a national cinema. Exacerbating the problem was the popularity of other forms of entertainment, such as pop music, which dominated the art scene at the time in Iran. A large segment of society (mostly the religious, traditional, and rural classes) did not attend the movies, as the religious authorities had declared film a corrupt and anti–Islamic institution. This collection of inhibiting forces did not allow Iran's art cinema the strength to stand alongside the commercial Film Farsi, which was patronized by the middle and working classes before the revolution.

The revolution of 1979 closed down both Film Farsi and art cinema. Apart from burning down theaters and summoning many actors and directors to the revolutionary court and forbidding them to work, the most damaging blow inflicted upon the film industry was the burning of hundreds of films (Iranian and foreign) in the middle of the yard of Ministry of Culture and Art. In the middle of this turmoil a few Film Farsi producers tried to change the face of their standard fare, presenting it this time not as Film Farsi but as revolution-related movies with a religious facade. *Mard-e Khoda* (*The Man of God*, 1979) and *Faryad-e Mojahed* (*The Cry of the Holy Warrior*, 1979) were examples of this opportunism. Their efforts met with opposition and soon failed. As most of the films made before the revolution did not meet the new regime's religious standards and thus could not be shown in theaters (due to their having female actors with no Hajab, violating the Islamic code of dress), foreign films and in particular those made in the former Soviet Union were shown. However, these films were so heavily censored that their length was cut to an hour, and practically every female character in the film was cut. Besides being dubbed the stories were also usually changed into what was buyable at the time of the revolution (a good guy stands against bad guys for the sake of the people's well being). These films failed to attract audiences into the theaters. As most forms of entertainment (music, concerts, opera, ballet, dance),[3] and leisure (bars, café-restaurants, social gatherings)[4] were banned or disappeared, and the state controlled television only broadcast religious and political lectures, a huge cultural vacuum was created, waiting to be filled by any form of entertainment. When this need was sensed by the authorities, they focused on the film industry as not only a cheap means of entertainment, but also a propaganda tool to spread the message of the revolution and their religious message to the masses. This change of attitude ushered in the first period of the new Iranian cinema after the revolution, which began in 1981 and continued till 1983.

The main function of the first period was to move the rusty wheels of the Iranian cinema into motion. As Behashti, the executive director of *Bonyad-e Farabi*, noted in an interview, in this period the "production growth of the Iranian cinema"[5] was the only agenda.

One factor that significantly helped the economic status of the Iranian film industry at this time and boosted cinematic production — albeit not a fortunate one for the country — was the invasion of Iran by Iraq in 1980. Although this war took several hundred thousand Iranians' lives, destroyed many cities and ruined the Iranian economy, it also forced the government to inject more money into the cinema to make films connected to the war. The aim was to praise the bravery of those who were fighting and to encourage young men to join the armed forces. Subsequently, in 1983, nine war movies were made, eight by government organizations. No doubt this act helped the economy of the industry, which at the time was in dire straits, to recover. The first attempts to make quality films in this period resulted in works such as *Hayolay-e Daroon* (*The Inner Beast*) directed by Khosroo Sinai and *Kamalolmolk,* directed by Ali Hatami. Still, both served the revolution's purpose in that they were critical of the previous royal regime, one in a direct way (*The Inner Beast*) and the other indirectly (*Kamalolmolk*).

The second period began in 1984 with the establishment of the Farabi Cinema Foundation; the improvement of the quality of films was its agenda, to be accomplished by implementing a plan known as "control, guidance and support"[6] for films to be made in line with the political and cultural values of the Islamic regime. In this period, which lasted until 1987, an opportunity was provided for some filmmakers and in particular those from the younger generations to learn and practice new techniques meant to result in films that didn't fall back on the familiar patterns of Film Farsi. Technique, or form, became the main preoccupation of many Iranian filmmakers during this period, although in most cases it mimicked or copied directly devices used in foreign films. Two successful examples are *The Peddler* directed by Mohsen Makhmalbaf and *Nar-o-Nai* by Said Ebrahimifar. One positive factor in the adaptation of technique was that it continued to evolve, and gradually most filmmakers found their own voice through experience. This became a very important element in developing the new Iranian cinema, especially in relation to its successes on the world stage. *The Runner* (Amir Naderi), *Where Is My Friend's Home?* (Abbas Kiarostami) and *Bashu* (Bahram Bayzai) are examples of works by filmmakers who had found their own, distinct voices as artists, while also incorporating concepts reflecting the culture of the nation. It is also in this period that symbolism began to gain prominence in films, partially as an answer to the harsh censorship imposed on the cinema. To escape the scissors of the censors, symbols were used to such an extent that the mix with the realism favored by many of the filmmakers gave the works surprisingly broader horizons, allowing for analysis and insight into the artist's conceptualization. In line with this development, children also found a significant place in many films, as they were less suspicious to the censors. In this way, a child in a film can be considered both as a character who the filmmaker is able to shape and develop with a greater degree of freedom, and at the same time the child as a symbol conveys meaning the director would be unable to express if the character were an adult. Again, a successful example of such a combination is *Bashu,* where the dark skinned little boy of the film is portraying the horror of the war and at the same time is seen as a symbol of reconciliation of two cultures.

The third period lasted from 1987 until 1997. This was the golden period of the new Iranian cinema after the revolution, when films like *Taste of Cherry* received the Golden Palm and *Children of Heaven* was nominated for an Oscar, and the Iranian cinema was praised the world over as a new and humanist outlet of expression. However, in this period the Iranian cinema began to struggle with two destructive forces, these being internal, rather than from outside the industry. One was familiar: economics. Most of the films still did not make a profit. A new problem was that many artists were making films only to win prizes at film festivals in the West. These films did not perform well domestically, as they were no longer representative of Iranian society and featured mostly misleading images of the people and the culture, meant to impress and shock juries and audiences with horrific stories. In *Rokod va Bohraan dar Cinemayeh Iran* (*Recession and Crisis in Iranian Cinema*), Ali Shidfar explains how most films were unable to perform at the box office, not even returning their costs, in 2001. The writer discusses how a successful film like *Maraal* (lauded at many international film festivals, such as the San Francisco Film Festival) failed to attract an Iranian audience.[7] F. Noor, on behalf of the Iranian Movie Theatre Owners, stated that most Iranian films had no domestic quality that merited their being shown in Iran, as they were made only to be shown at international festivals.[8] This problem is also acknowledged

Nezhad Ekhtiar-Dini in *A Time for Drunken Horses* (*Zamani ke Asbha Mast Misha-vand*), directed by Bahman Ghobadi in 2000.

by film critics outside Iran. The director of the Vienna Film Festival has pointed out to the problem in an interview: "Some of the Iranian film directors produce their works according to the directions and preferences of the international film festivals and this is a real danger for Iranian cinema."[9] Even Bahman Ghobadi, who made *Zamani ke Asbha Mast Misha-vand* (*A Time for Drunken Horses*), an award-winning film at the Cannes Film Festival, acknowledged that "his primary goal with the film was to win international acclaim."[10] A formula has been developed to create films to be exported to the foreign film festivals: it is built on the use of a real or semi-real event (often an isolated case that could happen anywhere in the world, but it is turned into a hot and critical social issue in the film), with the people actually involved in the story play themselves. A "new realistic" technique or technique of "film within film" served such stories and satisfied the expectations of those tired of the formal and repetitive narrative of commercial films. In the creation of this form of cinema, which was made for export, *Close-up* (Abbas Kiarostami) became an early model, while *Siib* (*Apple*, by Samira Makhmalbaf) and *A Time for Drunken Horses* (Bahman Ghobadi) have gained the reputation of being textbook examples of this style. This development has put the sense of national identity of Iranian cinema in danger. Another factor, one that had a great share in the improvement of the quality of films during this period, has been the greater control of filmmakers over their work — they began movies based on their own scripts, and in some cases produced and edited the films. The artists gaining complete control of a film's gradual development, has been most important in the growth of the number of quality works produced

Z. Naderi in *Apple* (*Siib*), directed by Samira Makhmalbaf in 1999.

Shaghayigh Jodat in *Gabbe* directed by Mohsen Makhmalbaf in 1996.

Delpak (right) and Majidi in *Color of Heaven* (*Rang-e Khoda*), directed by Majid Majidi in 1999.

Karimi (left) and Zarehe in *Two Women* (*Do Zan*), directed by Tahmineh Milani in 1999.

by the Iranian film industry. Mohsen Makhmalbaf (writer, editor and director in *Gabbe*) and Abbas Kiarostami (writer, art director, editor, director and producer in *Under the Olive Trees*) are among those Iranian directors who make their films with such freedom. This factor is critical in improving the quality of films and aiding the production of innovative works, not only in Iran, but in any country; putting such power in the hands of a director rarely happens anywhere.

And finally, the fourth period started in 1997 when a new reformist president (Mohammed Khatami) was elected and the Ministry of Culture and Islamic Guidance began to take a softer approach towards censoring films. The new atmosphere encouraged some filmmakers to put symbolic language aside and directly portray social issues. Two good examples of this type of cinema made in the new political environment are *Dayereh* (*The Circle*) directed by Jafar Panahi, and *Two Women* directed by Tahmineh Milani. In these films the status of Iranian women in the post-revolution period (and not that of the pre-revolution) was portrayed critically and the religion, the society and the system were confronted with their unjustified oppression of women.

There is no doubt that a new chapter will be added to the evolving

Delpak (center) in *Color of Heaven*.

story of Iranian cinema, as a new government with a conservative agenda came to power in 2005. Because the film industry and other cultural institutions are still controlled and supported by the state, what effect the shifting political climate will have on Iranian cinema remains to be seen. Because the government produces, promotes and supports films and filmmakers based upon its own political agenda, the future direction of Iranian cinema is an open question.

Notes

Preface

1. Sheila Johnston, *Sight and Sound,* January 1999, p. 18.
2. Desson Howe, *Washington Post,* April 28, 2002, p. G01.
3. Jamshid Malekpour, *The Islamic Drama* (London, Frank Cass Publishers, 2004): p. 158.
4. J. Shir-Mohammadi, *Cinemayeh badaz Enghelab* (Tehran: Navak Publishers, 1997).
5. M. R. Norai, "Cinemayeh pasaz Enghelab," *Sepidar* (Toronto) no. 3 (1992).
6. Translations by the author.

Introduction

1. The kinetoscope was a movie camera invented by W. K. Dickson in 1890. The patent was registered under the name of the Edison Company.
2. The cinematograph was invented by Louis and Auguste Lumière in 1895. It was a moving picture camera as well as a projector.
3. David Parkinson, *History of Film* (London: Thames and Hudson, 1995): p. 17.
4. Mosafaredin Shah (1853–1906) was one of the last powerful kings of the Qajar dynasty. TheQajar kings, including Mosafaredin Shah, undermined the political and cultural achievements of previous governments, and as a result Iran became so weak that it soon fell into the hands of foreign powers. Corruption, superstition and ignorance of the kings turned Iran from an independent power into a semicolonial state. Because of the level of destruction brought about by the Qajars, the nation was

ready for a revolution. The Constitutional Revolution in 1906 introduced the first Western parliamentary system to Iran. This was followed by a coup d'etat in 1921, which brought an end to the dynasty.
5. Mosafaredin Shah, *Safarnameh Mosafaredin Shah* (Tehran, 1982): p. 100.
6. Ibid., p. 107.
7. Although this trip had a profound effect on the introduction of the cinema to the Iranian people, it also had an impact on world cinema. Rene Claire, in the film *Silence is Gold,* made in 1947, portrayed Mosafaredin Shah's visit to Paris. In the film, Mosafaredin Shah is portrayed as a king from the East who accidentally visits the filming of one of the scenes. See Jamal Omid, *Tarihk-e-Cinemayeh Iran* (Tehran, 1990): p. 28.
8. A suburb of Tehran.
9. A square in Tehran.
10. Jamshid Malekpour, *Drama in Iran* vol. 1, (Tehran: Toos Publishers, 1983): p. 103.
11. M. A. Sahafbashi, *Safarnameh Sahafbashi* (Tehran, 1978): p. 14.
12. These films were probably of Georges Méliès.
13. Farrokh Ghaffari, "Farhang va Zendegi," *Tarikh-e Cinema-yeh Iran* (Tehran) no. 18 (1974): p. 10.
14. *Roosnameh Sobeh-Sadeq,* no. 166 (1907): p. 4.
15. "The Pathé Studios' greatest discovery was Max Linder (1882–1925), who shaped the future of film comedy.... Linder was given his own series, in which he gradually developed his screen character: the elegant young boulevardier with sleek hair, neatly rakish moustache, elegant cutaway, beautiful cravat, splendid silk hat and trim walking cane." David Robinson, *The History of World Cinema* (New

York: Stein and Day Publishers, 1973): pp. 48–49.

16. The month of Muharram is the most important period in the religious calendar of Iran. On the tenth day of this month, Ashura, Iranians mourn the death of their beloved Imam Hussein through public processions.

17. Omid, *Tarikh-e-Cinemayeh Iran*, p. 43.

18. *Etelaat* (Newspaper), 1916, no. 27, p. 3.

19. "In 1912 the Edison Company released the first American serial, *What Happened to Mary?* The following year the Selig Company began *The Adventures of Kathlyn*, starring Kathlyn Williams and assorted animals from the zoo which was a speciality of the particular company. From this point new serials came thick and fast, generally with female stars (Mary Fuller, Norma Phillips ... Ruth Roland...)." Robinson, *The History of World Cinema*, p. 76.

20. *Etelaat*, 10 May 1928, p. 2.

21. *Etelaat*, 10 May 1928, p. 3.

22. In an interview Motazedi claimed that he had sold his films to an American advisor named "Coleman" and that he took the films back to America. Attempts to determine the identity of this person have so far failed, and neither the US Department of State nor the National Archives have any record of an American official named Coleman in Iran at the time (as per their response to the author's inquiry). It is possible, however, that Motazedi mistook Coleman's nationality. If these films are found many aspects of the beginnings of Iranian cinema will be understood.

23. *The Thief of Baghdad*, starring Fairbanks in 1924.

24. After the Revolution of 1917, and particularly after Stalin took over power in Soviet Union, many Russians, including many Armenians, left Russia and took refuge in Iran. Okaniance was one of those refugees.

25. *Iran* (Tehran), 13 April 1930, p. 1.

26. See Chapter II.

27. *Setareh-Jahan* (newspaper), no. 274, 1930.

28. *Abi and Rabi* was an imitation of early silent French films. Abi and Rabi, the main characters, were the Iranian versions of Carl Schentron and Harold Madsen, who were known as Patte and Patachon in their films. *Abi and Rabi* did not have a particular plot; it was based on the comic actions of a tall and a short man, and was made up of a few comic scenes that were edited together.

29. On the making of this film, Sepanta writes in his diary: "Ardeshir Irani was the director of Imperial Film Company in Bombay, which was very famous. At that time this company was producing a film in Urdu (language of Pakistan).... Viewing this film gave me an opportunity to suggest making a Persian film to Ardeshir. In a short while a decision was made to produce the film. I wrote the screenplay of *The Dokhtare-Lur*, with the technical guidance of Ardeshir, who was a skilled editor. The film was produced in the Imperial Film Studios. I do not remember the exact date on which the film's production began. However, I remember that in April 1932 the first half of production was completed. The cinematography of this film was not an easy task as it was the first ever project for the cast, who for the first time were in front of the camera." A. Sepanta, "Memoir," *Fahang va Zendegi*, no. 18 (Tehran: Farhang va Honar, 1971): pp. 30–34.

30. Ferdowsi wrote the epic *Shahnameh* (The Book of Kings) at the order of Sultan Mahmood. This work took about 30 years to complete. However, upon its completion the King did not acknowledge Ferdowsi's great work, nor its high standard. The King realized his mistake too late. When the King's representative finally arrived at Ferdowsi's house, the body of the author was being taken to the cemetery.

31. The story is similar to Shakespeare's *Romeo and Juliet*.

32. Directed by Ali Darya-Baygi, 1948. See Chapter I for more details on this film.

33. Farrokh Ghaffari, "Abdol-Hussein Sepanata," *Farhang va Zendegi*, no. 18 (Tehran: Farhang va Honar, 1971): p. 43.

Chapter I

1. M. Zarabi, "Bazi Abi va Rabi dar Cinema Mayak," *Film* (Tehran) volume 1, (January 1999): p. 355.

2. There were however exceptions to this rule. There were filmmakers who tried very hard to create a cinema of Iranian character, one that could show on screen the clash between traditional values and alienating elements of society, most imported from the West. But the number and impact of these films were minimal compared to Film Farsi.

3. "The tradition of copying foreign films which was started in 1930 with *Abi and Rabi* reached its peak in (the 1970s). Looking at the films shows that not only the plot, but often the entire movie, was directly copied, with an Iranian cast." Massoud Mehrabi, *Tarikh-e Cinemayeh Iran* (Tehran: Nashre-Moalef, 1997), p. 143.

4. Abbas Shabaviz, "Moj-e No...," *Cinema* (Tehran) no. 442–444 (2000): p. 25.

5. *Ghamha va Shadiha* (directed by

Ahmad Safaie), *Ashq-e Gharon* (directed by Abrahim Bagheri), *Dokhtareh Eshvegar* (directed by Ferydoon Jorak), *Setareh Haft Asemon* (directed by Hussein Madani), *Gardesheh Rosegar* (directed by Ghodrat Bozorghie), *Dokhtareh Shah Parian* (directed by Shahpur Ghariab), *Donyayeh Poshali* (directed by Khosro Parvizi), *Paberehneah* (directed by Rahim Roshanian), *Charkheh Bazigar* (directed by Mehadi Amir Ghasem Khani), and *Poli besoyeh Behashy* (directed by Muhammad Zarin Dast).

6. *Ali Sorchi, Farar az Zendeghi, Ojobeha, Ghayeghranan, Fateh Delha*, and *Mykhakeh Sefeyed*.

7. B. Nik-Ahin, ed., *Gozasht-e Cheraghe Rahe Ayendeht*, (Tehran: Nilofar Publishers, 1983), p. 50.

8. "Before the Constitutional Revolution (1921) and much after that, Iranian women did not show their faces to any men other than their fathers, brothers and uncles. They did not even show their faces to their cousins.... Iranian women did not leave their houses except for going to the bathhouse or visiting their relatives." Y. Aryanpur, *Az Nima ta Rosegare Ma* (Tehran: Zavar Publishers, 1996): p. 4.

Furthermore, we read in *Jense Dovoom* (edited by N. Khorasani [Tehran: Nashr-e Towse, 2001]) that when two Iranian women, J. Sadiqi & Sh. Roosta, opened the first school for women, in 1921, both were arrested and sentenced to four years jail (p. 32).

9. *Shireen and Farhad* was made in 1935 with Muslim women, but it was produced in India, not in Iran.

10. Muhammad Tahami-Nejad, *Cinemayeh Roya-Pardaz-e Iran* (Tehran: Aks-e Moaser, 1986), p. 121.

11. Nilla Cram Cook went to Iran in 1941 to work in the Department of Theatre, but strangely, she was engaged in the Ministry of Interior and in 1942 took over the censorship of Iranian theatre and cinema!

12. Nilla Cram Cook, "The Theatre and Ballet Arts of Iran," *The Middle East Journal*, volume 3, no. 4 (October 1949): pp. 407–408.

13. The United States has recently publicly admitted its involvement in the coup d'etat of 1953. See "The C.I.A. in Iran" by James Risen, *The New York Times* (June 15, 2000). The CIA plotted the military coup that returned the Shah of Iran to power and toppled Iran's elected prime minister, an ardent nationalist.

14. Studio Artesh (Army Studio) made *Noql-Ali* (1954), the theme being the ability of the army to change disorderly people into orderly ones.

15. Nik-Ahin, *Gozasht-e Cheragh-e Rahe Ayendeh*, p. 89.

16. Ismael Koshan (1917–1983) studied economics in West Germany, earning a Ph.D. in the field. At the same time, he studied and worked for film companies and was involved with translation and dubbing of films for Iranian audiences. After returning to Iran, he established Mithra Film; its first production was *The Storm of Life*. As a producer, writer and director he made nearly one hundred films, most of them Film Farsis. He was one of the most influential producers in Iranian cinema during the Pahlavi reign and was largely responsible for creating the Film Farsi genre.

17. In an interview, Koshan described the process of the production: "First I established Mithra Film, and then with cooperation of Ali Darya-Baygi as director and Nezam-Vafa as writer, I made everything ready for *The Storm of Life*, the first Iranian film, to be filmed. We advertised the film and about fifty people came to work. We selected Farhad Motamedi, Onia Doshideh, Ziynat Moadeb and a few famous musicians among them. Khaleghi, a well-known composer, made the music and Banan, the beloved singer of Iran, sang the songs.... The film was about one hundred minutes and it was black and white. The film, however, did not have a good technique" *Mahnameh Cinemayi (1979–1983)* (Tehran, 1999), p. 452.

18. *Etelaat Haftegi*, no. 648, Tehran, 1953, p. 7.

19. Delkash, a popular singer of the time, played the role of Mariam in *Disgraced*.

20. "Film, Radio Report," *Unesco Press*, no. IV (1950): p. 4.

21. The cultural invasion did not happen only in Iran, but was part of a global phenomenon.

22. Apart from feature films, documentaries were another means that Americans used to impose their culture and political views upon Iranian society. Initially, American documentaries about health, sport, industry, and agriculture were imported and shown in Iran. In 1949, Americans established a Film Bureau with 36 mobile screening vehicles that screened documentaries in cities and villages. In 1951, Americans brought a group of ten film teachers (from Syracuse University) to Iran to train Iranians in filmmaking, as well as making documentaries about Iranian society. Even though these films were about agriculture, health and so on, they were also meant to sell the American way of life to people who were living in the most traditional parts of the country, and much of the foreign culture was in contrast with their longstanding beliefs.

23. Cram Cook, p. 408.

24. A chadoor is a long piece of fabric that a woman wears in order to conceal her hair and body.

25. Baba-Karam is usually a solo dance performed by a female who, comically, pretends to be a roughneck.

26. Kathryn Hansen, *Making Women Visible: Gender and Race Cross-Dressing in the Parsi Theatre* (India: 1992), pp.120–130.

27. Adding a song scene from a Film Farsi to a foreign film was the method of editing.

28. Delkas in *Sharmsar* (1950), *Mother* (1952) and *Dasiseh* (1954). Vigan in *Charah Havades* (1954), *Zalem Bala* (1958) and *Tapeh Eshgh* (1959).

29. Jamileh in *Khashme Koli* (1968) and *Khoshkeltarin Zan-e Alam* (1971). Shahrzad in *Haft Dokhtar barayeh Haft Pesar* (1968) and *Mardeh Ejarehyi* (1972).

30. Most Iranian films did not have their own composed music. It was only after the Islamic Revolution of 1979 and in the post-revolutionary cinema that films began to have their own compositions. The music in films made before the revolution consisted mainly of a few songs and some western classical and pop music, used illegally. Sometimes the melodies were played and repeated throughout a film and became the music of the film. The songs, sad or happy, had a vernacular language and were played and sung in common places like the bus, taxis and cafes. The text of these songs were printed and sold when the film was being shown in theaters.

31. "The contemporary change in Iran exhibits parallels to and differences from modern European and American history. The parallels lie in the challenge of science and technology to religious fundamentalism and in the changes in social consciousness encouraged by modern education and a more modern class structure or division of interest groups. The differences result from the suppression of the Constitutional Revolution at the turn of the century and a return, from 1925 to 1978, to an authoritarian, albeit modernizing, monarchy, as well as from a still very underdeveloped industrial economy and a demographic explosion. This last means an infusion into the national political arena of a very young population imbued with a popular religious culture and an enthusiastic attitude toward modern technology. The young people coming into the modern labor market from the villages and towns of Iran, literate and with modern education, retain a profound respect for Islamic morals and tradition, if not necessarily for the scholasticism of their religious leaders. Their cultural identity is rooted in the past, their vision turns toward the future. The social and cultural contradictions and tensions of modern Iran were dramatically catapulted into international attention by the 1977–1979 revolution, which ousted the Pahlavi dynasty." Michael Fischer, *Iran, From Religious Dispute to Revolution* (Cambridge, Mass: Harvard University Press, 1980), pp. vii-viii.

Chapter II

1. Amir Naderi and Naser Taqvai made films for commercial cinema as well as for the new wave movement. This will be discussed in detail in the next chapter.

2. Thirty-four new Iranian films were screened in 1999 at the National Film Theatre in London by the British Film Institute in a program titled *The New Iranian Cinema*. This clearly signaled world recognition of the new developments within the Iranian film community.

3. Mohsen Seif, *Kargardanan Cinemayeh Iran*, volume II (Tehran: Issargaran Association, 1998), p. 168.

4. T. Solhjo, "Bardasht-e Avaal," *Donyayeh Tasvir* (Tehran) no. 82 (2000): p. 49.

5. This film was finally released five years later, in 1963, with a change of title to *Reghabat dar Shahr* (Rivalry in the City).

6. Gholam Haydari, *Naqd Nevisi dar Cinemayeh Iran* (Tehran: Agha Publishers, 1989), p. 106.

7. Omid, p. 108.

8. It is worth mentioning that in 1953 Henry Georges, French filmmaker, made *Reward of Fear*, the theme of which is exactly the same. Ghaffari was acquainted with the French cinema and probably would have seen this film, and it subsequently may have had an impact on *The Night of the Hunchback*.

9. Hajir Daryoosh, "Shabe Qossi," *Majaleh Honar va Cinema*, (Tehran) no. 7 (1964): p. 10.

10. " In *The Bicycle Thieves* and *Umberto D*, the main characters were not professional actors, they were, respectively, a worker and a professor, both 'real protagonists of everyday life.'" Pierre Sorlin, *Italian National Cinema* (London: Routledge, 1996), p. 91.

11. Moshen, *Kargardanan Cinemayeh Iran*, volume II, pp. 358–359.

12. Pierre, *Italian National Cinema*, p. 91.

13. This thesis was translated into Persian and was published in Iran in 1972 under the title of *Vaghyat-Garahey Film* by Boff Publishers.

14. Free Cinema Movement was established in 1969 by experimental filmmakers like Basir Nasibi, Shahriar Parsipur, Abrahim Foroozesh, Behnam Jafari, Ferydoon Shybani and Abrahim Vahid-zadeh.

15. Hamid Sho-aie, *Ferydoon Rahnema* (Tehran: Sherkat Herminco, 1976), pp. 79–80.

16. Siavush was the son of Kai Ka'us, the Shah of Iran. His stepmother, Queen Saudabah, fell in love with him, but he rejected her because he did not want to bring shame upon his father. This rejection caused Saudabah to hate him and to accuse him of raping her.

17. Sho-aie, *Ferydoon Rahnema*, p. 86.

18. Ibid., pp. 94–95.

19. This, of course, was a very important issue in the '70s for different cinemas, such as Australia and West Germany.

20. Anthony Parsons, who was in Iran during this period (1970s), writes: "Iran in 1974 was a land of bewildering contrasts. I would visit a modern factory and come away feeling that I had seen something on a par with its equivalent in Western Europe—could it be that the Great Civilisation was possible? I would visit a teeming bazaar which left me with the impression that nothing had changed in this most traditional of countries.... I saw Persian villages rooted in the immemorial tradition of peasant life, contrasting with an area of massive, mainly foreign-owned agri-businesses where the old villages had been bulldozed to facilitate the use of agricultural machinery, leaving surly peasants grouped in centralised, landless collections of modern huts—there had been serious outbreaks of sabotage of the new machines in that place." Anthony Parsons, *The Pride and the Fall* (London: Jonathan Cape, 1984), pp. 8–9.

21. Hamid Sho-aie, *Noavaran-e Cinema* (Tehran: Sherkat Herminco, 1977), pp. 102–103.

Chapter III

1. In an interview with Iraj Saberi, Dariush Mehrjui explained why he left the cinema course to study philosophy: "At UCLA they only look at the cinema from a Hollywood perspective and they were not interested in cinema as an art form. Our school was a workshop that had equipment, and the purpose was to learn the equipment so that we might get a job as a cleaner at one of the studios. We could hardly find among the lecturers one who truly believed in cinema as art. All discussions were about who was where and who made what and who knocked down who, and how the big boss of that big company was all of a sudden kicked out, and who WB knocked down at MGM and so on. This was not tolerable for me, perhaps the choice of going toward philosophy was in a way

a reaction to those Hollywood-infected lecturers." *Dariush Mehrjui*, edited by Naser Zeraati (Tehran: Negha Publishers, 1996), p. 84.

2. Ibid., p. 36.

3. Close to Franz Kafka's *Metamorphosis.*

4. *Majaleh Ferdowsi*, no. 950, 1969, p. 15.

5. *The Observer*, 12/09/1971, p. 18.

6. *Soroush*, no. 524, 1990, p. 24.

7. Hoshang Kavosi writes in his review "When we see *Qasar* we can see its connection and closeness to Film Farsi. By this film Film Farsi all of a sudden is changed into an original Iranian cinema which after years of waiting was reborn." Kavosi viewed *Qasar* as a form of Film Farsi, with better technique and a better approach to Iranian culture. *Masoud Kimiai*, edited by Zavan Ghoukasian (Tehran: Agha Publishers, 1990), p. 102.

8. Najaf Daryabandari writes "For the first time Film Farsi has been shot and has been performed very well. *Qasar*' is a film which has been made in the process of evolution of the cinema industry. For this reason it might be viewed as a symbol of progress in the Iranian cinema industry." Ibid., 109.

9. This is in terms of Iranian cinema, as there had been such anti-heroes in American films. Characters played by James Dean and Marlon Brando are good examples.

10. M. Jafari, "Dar Barie Nakhl va Bad-e Jiin," *Setareh Cinema*, no. 219, Tehran, 1977, p. 23.

11. H. Bani-Hashemi, "Aramesh dar Hozor-e Digaran," *Ketab-e Cinema*, (Tehran) no. 1 (1970): p. 67.

12. An interesting point about Naser Taqvai is that despite being a novelist, most of his films are based on other writers' novels. His adaptations, however, were purely cinematic and not literary, so there is little similarity between the films and the novels. This of course is part of the cinematic quality of his films. Besides *Peace in the Presence of Others*, a novel by Sa'adi, *Curse* and *Captain Khorshid* are based on *Swamp* by Mika Valtry and *To Have and Have Not* by Ernest Hemingway, respectively. These three films in fact are among Taqvai's best films, and show how Iranian filmmakers adapt literary sources to make films with a recognizable Iranian quality.

13. "Goftegho ba Naser Taqvai," *Etelaat*, no.13287 (1971): p. 5.

14. *Be Ravayat-e Naser Taqvai*, edited by A. Talebi-Nejad (Tehran: Rozaneh-Kar Publishers, 1996), p. 35.

15. "Shahkari be Daqi Khorshid-e Jonob," *Film va Honar*, no. 433, (1973): p. 224.

16. "Filmi dar Sonat-e Hemingway," *Donyai Sokhan*, no. 9, (1987): p. 21.

17. *Bahram Bayzai*, edited by Zavan Ghoukasian (Tehran: Agha Publishers, 1992), p. 16.

18. Ibid., pp. 94–95.

19. *Ayandeghan*, no.17 (1972): p. 12.

20. *Bahram Bayzai*, p. 437.

21. *Bashu* was screened in January 1996 at the AFI Cinema in Melbourne, Australia.

22. N. Servizio, "L'iran Sututti," *Gazzetta di Parma*, 22 March 1974, p. 12.

23. *Naqd Nevisi dar Cinemayeh Iran*, p. 132.

24. *Tarikh-e Cinemayeh Iran*, p. 167.

25. "Man Film Misasam," *Cinema Panjah-o Seh* (Tehran, 1974): p. 11.

26. *The Village Voice*, November 17, 1998, p. 2.

27. Sadeq Hadayat (1903–1951), a well-known Iranian novelist. Among his works, *Bof-e Kor* (The Blind Owl) is regarded as a masterpiece in Persian literature. Loneliness, fear and death are the main themes of this novella.

28. Rene Maheu, *Iran, Rebirth of a Timeless Empire* (Paris: Editions J. A, 1976), p. 208.

29. *Cinemayeh badaz Enghelab*, p. 157.

30. When a man divorces his wife in the presence of a Mulla (Islamic priest) he says "I divorce you three times!" This manner of divorce shows the man's determination not to get together with that woman any more.

31. *Cinemayeh badaz Enghelab*, p. 165.

32. "Ghoftegoie ba Nosrat Karimi," *Cinema va Theatre* (Tehran) no. 2/3 (1972): p. 177.

33. Kimiavi finally succeeded in making another film in Iran in 1999, *Iran Saray-e Man Ast* (Iran is My Land).

34. *Cinema Panjah-o Seh*, p. 74.

35. *The Color of Pomegranate* was screened in 1972 in Tehran at the National Film Archive.

36. Zavan Ghoukasian, ed., *Dar barie Cheshmeh* (Tehran: Isfehan, 1972), p. 12.

37. "Seventh International Film Festival," Tehran, 1967, p. 34.

38. *Dar barie Cheshmeh*, p. 109.

39. Ibid., p. 73.

40. *Tarikh-e Cinemayeh Iran*, p. 163.

Chapter IV

1. "Mizegardeh Cinemayeh Iran," *Farhang va Zendagi* (1975): p. 75.

2. "The prime-ministership of Hoveyda, from 1965 to 1977, was marked by spectacular rise in Iranian prosperity due to exorbitant increases in oil prices and reckless foreign investments.... What the Shah's planners failed to solve was the problem of the vast gap between the foreign exchange earned by means other than oil exports—$385 million in 1975—and foreign exchange expenditure on importing consumer and capital goods which amounted to almost $19 billion. This was bound to destroy the country even if the Shah was not overthrown by revolution." S. A. A. Rizvi, *Iran, Royalty, Religion and Revolution* (Canberra, Ma'rifat Publishing House, 1980), pp. 265–271.

3. This "model character" typified requirements of art elsewhere too, notably socialist regimes in the former Eastern bloc.

4. *Mizegardeh Cinemayeh Iran*, pp. 81–82.

5. See *Velayat-e Faqi* by Imam Khomieni (Tehran: Amir Kabir Publishers, 1981), p. 292.

6. "Between 18 and 20 August (1978), cinemas in Abadan, Mashhad, Shiraz and Rezaeyeh were set on fire. About 400 people, including women and children, were burnt alive in the Rex Cinema in Abadan." Rizvi, *Iran, Royalty, Religion and Revolution*, p. 319.

7. Siavush Kasrai (poet), Bozorg-e Alavi (novelist), and A. H. Noshin (director of theatre), for example, were members of the Communist Party of Iran (Todeh), while many more had connections with other Marxist organizations. See: *Adabiyat-e Novin Iran*, edited by Y. Ajand (Tehran: Amir Kabir, 1985), pp. 359–367.

8. *The Times*, London, July 12 1999, p. 7.

9. *The Chronicle*, Canberra, July 11, 2000, p. 27.

10. *Kayhan*, no. 10663, Tehran, 1978, p. 2.

11. *Cinemayeh Iran badaz Enghelab*, p. 194.

12. He means those who made Film Farsi.

13. Mojahedin-e Khalq is known as a guerrilla organization opposed to the Islamic regime.

14. The Todeh Party was the communist party of Iran.

15. *Cinemayeh Iran badaz Enghelab*, pp. 217–220.

16. *Islamic Cinema* is a title that after the revolution was used widely by authorities to describe the cinema of the new regime. However, no one explained what exactly it meant or what were its characteristics except being in line with the revolution, having moral messages and so on. "If in a film you teach children to brush their teeth, that film is an *Islamic Film*." *Dar Hozor-e Cinema*, p. 22.

17. Another activity of this group of young revolutionary artists was attacking and removing those artists who worked before the revolution. Those artists were accused by the group belonging to the Islamic Propaganda Organization of being either royalist, communists or pro–Western and their works were attacked;

they were also subjected to personal attacks, and their works removed from the stages. In theatre and cinema Mohsen Makhmalbaf attacked many artists who he believed were not Islamic, asking that the Iranian art scene be cleared of them.

18. S. Mohammed Behashti, "Movafaqiyat-e Ma," *Majaleh Film* (Tehran, 1998): p. 35.

19. There was a blacklist which meant that some artists were able to work and others not. Mohammed Behashti, the executive director of *Bonyad-e Farabi* in response to a question said that, "I am not saying that such a list exists or does not exist." If in fact such a blacklist did not exist, he could easily have denied it. *Movafaqiyat-e Ma*, p. 42.

20. *Haftomin Jashnvareh Film-e Fajr* (Tehran, 1989): p. 2.

21. Parviz Davai, "Khaste Nabashi Rafiq," *Sepid va Siah*, (Tehran) no. 941 (1971): p. 65.

22. *Amir Naderi*, edited by Gholam Haydari (Tehran: Nashr-e Sohail, 1991), p. 232.

23. Kiumars Pour-Ahmad, "Sazeh Dahani, Gami Arseshmand," *Film va Honar*, no. 256 (1974): p. 38.

24. In fact, Naderi first came to Australia. After a while when he realized that he couldn't make films there, he left for America.

25. Hoshang Golmakani in a review on *Search 1* writes: "if this film did not have the signature of Amir Naderi, and if he didn't have a few legitimately timeless films like *Deadlock*, then it would be possible to compare *Search 1* with one of those easily made, easily consumed television programs." This is only one example exemplifying the harsh critical commentary heaped upon *Search 1*, much of which was unkind to Naderi's films for no apparent reason. *Amir Naderi*, p. 448.

26. *The Washington Post*, January 25, 1991, p. 20.

27. A similarity can be found here with road movies. Wim Wenders, in *Alice in the Cities*, looks for every possible means of transport to sustain the "kinetic energy" for his story.

28. *Mahnameh Film*, no. 33 (1985): p. 37.

29. *Iran Media*, March 15, 1998, p. 2.

30. The run that the director himself finally performed was to leave Iran for the United States, where he made *Manhattan by Numbers* (1992), and *ABC Manhattan* (1997) with no connection to Iran and the Iranian people. Both films are about Manhattan and its residents. Although in both films the theme of running is used, there is no sign of the little boy (Amiro) from the south of Iran in the films. In *ABC Manhattan*, Naderi shows a relationship between three women: Colleen, who is forced to

abandon her daughter; Kacey, a bisexual who exchanges her boyfriend for a girlfriend; and Kate, who like Naderi himself has come to New York to try her luck, though in music.

31. However there was again an exception: Khosroo Dehghan, the same critic who insulted Naderi by accusing him of not knowing the basics of filmmaking, this time suggested in a review that Naderi leave cinema altogether.

32. *Amir Naderi*, p. 548.

33. "Car-seat Conversations Inspire Iranian director," *The Christian Science Monitor*, July 28, 2000, p. 16.

34. "No Sex, No Violence, Just film," *The Times*, London, July 12, 1999, p. 7.

35. "Sahal va Jazab," *Rodaki* (Tehran) no. 37–38 (1974): p. 52.

36. Zaven Ghoukasian ed., *Abbas Kiarostami* (Tehran: Nashr-e Didar, 1997), p. 182.

37. "Morality Tale Told with Class," *The Toronto Sun*, 23 July 1997, p. 3.

38. *Cinemaya*, no. 16 (1992): p. 59.

39. *Abbas Kiarostami*, p. 176.

40. *2000 San Francisco International Film Festival*, WSWA, p. 4.

41. *Sight and Sound*, February 1997, p. 24.

42. In the film there is no mention of cherries, so the filmmaker's reasons for choosing the title that he did when the story of Mr. Bagheri is about a mulberry tree are a mystery.

43. *The Christian Science Monitor*, July 28, 2000, p. 12.

44. *Bad Mara Ba Khod Khahad Bord* (The Wind Will Carry Us, 1999) is about a filmmaker who comes to a small town in Kurdistan to document a funeral ritual that is supposed to take place after the death of a very old woman.

45. "The Wind Will Carry Us," a poem by Foroogh Farookhzad from which Kiarostami took the title of his film.

46. Makhmalbaf was one of the artists who were strong backers of the Islamic revolution and who were going to purge the Iranian art scene of any artists who did not share their beliefs, violently if necessary. Of non–Islamic artists he said, "I am not ready to be with these artists even by a long shot" (*Soroosh*, 1987). Thirteen years later he said, "I started to criticise myself, as part of a generation who—at the time—thought we could save the world through violence." (*The Japan Times*, July 21, 2000, p. 12.)

47. This, however, was a very expensive workshop as each of these revolutionary young men made two or three feature films to learn the basics of filmmaking. They were given a golden opportunity not available to anybody outside of the organization.

48. *International Film* (Tehran) vol. 2, no. 2 (1994): p. 6.

49. *Film, Goftegoha,* vol. I (Tehran, 1988): p. 132.

50. *Donyayeh Sokhan,* no. 11 (Tehran, 1987): p. 12.

51. *Cinemayeh badaz Enghelab,* p. 339.

52. *Mohsen Makhmalbaf,* pp. 335–36.

53. *Cinemayeh badaz Enghelab,* p. 353.

54. *Harram,* something which is against the Islamic law.

55. He means that if a film is not criticising a political or social issue, it is not a film at all. *Majaleh Film, Goftegoha,* vol. I (Tehran, 1997): p. 125.

56. Ibid., p. 131.

57. *Variety,* Cannes, May 12, 1996, p. 3.

Chapter V

1. "From 524 active cinemas in the last years of the previous regime (Pahlavi) nearly 200 were burnt down or destroyed during the revolution." *Dar Hozor-e Cinema,* p. 6. This number alone is indicative of the havoc wreaked upon the whole Iranian cinema during and after the revolution. The new Iranian cinema, therefore, can be considered a phoenix that arose from the fire of the revolution.

2. There were a few producers like M. Misaghiyeh and A. Abbasi who made art-house as well as commercial films.

3. Literature too suffered the same fate as other forms of art. Most works by poets and novelists were banned and no new work could be published.

4. People did not have even the right to use music at their wedding parties or dance at such gatherings. If they were caught they would have been prosecuted.

5. *Adabestan,* no. 1. (Tehran, 1989): p. 51.

6. Ibid., p. 52.

7. *Hamshari,* Tehran, September 27, 2001, p. 14.

8. *Iran,* Tehran, December 8, 2001, p. 7.

9. *Payvand's Iran News,* August 10, 2000, p. 1.

10. *The New York Times,* March 11, 2001, p. 12.

Filmography

Abi and Rabi (*Abi va Rabi*), written and directed by Avance Okaniance, produced by S. Lidzeh, starring Zarabi and Sohrabi-Fard, 1930. The first film of the Iranian cinema. Based on the comic actions of a tall and short man, the film was a copy of the early silent French films.

Adamak, written and directed by Khosroo Haritash, produced by R. Golzar, starring Doolatshahi and Khoshkam, 1971. A film directed by a graduate of UCLA. A rebellious young aristocrat, Babak, escapes from his family and their social values.

Aghayeh Heroglif, written and directed by Gholam Ali Erfan, produced by H. Kabir, starring Rashidi and Valli, 1981. A leftist film about a group of miners. The film was never shown in Iran.

Amo-Sibilo, written by B. Bayzai (based on F. Hadayatpour), directed by Bahram Bayzai, produced by K.P.F.K.N., starring Bahrami, 1970. A short film about the loneliness of an old man and the necessity of having contact with others.

And Life Goes On (*Va Zendegi Edameh Darad*), written and directed by Abbas Kiarostami, produced by K.P.F.K.N., starring Kheradmand and Payvar, 1992. A real earthquake in northern Iran causes the director, Kiarostami, to take his camera and go in search of two actors who lived in that area. The search (performed by a father and son) becomes an exploration of the meaning of existence as well.

Apple (*Siib*), written by Mohsen Makhmalbaf, directed by Samira Makhmalbaf, produced by M. Karmitz, V. Cayla and I. Sarbaz, starring M. Naderi and Z. Naderi, 1999. A father locks his two daughters in the house for 11 years, not allowing them outside in order to protect them from being corrupted. Finally a neighbor informs the welfare department.

Arbai'in, written and directed by Naser Taqvai, produced by IRTV, 1970. A documentary about a religious ceremony.

Aroos-e Dejleh, written by M. Shab-Pareh, directed by N. Mohtasham, produced by M. Shab-Pareh, starring Jaleh and Rakhshani, 1955. A story of love and jealousy taken from history. The chancellor is in love with the sister of the king and marries her in secret. The queen — who is also in love with the chancellor — finds out, and causes the death of the chancellor and his two children.

Bad-e Jiin, written and directed by Naser Taqvai, produced by IRTV, 1969. A documentary about the ritual of Zar and its psychological and social effects.

The Ballad of Tara (*Cherikeh Tara*), written, directed and produced by Bahram Bayzai, starring Taslimi and Fariid, 1979. A film dealing with mythology and philosophy. Tara, a widow, meets a strange man who gives her a sword to fight unknown forces of destruction.

Baluch, written and directed by Masoud Kimiai, produced by M. Misaghiyeh, starring Vosooghi and Erane, 1972. A proud ethnic man of Baluchestan leaves his village for the city to find and kill those who raped his wife. Family honor is the theme of the film, which was very close to Film Farsi.

Barzakhiha, written by Said Motalebi, directed by Eraj Ghaderi, produced by A. Mohammadzadeh, starring Fardin and Malekmoteai, 1981. During the Islamic revolution, the doors of prisons are opened and prisoners, including criminals, escape. A group of them is planning to leave the country but they are stopped by a member of the revolution. A "revolutionary" Film Farsi.

Bashu, the Little Stranger (*Bashu, Gharibeh Kuchak*), written and directed by Bahram Bayzai, produced by K.P.F.K.N., starring Taslimi and Ofravian, 1986. A boy, lost in the war between Iraq and Iran, finds a new home. However, he feels he is a stranger there, unable to communicate with anybody. A beautiful film about war and its innocent victims.

Behind the Mist (*Ansoyeh Meh*), written by S. Mohammad Beheshti, directed by

M. Asghari Nasab, produced by Farabi, starring Shojanoori and Tahmasb, 1986. Three terrorists are after the governor, but kill another man by mistake. They come back to finish the job but are buried under a landslide.

Bells (*Zangha*), written by M. Makhmalbaf, directed by M. R. Honarmand, produced by Hozeh Honari, starring Kassebi and Sultanian, 1985. A number of people are threatened with death by an anonymous telephone caller and then are killed one after another. A journalist tries to find the killer or killers, however, he is more interested in headlines than the truth.

Blade and Silk (*Tigh va Abrisham*), written, directed and produced by Masoud Kimiai, starring Seddighi and Farjami, 1986. An action film about the distribution of drugs among young people in Iran. A poor film, made after the revolution, from the director who made good films like *Qasar* before the revolution.

A Boat Toward the Coast (*Balami besoyeh Sahel*), written and directed by R. Mulla-Gholipur, produced by Hozeh Honari, starring Ziyai and Salmanian, 1985. A war film: The port of Khoramshahr is surrounded by the Iraqi army. A group of volunteers arrives from Tehran and finally succeeds in breaking the enemy line.

The Boycott (*Baykot*), written and directed by Mohsen Makhmalbaf, produced by Hozeh Honari, starring Majidi and Sarmadi, 1985. Vale, a left-wing activist, is arrested and jailed by the Shah's regime. In jail, he starts questioning his ideology and, ultimately, comes to believe in God just before the bullets penetrate his chest. A politically and religiously motivated melodrama about Marxism.

The Bread and the Alley (*Nan va Kocheh*), written by Taqi Kiarostami, directed by Abbas Kiarostami, produced by K.P.F.K.N., starring Hashemi and Shahrvanfar, 1970. A short children's film about self-confidence and the ability to solve problems. A boy is returning home after buying bread, but is stopped by a dog. The boy does not dare to pass the barking dog. At the end he finds a solution: he throws a piece of bread to the dog and continues on his way.

Brehan-e ta Zohr ba Soraat, written and directed by K. Haritash, produced by M. Misaghiyeh, starring Seddighi and Erane, 1976. Murder and sex appear in the Iranian cinema, which caused outrage and criticism. A young man kills his creditor and is forced to live with a woman who has witnessed the murder.

Captain Khorshid (*Nakhoda Khorshid*), written and directed by Naser Taqvai, produced by H. Yashayai and Associates, starring Arjmand and Maasomi, 1987. A well-made film loosely based on *To Have and Have Not* by Hemingway. Captain Khorshid is paid by a group of people who want to leave the country illegally. A fight breaks among them, but Captain Korshid regains control, only to be thwarted just as he is about to complete his mission.

The Circle (*Dayereh Mina*), written by G. H. Sa'adi and D. Mehrjui, directed by Dariush Mehrjui, produced by M. Sassan-Viasi, B. Farmanara and P. Sayyad, starring Forozan and Kangarani, 1976. A young man in need of money for treatment of his ill father is dragged into a gang that buys and sells blood for hospitals. A horrific picture of poverty in a country that was second in the world in oil production.

The Circle (*Dayereh*), written by J. Panahi and K. Partovi, directed and produced by Jafar Panahi, starring Mamizadeh and Almani, 2000. Three women, each with a secret, are released from prison. They struggle to survive in a male dominated society.

Close-up (*Namaye Nazdik*), written and directed by Abbas Kiarostami, produced by Ali Reza Zarin, starring Sabzian and Ahankha, 1990. A drama/documentary about a young man who introduces himself to a family as Makhmalbaf, the famous film director, and forms a close bond with them.

Color of Heaven (*Rang-e Khoda*), written and directed by Majid Majidi, produced by M. Karimi and Associates, staring Delpak and Mahjub, 1999. After deciding to remarry, a father tries to get rid of his blind son.

Come Stranger (*Biganeh Biya*), written and directed by Masoud Kimiai, produced by M. and N. Akhavan, starring Vosooghi and Sajedi, 1968. A man leaves his fiancée and her child to go overseas to continue his education, not caring about the fate of the mother and child left behind. The woman attempts suicide but is saved by another man.

Concierge (*Saraydar*), written by K. Haritash and H. Sharifimehr, directed by Khosroo Haritash, produced by H. Sharifimehr, starring Nasiriyan and Kangarani, 1975. A good and timely film about the economic capitalization of a traditional society without regard to social justice. A concierge of a company, in competition with his neighbor and to solve his financial problems, is forced to rob his own company. His amateur filmmaker son, however, films his illegal action.

The Cow (*Gav*), written by G. H. Sa'adi and D. Mehrjui, directed by Dariush

Mehrjui, produced by D. Mehrjui and Farhang va Honar, starring Entezami and Nasiriyan, 1969. The first important film of the new wave in Iranian cinema before the revolution; the movie is about a metamorphosis of a man into a cow. Mash Hassan leaves his village and his cow (the only cow in the village) to do business in the city. On his return he is told that his cow has escaped. Not believing the story, he enters the stable and comes out as if he has become the cow, to the consternation of his fellow villagers.

The Crow (*Kalagh*), written and directed by Bahram Bayzai, produced by B. Farmanara, starring Maasomi and Parvaresh, 1977. An advertisement and a photo in a newspaper attract the attention of a television newsreader and his wife. At the end, his wife, finds out that the photo is of her mother in her youth. From a filmmaker whose examination of the unknown past in a quest to give a meaning to the present existence is his cinematic preoccupation.

Cry at Midnight (*Faryad-e Nimeh-Shab*), written and directed by Samuel Khachekian, produced by M. Misaghiyeh, starring Fardin and Arman, 1961. One of the better gangster films. Just married, a young man finds no other way to make money but to join a gang. Being good of heart and in love with his wife, he returns to a normal and decent life at the end.

The Cry of the Holy Warrior (*Faryad-e Mojahed*), written and directed by Mahdi Madanian, produced by Satar Harris, starring Firooz and Bayat, 1979. The secret police attack a mosque where some clergymen are active in opposition to the royal regime.

Curse (*Nafrin*), written and directed by Naser Taqvai, produced by M. T. Shokrai, starring Vosooghi and Khorvash, 1973. On suspicion of their having an affair, an alcoholic husband kills his wife and her friend. An attempt at a psychological drama before the revolution.

The Cyclist (*Baicykelran*), written and directed by Mohsan Makhmalbaf, produced by Bonyad-e Mostazafan, starring Zinalzadeh and Sultanian, 1989. Nasim is forced to participate in a race, riding a bike non-stop day and night, in order to raise money for the treatment of his ill wife.

Dalshodeghan, written, directed and produced by Ali Hatami, starring Seddighi and Abddi, 1992. A film dedicated to traditional music of Iran, portraying a master musician in the era of Qajars.

The Dancer of the Town (*Raghase Shahr*), written by Reza Mirlohi, directed by Shahpour Gharib, produced by Homayoun and Sadeghpour, starring Forozan and Malekmoteai, 1971. A married middle-aged man falls in love with a dancer. When the dancer realizes that her affair is damaging his family, she starts ignoring him.

Dash Akol, written by M. Kimiai (based on the novel by Sadeq Hadayat), directed by Masoud Kimiai, produced by H. Kaveh, starring Vosooghi and Apyk, 1971. An unsuccessful adaptation of a famous novel. A man of honor is driven to the verge of insanity by his desire for a young girl.

Dead Nature see **Still Life**

Deadlock (*Tangna*), written by A. Naderi and M. Aslani, directed by Amir Naderi, produced by Ali Abbasi, starring Raad and Kasrai, 1973. Ali, a street man, fights with three brothers. One of them is killed and Ali is forced to flee.

The Death of Yazdegard (*Margeh Yazdegard*), written, directed and produced by

Bahram Bayzai, starring Taslimi and Hashemi, 1979. More theatre than cinema, this is an adaptation of a play based on a historical event. The last king of Persian Empire is defeated by Arabs and takes refuge in a mill, where he is finally discovered by his enemies and killed.

The Deer (*Gavaznha*), written and directed by Masoud Kimiai, produced by M. Misaghiyeh, starring Vosooghi and Gharibian, 1975. A cursed film in Iranian cinema. First the public screening of the film was banned by the government, and when it was finally released with some changes, the cinema (Rex) that was showing the film was set on fire in the midst of the revolution and 600 people burned alive inside. A political activist is on run from security forces and is forced to seek the help of his old friend, whose life is in a mess due to his addiction.

Diamond 33 (*Almas-e Siose*), written by D. Mehrjui and R. Fazeli, directed by Dariush Mehrjui, produced by N. Montakheb and M. R. Fazeli, starring Fazelli and Zohori, 1967. A James Bond–style film. A professor discovers how to make diamonds from oil, and gives the formula to his niece who is to take it to Iran. But members of a gang are waiting for her, hoping to steal the formula.

Disgraced (Sharmsar), written by Ali Kasmai, directed and produced by Ismael Koshan, starring Delkash and Daneshvar, 1950. City social values versus country social values. A country girl is deceived by a man from city. Disgraced, the girl is forced to leave the village and go to the capital, where luckily by her good voice she becomes a famous singer. One of the first films to bring songs into Iranian films.

Doroshkehchi, written and directed by Nosrat Karimi, produced by M. Sadeqpour, starring Karimi and Shahla, 1971.

A comedy of love and traditions. A man is in love with a woman but cannot marry her due to the opposition of the woman's brother. They marry other people instead, but sadly, after years of marriage both lose their partners. The man wants to try to marry his old love, but this time the woman's son is opposed to their marriage.

Downpour (*Ragbar*), written and directed by Bahram Bayzai, produced by B. Taheri, starring Maasomi and Fanizadeh, 1971. The first feature film by Bayzai, and his best one. A young teacher, Mr. Hakmati, is transferred to a school in a small community where he falls in love with the sister of one of his students. The butcher is also in love with the girl. A good film which shows the social and psychological structure of a small community.

The Earth (*Khak*), written by M. Kimiai (based on M. Dolatabadi), directed by Masoud Kimiai, produced by M. Misaghiyeh, starring Vosooghi and Taaydi, 1973. Based on a novel by Dolatabadi, this is a film about land and the invasion of foreigners, which changes the structure of society. A landlord dies and his wife asks a farmer to leave the land that he has worked on for years.

Elegy (*Marsiyeh*), written and directed by Amir Naderi, produced by Ali Mortazavi, starring Ahmadi and Basiri, 1975. A man is released from a prison after eight years. He tries to adapt himself to the new environment and learn to stand on his own two feet.

Ferdowsi, written and directed by Abdul-Hussein Sepanta, produced by Ardeshir Irani, starring Sepanta and Mohtasham, 1934. Based on the life of Ferdowsi, a great Persian poet. By order of the king, he spends thirty years of his life to write the epic of *Shahnameh* yet hears nothing in return. He dies in poverty and isolation.

Fickle (*Bolhavas*), written and directed by Abrahim Moradi, produced by A. Dehghan and M. A. Ghotbi, starring Amir-Fazli and Tabesh, 1935. One of the first Iranian detective films. A gang of jewelry thieves is finally caught with the help of a young member of the gang.

Gabbe, written and directed by Mohsen Makhmalbaf, produced by Doroodchi and Mahmmodi, starring Jodat and Sayahi, 1996. Finally, a beautiful and colorful film by Makhmalbaf, and not related to politics or religion. A love story, told through the colors of a carpet, between a boy and a girl from a nomadic tribe.

Goodbye, My Friend (*Khoda Hafez Rafiq*), written by A. Naderi and N. Navidar, directed by Amir Naderi, produced by A. Shabaviz and B. Taheri, starring Raad and Hashemi, 1971. Naser wants to perform one last robbery and retire from a life of crime, but all the jewels are taken by one of his partners. Three robbers are killed at the end, and Naser's efforts to regain his share of the jewels are in vain.

Haji Agha Becomes an Actor of Cinema (*Haji Agha Actor Cinema Mishavad*), written and directed by Avance Okaniance, produced by Perse Film, starring Morad and Ghostanian, 1932. A first attempt to convince Iranians that cinema was not a corrupt institution. Haji-Agha, an enemy of cinema, is filmed secretly by his son-in-law and is taken to a theater to see himself on the screen and decides that cinema is not that bad after all.

Haji Washington, written, directed and produced by Ali Hatami, starring Entezami and Harrison, 1982. The comic/ tragic life of the first Ambassador of Iran, known as Haji Washington, in the United State of America.

Hamoon, written, directed and produced by Dariush Mehrjui, starring Shakibai and Entezami, 1990. Philosophy and cinema. Depressed by the revolution and a long war, Hamid is forced to turn inward in search of the meaning of his existence. One of the best films that Mehrjui made after the revolution.

Harmonica (*Sazeh Dahani*), written and directed by Amir Naderi, produced by K.P.F.K.N., starring Godarzi and Javadi, 1974. A boy who has a harmonica uses it to make other boys serve him like slaves.

Hassan Kachal, written and directed by Ali Hatami, produced by Ali Abbasi, starring Sayaad and Katayoun, 1970. A comic/fantasy film taken from a fable; a musical. A lazy boy meets a jinnee and falls in love with her.

Hello Cinema (*Salaam Cinema*), written and directed by Mohsen Makhmalbaf, produced by Abbas Ranjbar, starring Kayhan and Ashraghi, 1995. Makhmalbaf puts an advertisement in newspapers for a few actors for his new film. Hundreds turn up at the door and the director starts interviewing them while the camera is rolling.

Hezardastan, written, directed and produced by Ali Hatami, starring Rashidi and Mashayikhi, 1988. A television series based on historical characters and events.

Homework (*Mashq-e Shab*), written and directed by Abbas Kiarostami, produced by K.P.F.K.N., 1989. A documentary about the psychological consequences of children having to do homework.

The Husband of Ahoo-Khanom (*Sho-whar-e Ahoo-Khanom*), written, directed and produced by Davood Mula-Qolipour, starring Eshragh and Meshkin, 1968. Based on a novel by Afghani, the film failed to transform the words into images. A married middle-aged man falls in love with a widow. There ensues a struggle between his love for the woman and his responsibility for the family.

The Inner Beast (*Hayolay-e Daroon*), written and directed by Khosroo Sinai, produced by Bonyad-e Mostazafan, starring Rashidi and Mirbakhtyar, 1985. During the Islamic revolution, a senior member of the secret police hides from his memories in a rural village, but he starts to recall his past life.

Jafar-Khan Is Back from Europe (*Jafar-Khan az Farang Bargashteh*), written by A. Hatami (based on H. Moghadam), directed by Ali Hatami, produced by Ali Abbasi, starring Sarshar and Keshavarz, 1984–1989. Based on a play by Moghadam, this is a comic portrayal of a young Iranian man returning home from France. The clash of cultures is the central theme.

Journey of the Stone (*Safare Sangh*), written by M. Kimiai (based on B. Farahani), directed and produced by Masoud Kimiai, starring Raad and Taaydi, 1978. The landlord owns the only mill in the village and imposes his power over the farmers. A gipsy comes to the village and makes the farmers to stand against the local tyrant.

Kamalolmolk, written and directed by Ali Hatami, produced by H. Ghafori, starring Mashayikhi and Entezami, 1984. The story of Kamalolmolk, one of the best painters in Iran in late 19th century. The movie features a good performance by Mashayikhi in the role of Kamalolmolk.

Laila and Majnun (*Laila va Majnun*), written and directed by Abdul-Hussein Sepanta, produced by Lamka, starring Sepanta and Vaziri, 1937. Based on a classic love story by Ganjavi. Laila and Majnun fall in love but cannot have each other as Liala's father is opposed to their marriage.

The Lead (*Sorb*), written by M. Kimiai (based on T. Sakhai), directed by Masoud Kimiai, produced by M. H. Saboki, starring Islami and Mashayikhi, 1989. On surface, a detective film with some political spice, but deep down, it is a film about the love of movies from a child's (the director) view point.

The Lur Girl (*Dokhtar-e Lur*), written and directed by Abdul-Hussein Sepanta, produced by Ardeshir Irani, staring Rohangiz and Sepanta, 1933. Made in India and in Persian by an Iranian director, this is the first Iranian sound film. Golnar is kidnapped by a group of thieves and is forced to dance in teahouses. Her lover, Jafar, finally rescues her and brings law and order to the region.

Made in Iran (*Sakht-e Iran*), written and directed by Amir Naderi, produced by Ali Mortazavi, starring Raad and Bergen, 1979. A young Iranian boxer goes to America to become a champion, but is dragged into arranged fights.

The Man of God (*Mard-e Khoda*), written by Mahdi Madanian, directed and produced by Reza Safai, starring Vosoogh and Shirandami, 1979. Morteza, a devoted religious man, is against the marriage of his younger brother to a woman who once had to work as a prostitute. At the end Morteza realizes that nothing is better than helping someone to get back to a decent life.

Marriage of the Blessed (*Arusi-e Khuban*), written and directed by Mohsen

Makhmalbaf, produced by Hozeh Honari, starring Bigham and Nonahali, 1991. A young photographer suffers a nervous breakdown due to an explosion in the war. He comes back to Tehran and sees that many people, including his father-in-law, are benefiting from the war. A first film criticizing an unjust system and an ignorant society in the time of war.

Maybe Some Other Time (*Shayed Vaghti Digar*), written and directed by Bahram Bayzai, produced by M. A. Farajolahi and Associates, Taslimi and Farhang, 1988. A search for identity. A narrator of documentary films sees his wife, dressed in greenish yellow, sitting in a stranger's car in one of the films. At home, he asks her to explain. She denies everything, including having a greenish yellow dress.

Mr. Simpleton (*Aghayi Haloo*), written by A. Nasirian and D. Mehrjui, directed by Dariush Mehrjui, produced by Tabibiyan, starring Nasiriyan and Khorvash, 1971. A simple man from a small town comes to the capital in search of a wife.

Mohalel, written and directed by Nosrat Karimi, produced by M. Misaghiyeh, starring Karimi and Erane, 1971. A religious law creates a comic/tragic situation for a man who, in anger, divorces his wife three times and cannot remarry her again unless she marries another man first. She must then get a divorce from her new husband to remarry her ex-husband. The filmmaker went to jail after the revolution for making fun of a religious law in a film made before the Islamic revolution.

The Mongols (*Mogolha*), written and directed by Parviz Kimiavi, produced by Tel Film, starring Rastgar and Chamani, 1973. A television director is sent to a poor area to install a relay station in order to bring television to the local people. A good and timely film about cultural invasion.

The Morning of the Fourth Day (*Sobeh Rooz-e Chahrom*), written by K. Shirdal and M. Aslani, directed and produced by Kamran Shirdal, starring Raad and Vajesta, 1972. A poor film from a good documentary maker. Amir accidentally kills someone and runs away till he is killed on "the morning of the fourth day." During his flight, he doesn't receive a helping hand from anyone.

Mud-brick and Mirror (*Khasht va Ayineh*), written, directed and produced by Abrahim Golestan, starring Taji-Ahmadi and Hashemi, 1965. A neo-realistic film, one of the first films of the Iranian New Wave. A woman leaves her newborn baby in a taxi and vanishes. The baby takes the man and his lover to a journey of self-discovery.

Nar-o-Nai, written and produced by S. Ebrahimifar, H. Eri and A. Tarseh, directed by Said Ebrahimifar, starring Almasi and Garmsiri, 1989. Visually, one of the best films of Iranian cinema. The film is about a photographer who meets an ill old man. The photographer puts everything aside to get to know and help the old man.

Nassouh's Repentance (*Tobeh Nassouh*), written and directed by Mohsen Makhmalbaf, produced by Hozeh Honari, starring Salahshor and Kasebi, 1982. During a man's funeral it is realized that he is still alive. Shameful of his past life, he decides to change himself for the better.

The Night of the Hunchback (*Shabe Qossi*), written by J. Moghadam, directed and produced by Farrokh Ghaffari, starring Keshavarz and Ghaffari, 1964. A provocative film, which had roots in the Iranian culture. A death of an actor in a theatre group creates fear and causes people around him to distance themselves from the corpse.

Nights on Zayandeh Rud (*Shabhay-e Zayandeh Rud*), written and directed by Mohsen Makhmalbaf, produced by Shahed and Film Khaneh, starring Esmaeli and Naderi, 1991. A professor of anthropology loses his wife in a car accident while he himself is paralysed. He does not see much compassion or help from people at the time, so he alienates himself from society. This only lasts till the revolution, when he witnesses the ways in which people are helping each other.

Noql-Ali, written by Golesorkhi, directed by Parviz Khatibi, produced by Golesorkhi, starring Tafakori and Mosadegh, 1954. A comic-patriotic film made by the army to show how army training can change people for the better. The hapless Noql-Ali joins the army only to graduate as a skillful and disciplined man.

One Step to Death (*Yek Ghadam ta Margh*), written and directed by Samuel Khachekian, produced by J. Vaesian, starring Botimar and Sohaila, 1961. A gangster film by Khachekian, who is considered the Alfred Hitchcock of Iranian cinema. A female member of a gang falls in love with a detective. Technically, the film was far ahead of the rest of Iranian films made in the '50s and '60s.

P for Pelican (*P mesleh Pelikan*), written and directed by Parviz Kimiavi, produced by Tel Film, 1972. A semi-documentary about an old man living on the edge of a desert whose solitary life is interrupted by the arrival of a migrating pelican.

A Party in Hell (*Shab Neshini dar Jahanam*), written by H. Madani, directed by M. Sarvari, produced by M Misaghiyeh, starring Vosoogh and Sadr, 1957. A greedy wealthy man decides to marry his daughter to a rich old man, without caring that she is in love with a young man.

Patriotic (*Mihan-Parast*), written by Mohammad Deram-Bakhsh, directed by Gholam Hussein Naghshineh, produced by M. Deram-Bakhsh, starring Naghshineh and Nadereh, 1953. A bad melodrama of war and patriotism. When a retired colonel finds out that his own son is not willing to go to the front to defend the motherland, he, with his daughter, joins the army to defeat the enemies. There was no chance for an Iranian woman to join the army in that time.

Peace in the Presence of Others (*Aramesh dar Hozor-e Digharan*), written by N. Taqvai and G. H. Sa'adi, directed by Naser Taqvai, produced by IRTV, starring Meshkin and Ghasimi, 1970. A retired colonel goes to a small town to live in peace for the rest of his life. After a while he marrys a young girl and soon returns to his city where he ends up in a mental institution. The colonel carries a secret that he hides from others. The secret that caused the film to be banned for years: the censor's interpretation was that the film was about the life of a member of the secret police responsible for torturing political opponents of the Royal regime.

The Peddler (*Dastforoosh*), written and directed by Mohsen Makhmalbaf, produced by Hozeh Honari, starring Zarabi and Zinalzadeh, 1987. A film with three episodes. A poor couple decides to give away their fourth child; a mentally disabled young man is taking care of his mute mother; and the killing of a member of a gang who tries to run away.

The Pleasure of the Sin (*Lezat-e Gonah*), written, directed and produced by Siamak Yasami, starring Forozan and Jafari, 1964. The first film in Iranian cinema to show a sex scene, which made the actress a superstar overnight. A mute country girl is raped. Later the rapist tries to kidnap the child from the woman but in the struggle the child is dropped into the river, which causes the mother to scream for help. Help arrives, the child is saved, and the rapist gets what he deserves.

The Postman (*Postchi*), written and directed by Dariush Mehrjui, produced by M. Misaghiyeh, starring Nasiriyan and Entezami, 1972. A postman who is seeking treatment for his sexual disability kills his wife for having an affair with his employee.

Prince Ehtejab (*Shazdeh Ehtejab*), written by H. Golshiri and B. Farmanara, directed by Bahman Farmanara, produced by B. Farmanara and M. Sassan Vaisi, starring Mashayikhi and Khorvash, 1974. Based on a novel by Golshiri, this is about the fall of a dynasty. The last member of an aristocratic family is dying of tuberculosis in isolation. He remembers the glorious past and his sins at the same time.

Qasar, written and directed by Masoud Kimiai, produced by Abbas Shabaviz, starring Vosooghi and Malekmoteai, 1969. A quality commercial film, *Qasar* is a drama of honor and revenge. A girl is raped, and her elder brother is killed, too. The younger brother, Qasar, pulls his knife and kills those men responsible for the death of his sister and brother. Bleeding, Qasar takes refuge in an abandoned train car where he is shot by police.

Qazal, written and directed by by Masoud Kimiai, produced by K. S. P, starring Fardin, Banai and Gharibian, 1975. Two brothers fall in love with a prostitute.

The Red Line (*Khat-e Ghermez*), written by M. Kimiai (based on B. Bayzai), directed by Masoud Kimiai, produced by Ali Homani, starring Raad and Farjami, 1982. During the revolution, a woman becomes suspicious of her husband's profession and discovers that he is a member of the secret police.

Red Wind (*Bad-e Sorkh*), written and directed by Jamshid Malekpour, produced by A. Montazeri, starring Mirbakhtyar and Almasi, 1990. Due to superstitions, a pregnant woman is forced to give birth into the sea. The film has been banned in Iran despite being shown at many international festivals, including the Montreal Film Festival and National Film Archive in Australia.

The Report (*Gozaresh*), written and directed by Abbas Kiarostami, produced by B. Farmanara, starring Aghdashlou and Tari, 1978. After having a fight with his wife, Mohammad leaves the house with his child. When he returns he finds out that his wife has committed suicide.

Reza Motori, written and directed by Masoud Kimiai, produced by Ali Abbasi, starring Vosooghi and Khatami, 1970. The impersonation of Farrokh who is researching mental patients, by Reza, who looks like him and then, pretends to be a mental patient in a hospital. Two very different lives depicted, with tragedy at the end for Reza.

The Runner (*Davandeh*), written by A. Naderi and B. Qaribpour, directed by Amir Naderi, produced by K.P.F.K.N., starring Niroomand and Tarekizadeh, 1985. This film opened the doors of many international film festivals to Iranian films. The life of an orphaned boy who lives alone in an abandoned ship, dreaming that one day he will be able to run away to his utopia.

Sadeq Kurdeh, written and directed by Naser Taqvai, produced by M. Misaghi-yeh, starring Raad and Entezami, 1972. The wife of a tea house owner, Sadeq, is raped by a driver on a particular road. Sadeq becomes a serial killer, targeting people who drive on the same road.

Search 1 (*Josteju Yek*), written and directed by Amir Naderi, produced by IRIB, 1981. A documentary about people who vanished during the revolution.

Search 2 (*Josteju Do*), written and directed by Amir Naderi, produced by IRIB, 1983. A documentary about the war between Iraq and Iran in 1981.

Shirak, written by K. Partovi and D. Mehrjui, directed by Dariush Mehrjui, produced by M. Kimiai and D. Mehrjui, starring Entezami and Kaboli, 1989. The struggle of a young man to keep his father's farm safe from wild boars. A simple film suitable for a young audience.

Shireen and Farhad (*Shireen va Far-had*), written and directed by Abdul-Hussein Sepanta, produced by Ardeshir Irani, starring Vaziri and Sepanta, 1935. A love story taken from classical Persian literature. Farhad, to reach her beloved Shireen, challenges and changes even nature.

Siavush in Persepolis (*Siavush dar Takht-e Jamshid*), written, directed and produced by Ferydoon Rahnema, starring Moayeri and Farjad, 1967. Taken from Persian mythology, this is an avant-garde film about the struggle between right with wrong and the martyr-dom of Siavush, who is unable to escape his destiny.

A Simple Event (*Yek Etefagh-e Sadeh*), written and directed by Sohrab Shahid

Saless, produced by Farhang va Honar, starring Zamani and Tarikhi, 1973. One of the first films of the Iranian cinema which earned recognition outside the country, it was praised as a simple but effective film. The boring life of a boy who lives with his parents; even the death of his mother does not bring much change. Acted by ordinary people and filmed in real locations, the film was semi-documentary in nature.

Snake Fang (*Dandan-e Mar*), written by M. Kimiai (based on A. Talebinejad), directed by Masoud Kimiai, produced by Majid Modaresi, starring Seddighi and Sajadiyeh, 1990. The fourth and the best film made by Kimiai after the revolution. With this film he turns back to the genre that he created before the revolution with films like *Qasar* and *Reza Motori*. A lack of social justice and loneliness drive his characters inexorably towards a tragic destiny. After the death of the mother, Reza goes to live in a motel to forget about his past, but he cannot find escape.

The Son of Iran Does Not Know His Mother (*Persar-e Iran az Modarash bi Khabar ast*), written, directed and produced by Ferydoon Rahnema, starring Jiyan and Kheradmand, 1976. Once we were superpower too. Nostalgia for a glorious past and mourning for a defeated present. A director of theatre, in search of a sense of identity, wants to stage a play about Iran.

Sotehdelan, written, directed and produced by Ali Hatami, starring Vosooghi and Aghdashlou, 1977. A mentally disabled young man goes after women one after another. His elder brother decides to find him a woman. He brings a prostitute into the house to be with his young brother, but after a while, the woman and the young man fall in love with each other.

South of the Town (*Jonobe Shahr*), written by J. Moghadam, directed by Farrokh Ghaffari, produced by Ghaffari and Emad, starring Asvadi and Homayoun, 1958. A woman causes two men fight with each other over her. The realistic portrayal of the people and the environment of the region south of Tehran caused censors to ban the public screening of the film.

Speak Out, Turkman (*Harfbezan Turkman*), written, directed and produced by Reza Alameh-Zadeh, 1980. A documentary about an ethnic group in Iran.

Spring (*Cheshmeh*), written and directed by Arbi Avanesian, produced by Tel Film, starring Arman and Nojomi, 1972. Technically and conceptually, a controversial film. Jalizban falls in love with the wife of his friend, not knowing that the woman has a lover. Tragedy strikes as the woman cannot have three men at the same time. The camera moves very little, and lingers over every scene.

Still Life (*Tabiat-e Bijan*), written and directed by Sohrab Shahid Saless, produced by Pishroo and Tel Film, starring Yazdani and Bonyadi, 1974. A simple portrayal of a quiet life. A signal operator and his wife live in peace for years in a house attached to the railway, where they see only trains passing by. One day a letter informing the man of his forced retirement and consequent need to vacate their home arrives.

The Storm of Life (*Tofan-e Zandeghi*), written by Nezam Vafa and Ziyai, directed by Ali darya-Baygi, produced by Ismael Koshan, Khaje-Noori and Chahr-Azad, 1948. The first step towards creation of a popular genre in Iranian cinema known as Film Farsi. A rich father does not allow his daughter to marry her lover, who lacks wealth but has

other virtues. Destiny, however, has something else in store for them.

The Stranger and the Fog (*Gharibe va Meh*), written and directed by Bahram Bayzai, produced by M. T. Shokrai, starring Maasomi and Shojazadeh, 1973. More Japanese than Iranian, the film shows the influence of Kurosawa. A wounded stranger comes into a village, not knowing who he is or where he came from. But he senses that he is escaping from something.

Tangsir, written by Amir Naderi (based on Sadeq Chobak), directed by Amir Naderi, produced by Ali abbasi, starring Vosooghi and Kasrai, 1974. Based on a novel by Chobak, Zar Mohammad picks up his rifle to fight with people who have taken his money unjustly.

Taste of Cherry (*Ta'me Gilass*), written, directed and produced by Abbas Kiarostami, starring Ershadi and Bagheri, 1997. Winner of the Golden Palm of the Cannes Film Festival in 1997. Mr. Badii, a middle-aged man, is planning to commit suicide and is seeking someone to help him. A good example of "incomplete cinema" in which the story's conclusion is left to the viewer's imagination.

The Tenants (*Ajareh-Neshinha*), written and directed by Dariush Mehrjui, produced by H. Yashayai and H. Soltanzadi, starring Entezami and Abdi, 1987. An old building, desperately in need of renovation, is occupied by four families who stand against a real estate agent who is trying to kick them out. A good comedy with a tragic subtext.

A Time for Drunken Horses (*Zamani Baray-e Masti Asbha*), written, directed and produced by Bahman Ghobadi, starring Ahmadi and Younessi, 2000. After the death of the father, a 12-year-old boy becomes the head of a family in a Kurdish village. To support his family he starts working to import goods from Iraq into Iran in a very tough and hostile environment so that even horses are given liquor in order to work.

Time of Love (*Nobat-e Asheghi*), written and directed by Mohsen Makhmalbaf, produced by Shahed and Darsib, starring Gordeh and Yalmas, 1991. A love triangle story repeated in three episodes. An old man who is in love with the woman reveals the affairs twice, causing two deaths. In the third episode, the two men (husband and lover) refuse to kill each other.

Topoli, written and directed by Reza Mirlohi, produced by E. Sadeqpour and A. Homayoun, starring Homayoun and Aghili, 1872. A successful adaptation of *Of Mice and Men* by Steinbeck; Topoli kills a woman and is killed by his best friend.

Traveller (*Mosafer*), written by Abbas Kiarostami (based on Hassan Rafiai), directed by Abbas Kiarostami, produced by K.P.F.K.N., starring Zand-Pegeleh and Tari, 1972. A young man's dream is to go to the capital and see a football match in the main stadium. He finally earns the money, in part by cheating, and goes to Tehran by a bus. When he arrives at the stadium, he is so tired that he falls asleep immediately. When he wakes up the match is over.

The Treasure of Gharoon (*Ganj-e Gharoon*), written by S. Yasami and A. Z. Ashtiani, directed and produced by S. Yasami, starring Fardin and Forozan, 1965. The most successful of all Film Farsis (commercial films), and a model for many other films. A decent and hardworking man, Ali, is accidentally thrown into the life of a girl from a very rich family. He rescues her from her evil fiancé who is only after her money.

Love, song, dance, action, comedy and drama made the film popular. A handsome and charismatic actor with a magic smile, Fardin, made the film unforgettable, too.

Two Sightless Eyes (*Do Chashmeh Bisou*), written and directed by Mohsen Makhmalbaf, produced by Hozeh Honari, starring Kasebi and Majidi, 1983. A villager takes his blind son to the Holly City of Mashhad to be healed by a miracle.

Two Women (*Do Zan*), written and directed by Tahmineh Milani, produced by Arta Film and Arman Film, starring Karimi and Zarehe, 1999. Despite the opposition of her father, a young girl goes to a college in Tehran. Soon she is followed and harassed by a young man who is in love with her and who makes her life a living hell.

Under the Olive Trees (*Zir-e Darakhtan-e Zieton*), written, directed and produced by Abbas Kiarostami, starring Keshavarz and Kheradmand, 1994. Two love stories, one real and another based on a script, are mixed together in front of the camera.

Waiting (*Entezar*), written and directed by Amir Naderi, produced by K.P.F.K.N., starring Haydari and Ghahremani, 1974. A boy has to deliver a pot of ice every day to a house. Every time a hand comes out and takes the pot. The boy has no desire other than to see the face belonging to the henna-stained hand.

Water, Wind, Dust (*Ab, Bad, Khak*), written and directed by Amir Naderi, produced by IRIB, starring Niroomand and Moghsodlou, 1989. In the middle of a dust storm, a boy returns to the desert to find his family who are living there. The third part of a trilogy, following *The Winner* and *The Runner*.

Where Is My Friend's Home? (*Khaneyeh Dost Kojast?*), written and directed by Abbas Kiarostami, produced by K.P.F.K.N., starring Ahmadpours and Defai, 1987. Mohammed Reza, a primary school student, is threatened with expulsion from school for not doing his homework. His classmate, Ahmad, finds out that he has brought home Mohammd's notebook by mistake. Not knowing Mohammad's address, Ahmad does everything he can to return Mohammad's notebook. A good example of simplicity and power in an Iranian movie.

The Wind Will Carry Us (*Bad Mara Ba Khod Khahad Bord*), written by A. Kiarostami (based on M. Aydin), directed by Abbas Kiarostami, produced by M. Kamitz and A. Kiarostami, starring Doorani and Sohrabi, 1999. A film-maker comes to a village to film a funeral after the death of a old woman.

The Winner (*Barandeh*), written and directed by Amir Naderi, produced by K.P.F.K.N., 1979–1983. A short film about a group of children who buy a watermelon and place it on an empty barrel. Whoever reaches it first will be the winner. The race starts but a man riding a bike grabs the melon and rides away.

World Champion Takhtie (*Jahan Pahlevan Takhtie*), written by A. Hatami, directed by Ali Hatami and Behrooz Afkhami, produced by Hadayat Film, starring Entezami and Gharibiab, 1996. Portraying the life of a great wrestler, Takhtie, whose body was found in a motel room. The question is whether it was death by suicide or assassination by the secret police.

Bibliography

Abbasi, Ali. "Mizegardeh Cinemayeh Iran." *Farhang va Zendegi* no. 18. Tehran, 1975.

Ajand, Y, ed. *Adabiyat-e Novin Iran*. Tehran: Amir Kabir Publishers, 1985.

Akrami, Jamshid. "Sahal va Jazab." *Rodaki* no. 37–38, Tehran, 1974.

Albert, Lisa. "The Runner." *Iran Media,* March 15, 1995.

Anvar, Fakhrodin. *Haftomin Jashnvareh Film-e Fajr*. Tehran, 1989.

Arjomand, Jamshid. *Dar Bareh Cinema*. Tehran: Jar Publishers, 1972.

_____. *Naqd-e Film*. Tehran: Farzan Publishers, 1999.

Aryanpur, Y. *Az Nima ta Rosegare Ma*. Tehran: Zavar Publishers, 1996.

_____. *Az Saba ta Nima,* 2 volumes. Tehran: Jibi Publications, 1976.

Asadi, Ali. "Daramadi bar Jameh Shenasi Cinemayeh Iran." *Farhang va Zendegi* no. 13–14. Tehran: Farhang va Honar, 1973.

Azadivar, H. "Dar Jostejoi Hoviyat." *Bahram Bayzai*. Edited by Z. Ghoukasian. Tehran: Agha Publishers, 1992.

Bahrlo, Mohammed. "Yek Mard Tanha Nemitavanad." *Film* no. 60. Tehran, 1987.

Bani-Hashemi, H. "Aramesh dar Hozor-e Digaran." *Ketab-e Cinema* no.1. Tehran, 1970.

Behashti, S. Mohammed. *Adabestan* no. 1. Tehran, 1989.

_____. "Movafaqiyat-e Ma." *Majaleh Film*. Tehran, 1998.

Bojnoordi, Neda. *Dar Ghorbat*. Tehran: Nashr-e Nay, 2000.

Brown, Geoff. "No sex, No Violence, Just Film." *The Times,* London, July 12, 1999.

Camhi, Leslie. "A Still Life." *The Village Voice* (November 17, 1998).

Cheshire, Godfrey. *Variety*. (May 12, 1996).

Cram Cook, Nilla. "The Theatre and Ballet Arts of Iran." *The Middle East Journal,* vol. 3 (October 1949).

Dabashi, Hamid. *Close-Up: Iranian Cinema, Past, Present and Future*. New York: Verso, 2001.

Daryoosh, Hajir. "Shabe Qossi." *Majaleh Honar va Cinema* no. 7. Tehran, 1964.

Davai, Parviz. "Gav." *Sepid va Siah* no. 30. Tehran, 1969.

_____. "Khaste Nabashi Rafiq." *Sepid va Siah* no. 941. Tehran, 1971.

Davalkoh, S. "Kharashhai bar Chehrai Vaqiyat." *Abbas Kiarostami*. Edited by Z. Ghoukasian. Tehran: Nashr-e Didar, 1997.

Dehbashi, Ali, ed. *Sohrab Shahid Saless*. Tehran: Saqeb & Sokhan Publishers, 1999.

Dehghan, Khosroo. *Mahnameh Film* no. 33. Tehran, 1985.

"Film, Radio Report." *Unesco Press* no. IV. 1950.

Fischer, Michael. *Iran, From Religious Dis-*

189

pute to Revolution. Cambridge, Ma.: Harvard University Press, 1980.

Frasati, M. "Mohsen Makhmalbaf, Montor-e Cinema." *Soreh Cinema* no. 1 (1991).

Ghaffari, Farrokh. "Abdol-Hussein Sepanta." *Farhang va Zendegi* no. 18. Tehran: Farhang va Honar, 1971.

Ghobadi, Ali. "Hamoon va Mehrjui." *Farhang va Cinema* no. 13 (1991).

Ghobadi, Bahman. *The New York Times* March 11, 2001.

Ghoukasian, Zavan, ed. *Abbas Kiarostami*. Tehran: Nashr-e Didar, 1997.

_____, ed. *Bahram Bayzai*. Tehran: Agha Publishers, 1992.

_____, ed. *Banoyeh Ordibehasht*. Tehran: Saless & Yoshij Publishers, 1999.

_____, ed. *Dar Barie Cheshmeh*. Tehran: Isfehan, 1972.

_____, ed. *Masoud Kimiai*. Tehran: Agha Publishers, 1990.

Golmakani, H. "Ensan va Shaytan." *Film* no. 20. Tehran, 1974.

Golshirie, Hoshang. "Gozaresh." *Abbas Kiarostami*. Edited by Z. Ghoukasian. Tehran: Nashr-e Didar, 1997.

Haji-Mashadi, A. "Arusi-e Khuban." *Mohsen Makhmalbaf*. Edited by G. Haydari. Tehran: Negah Publishers, 1997.

Hansen, Kathryn. *Making Women Visible: Gender and Race Cross-Dressing in the Parsi Theatre*. India: 1992.

Hatami, Ali. *Majmoe Assar*, 2 volumes. Tehran: Nasr-e Markaz, 1997.

Haydari, Gholam, ed. *Amir Naderi*. Tehran: Nashr-e Sohail, 1991.

_____, ed. *Foroogh Farokhzad va Cinema*. Tehran: 1998.

_____, ed. *Mohsen Makhmalbaf*. Tehran: Negah Publishers, 1997.

_____. *Naqd Nevisi dar Cinemayeh Iran*. Tehran: Agha Publishers, 1989.

_____, ed. *Naser Taqvai*. Tehran: Benegar Publisher, 1991.

Herzog, Werner. *International Film*. (Tehran) vol. 2, no. 2 (1994).

Hesami, Hoshang. *Donyayeh Sokhan* no. 11 (Tehran, 1987).

_____. "Gav." *Mahe No* no. 59 (1969).

Hinson, Hal. "The Runner." *The Washington Post*, January 25, 1991.

Howe, Desson. *Washington Post*, April 28, 2002.

Issa, Rosa & Whitaker, ed. *Life and Art....* London: The British Film Institute, 1999.

Jafari, M. "Dar Barie Nakhl va Bad-e Jiin." *Setareh Cinema* no. 219. Tehran, 1977.

Jahad, Parviz. "Gabbe." *Donyai Sokhan* no. 68. Tehran, 1995.

Jahanbglou, Ramin. "Kiarostami ya Haqiqat Joi." *Abbas Kiarostami*. Edited by Z. Ghoukasian. Tehran: Nashr-e Didar, 1997.

Johnston, Sheila. *Sight and Sound* (January 1999).

Karimi, N. "Ghoftegoie ba Nosrat Karimi." *Cinema va Theatre* no. 213. Tehran, 1972.

Kavosi, H. "Sepanta-e Pishgam." *Ayendegan Newspaper* Tehran, 22 August 1971.

Khaksar, Elham. "Zan va Zendeghi va Zayton." *Zanan* no. 21. Tehran, 1994.

Khomieni, R. *Velayat-e Faqi*. Tehran: Amir Kabir Publishers, 1981.

Khorasani, N. ed. *Jense Dovoom*. Tehran: Nashr-e Towse, 2001.

Kiarostami, Abbas. *Cinemaya* no. 16 (1992).

_____. *Sight and Sound* (February 1997).

Kirkland, Bruce. "Morality Tale Told with Class." *The Toronto Sun*, July 23, 1997.

Koshan, Ismael. *Mahnameh Cinemayi (1977–1983)*. Tehran: 1999.

Lahiji, Shahla. *Cimayeh Zan dar Assar-e Bahram Bayzai*. Tehran: Roshangaran Publishers, 1988.

Maheu, Rene. *Iran, Rebirth of a Timeless Empire*. Paris: Editions J. A., 1976.

Majaleh Ferdowsi no. 950 (1969).

Makhmalbaf, Mohsen. *Film, Goftegoha* (Tehran) vol. I (1988).

_____. *Gabbe*. Tehran: Nashr-e Nay, 1996.

_____. *Japan Times*, July 21, 2000.

_____. *Majaleh Film, Goftegoha* (Tehran) vol. I (1997).

_____. *Soroosh*, Tehran, 1987.

Malekpour, Jamshid. *Adabiyat-e Namayishi dar Iran*, volume I. Tehran: Toos Publishers, 1983.

_____. *The Islamic Drama*. London: Frank Cass Publishers, 2004.

Manteqi, Aman. "Mizegaredeh Cinemayeh Iran." *Farhang va Zendegi* no. 18. Tehran, 1975.

Mehrabi, Massoud. *Tarikh-e Cinemayeh Iran.* Tehran: Nashre Moalef, 1997.

Milne, Tom. "The Cow." *Dariush Mehrjui.* Edited by Naser Zeraati. Tehran: Negha Publishers, 1996.

Moazazi-Nia, Hussein. *Abrahim Hatami-Kia.* Tehran: Issargaran Publishers, 1997.

Mohasani, Mitra. *Bist Sal Akasi dar Iran.* Tehran: Mosiyeh Cinema, 2000.

Moradi-Kochi, Shahnaz. *Zanan-e Cinemagareh Iran.* Tehran: Now Rowz Honar Publishers, 2000.

Mosafaredin Shah. *Safarnameh Mosafaredin Shah.* Tehran, 1982.

Moslimi, D. "Namayesh-e Vaqiyat." *Bahram Bayzai.* Edited by Z. Ghoukasian. Tehran: Agha Publishers, 1992.

Motevaselani, M. *Kayhan* no. 10613 (1978).

Naffisi, Hamid. "Neghahi be Arbai'in." *Film Mostanad.* Tehran, 1978.

Nasibi, Basir. "Chehriyeh Digar-e Cinemayeh Iran." *Negin* (Tehran) no. 68 (1970).

Nasir Muslim, F. "Hamoon." *Dariush Mehrjui.* Edited by Naser Zeraati. Tehran: Agha Publishers, 1996.

Nik-Ahin, B, ed. *Gozasht-e Cheragh-e Rahe Ayendeh.* Tehran: Nilofar Publishers,1983.

Noor, F. *Iran.* Tehran, December 8, 2001.

Noori, Parviz. "Gav." *Dariush Mehrjui.* Edited by Naser Zeraati. Tehran: Agha Publishers, 1996.

Norai, M. R. "Cinemayeh pasaz Enghelab." *Sepidar* no. 3 (Toronto, 1992).

Nori-Ala, Ismail. "Dar Jostejoie Cinemayeh Meli." *Cinema va Theatre* no. 2–3 (Tehran, 1973).

Nori-Ala, Parto. "Naqsh-e zan dar Cinemayeh Kimiai." *Doo Naqd.* Tehran: Agha Publishers, 1983.

Okaniance, Avance. "International Federation for Scientific Research Report." Bombay, 1941.

Omid, Jamal. *Farhange Film va Cinemayeh Iran.* 2 volumes. Tehran: Negah Publishers, 1987.

_____. *Tarikh-e-Cinemayeh Iran.* Tehran: Negah Publishers, 1988.

Parkinson, David. *History of Film.* London: Thames and Hudson, 1995.

Parsons, Anthony. *The Pride and the Fall.* London: Jonathan Cape, 1984.

Pour-Ahmad, K. "Hasrat-e Kodaki." *Setareh Cinema* no. 823. Tehran, 1972.

_____. "Sazeh Dahani, Gami Areshmand." *Film va Honar* no. 256. Tehran, 1974.

_____. "Shahkari be Daqi Khorshid-e Jonob." *Film va Honar* no. 433. Tehran, 1973.

Rabihavi, G. "Filmi dar Sonat-e Hamingway." *Donyai Sokhan* no. 9. Tehran, 1987.

Rahnema, Ferydoon. "Film va Cinema dar Iran." *Setareh Cinema* no. 230. Tehran, 1959.

_____. *Vaghyat-Garahey Film.* Tehran: Boff Publishers, 1972.

Risen, James. "The C.I.A. in Iran." *The New York Times,* June 15, 2000.

Rizvi, S. A. A. *Iran, Royalty, Religion and Revolution.* Canberra: Ma'rifat Publishing House, 1980.

Sahafbashi, M. A. *Safarnameh Sahafbashi.* Tehran: 1978.

"Sanadhayeh Zandeh Tarikhe Cinemayeh Iran." *Mahnameh Cinemayi* (1979–1983). Tehran: 1999.

Seif, Mohssen. *Kargardanan Cinemayeh Iran,* 2 volumes. Tehran: Issargaran Association, 1998.

Sepanta, A. "Memoir." *Farhang va Zendegi* no.18. Tehran: Farhang va Honar, 1971.

Servizio, N. "L'iran Suttutti." *Gazzetta di Parma* no. 22 (1974).

Shabaviz, Abbas. "Moj-e No...." *Cinema* no. 442–444. Tehran, 2000.

Shahid-Saless, S. "Man Film Misasam." *Cinema Panjah-o Seh.* Tehran, 1974.

Shidfar, Ali. "Rokod va Bohraan dar Cinemayeh Iran." *Hamshari.* Tehran, September 27, 2001.

Shir-Mohammadi, J. *Cinemayeh badaz Enghelab.* Tehran: Navak Publishers, 1997.

Sho-aie, Hamid. *Ferydoon Rahnema.* Tehran: Sherkat Herminco, 1976.

_____. *Namayeshnameh va Filmnameh dar Iran.* Tehran: Sherkat Herminco, 1976.

_____. *Noavaran-e Cinema*. Tehran: Sherkat Herminco, 1977.

Solhjo, T. "Bardasht-e Avaal." *Donya-yeh Tasvir* no. 82. Tehran, 2000.

Sorlin, Pierre. *Italian National Cinema*. London: Routledge, 1996.

Soroush no. 524 (1990).

Sterritt, David. "Car-seat Conversations Inspire Iranian director." *The Christian Science Monitor,* July 28, 2000.

Taavoni, Shirin. *Ketabshenasi Theatre va Cinema*. Tehran: Asian Cultural Center, 1976.

Tahami-Nejad, M. *Cinemayeh Roya-Pardaz-e Iran*. Tehran: Aks-e Moaser, 1986.

_____. *Filmnameh Tarikhe Cinemayeh Iran*. Tehran: Cinema Publications, 1993.

_____. "Chelosesal Naqd-e Film dar Iran." *Cinema va Theatre*. Tehran, February 1973.

Talebi-Nejad, A, ed. *Be Ravayat-e Naser Taqvai*. Tehran: Rozaneh-Kar Publishers, 1996.

_____. *Dar Hozor-e Cinema*. Tehran: Farabi Publishers, 1998.

Taqian, Laleh. "Zan dar Cinemayeh Iran."

Farhang va Zendegi no. 19–20. Tehran: Farhang va Honar, 1975.

Taqvai, Naser. "Goftegho ba Naser Taqvai." *Etelaat* no.13287. Tehran, 1971.

Taylor, John Russell. "Downpour." *Ayandeghan* no. 17. Tehran, 1972.

"Tofan-e Zandeghi." *Etellaat Haftegi* no. 648. Tehran, 1953.

Toosi, Javad. "Dar-e Baq-e Fardoos." *Film* no. 184. Tehran, 1994.

_____. "Hoviyet-e Penhan...." *Donyayeh Tasvir* no. 13. Tehran, 1994.

Trapper, Richard, ed. *The New Iranian Cinema: Politics, Representation and Identity*. London: I. B. Tauris, 2002.

Wilson, David. "The Mongols." *Cinema Panjah-o Seh*. Tehran, 1974.

Yazdanian, Hassan. *Dokani be Nameh Cinema*. Tehran: Sepehr Publishers, 1968.

Yimou, Zhang. *The Chronicle*. Canberra, July 11, 2000.

Yosofi, Akbar. "Dar Bareh Hamoon." *Mahnameh Film* no. 95. Tehran, 1990.

Zarabi, M. "Bazi Abi va Rabi dar Cinema Mayak." *Film* (Tehran), vol. I. (January 1999).

Zeraati, Naser, ed. *Dariush Mehrjui*. Tehran: Negha Publishers, 1996.

Index

193